NO WAY BACK
REVOLUTION AND EXILE
RUSSIA AND BEYOND

by

Nathalie Apouchtine

Riverton
Press

Nathalie Apouchtine is a print and broadcast journalist and historian. She worked as a news reporter, sub-editor and producer in radio and television for the Canadian and Australian Broadcasting Corporations and Australia's Special Broadcasting Service. Later Nathalie turned to history, focussing on media and immigration in the twentieth century. Her research culminated in a PhD and provided the foundation for *No Way Back*. Nathalie was born a refugee in France, emigrated to Canada as a child and to Australia as an adult. She now lives in Sydney.

No Way Back: Revolution and exile, Russia and beyond
by Nathalie Apouchtine

Cover Photographs:
Front Cover:
The author's great-grandmother Nadezhda (Galitzine) Popov in traditional costume, 1880s.
Piatnitskoe, the estate of the Popov family.
Back Cover:
The author's mother Irene with her mother Natalia, 1920s.
The author's father Dimitri at left, with siblings Sasha, Seriozha and Nadia, 1926.

ISBN paperback: 978-0-6450335-4-0
ISBN e-book: 978-0-6450335-5-7
© Copyright Nathalie Apouchtine 2024

Book design by Petr Kovarik
Cover design by Leonie Lane, Booyong Design
First published by Riverton Press 2024
Sydney, Australia
Printed by Breakout Media Communications

Table of Contents

Preface 1
Family Trees 5
Prologue – Traces of the Past 8
Chapter 1 – Foundation Stories 15
Chapter 2 – Protest and Patriotism 36
Chapter 3 – "Some sort of new life was beginning…" 64
Chapter 4 – "We've taken power and we won't give it up…" 83
Chapter 5 – Former People 105
Chapter 6 – Reluctant Exiles 125
Chapter 7 – Divergent Paths 153
Chapter 8 – Heading West 175
Illustrations 189
Chapter 9 – Faltering New Beginnings 205
Chapter 10 – The Paris Years 224
Chapter 11 – Russia Abroad 239
Chapter 12 – Troubled Ties 265
Chapter 13 – War and Occupation 290
Chapter 14 – Bombs and Punishment 307
Chapter 15 – "The world is big…" 333
Chapter 16 – New World 355
Chapter 17 – "Citizens of the world…" 370
Epilogue – Moving on 385
Acknowledgements 390
Sources and Further Reading 393

*To the memory of Irene and Dimitri –
and all those who came before them.*

Any good history begins in strangeness. The past should not be comfortable... The past should be so strange that you wonder how you and the people you know and love could come from such a time.

    Richard White, *Remembering Ahanagran: Storytelling in a Family's Past.*

The Russian nation is so heterogeneous in its ethnical (sic) and moral composition... it has always developed in such defiance of logic, through such a maze of clashes, shocks and inconsistencies, that its historic evolution utterly defies prophecy.

    Maurice Paléologue, *An Ambassador's Memoirs.*

Preface

Years ago, as a young post-graduate student in Canada about to embark on further studies, I had a very unsettling experience. Nervously arriving at a new university, in a new city several thousand kilometres from my hometown, I set out to my first meeting with the head of the Russian Department, in which I was enrolled.

As I entered a small, cluttered office, a tall thin man, his bony face topped with a heavy dollop of wavy white hair, rose to shake my hand. He wore a welcoming smile, but his words made my own half-formed smile freeze.

"I wonder," he said, glancing at the over-sized, dangly earrings I favoured then, "are those heirlooms that were seized when your ancestors were oppressing my ancestors?"

The professor came from Poland and my first thought was to question why he had become the head of Russian studies if he harboured such bitterness towards Russians. But of course he was joking. All the same, I knew that many jokes reflect some truth about the teller's feelings.

My sensitivity probably had more to do with my political evolution than with any intended malice on the professor's part. As a child in a Russian migrant family, I had imagined a storied past of palaces, servants and balls, visions gleaned from classic novels – and my family's equally improbable noble origins. In the history lessons I had attended at weekend Russian School, the centuries' long litany of conquest by Russia of neighbouring lands like Poland had been presented as glorious, rather than brutal. The repression of fellow citizens, meanwhile, had been discussed as a Soviet crime, not as the continuation of a well-worn tradition from before the 1917 Revolution. But as I grew older, I learned other versions of the history of the land of my ancestors, and my image of it soured. I could not shake the feeling that I was linked to all the wrongs – past and continuing – of those with whom I shared my ethnicity and social origins. And to some sort of responsibility for them.

It was a long time later that I set out to discover more about my forebears, especially my grandparents and people of their generation. I wanted to search behind the myths and counter-myths, to dig past stereotypes to the many layers of their existence in Russia and beyond. Through the story of the migrations of this group and their descendants, I also wanted to explore how such origins, along with subsequent dislocation, can impact on identity – individual and collective – as it is continuously re-evaluated. Among these questions was the puzzle over why Russia – with its violent past and continuing brutality – could continue to exert a hold on a descendant of those early twentieth century refugees, three generations on.

The result is this narrative of my extended family and its wider community in the context of turbulent historical times, and of the echoes of cataclysmic events across three generations. The story stretches from Russia to Western Europe to Canada and Australia. It is at one level a family history, at another a history of a central and now all too familiar experience: violent disruption to traditional ways of life, the mass movement of peoples and exile.

Many stories of Russian migration deal in depth with mainly one generation. I have been able to span a longer period due to the fortuitous existence of extensive memoirs, especially in my father's family. Also the archive that I have collected includes material from my extended family. Most of it has never been published and was produced in languages other than English; I have translated it for the purposes of this book.

So this account is based on a range of sources: diaries and memoirs by several of my relatives, interviews of others, family letters and photographs dating back to the late nineteenth century, official documents and archives pertaining to the 1870s onwards, other auto/biographies and historical texts, and travel for further exploration to sites of historical importance to my family.

The result is a combination family history, auto/biography and memoir. It is the story of one family, but at the same time, it is an example of the impacts of wider events on individuals and families, and how these impacts continue to echo.

In the twentieth century and continuing in the twenty-first, war and civil conflict, and the associated dislocation and displacement, have been widespread. Many issues in this story remain highly relevant today.

A note on transliteration and dates:
The transliteration system used in this book for words in Cyrillic is the Modified Library of Congress system. Exceptions are made in a number of cases: where there are accepted English versions of names of people or places (for example Tchaikovsky, Moscow) or where the people named have themselves adopted or been given a particular transliteration of their names which they then have continued to use. Sometimes these transliterations reflect time spent in non-English speaking countries, where conventions for conversion of Cyrillic are different.

PREFACE

Russia used the Julian calendar until February 1918, when it fell into line with the rest of Europe, adopting the Gregorian calendar. Dates relating to the period before then are given in so-called Old Style in this book, except where dates had significance for both Russia and the West (for example, the date of Germany's declaration of war on Russia) where the Old Style date is given first, followed by the New Style date in parentheses.

Note on family trees

The family trees on the following pages are summaries of the last three generations of my family, from my great-grandparents to my parents: the main players in this family history. The many question marks in my maternal line demonstrate how much is unknown in my family about that side of our relatives. There is even a question over my mother's exact birth date.

Parentheses indicate place of birth and place of death. These point to the way the family was scattered after the Revolution (other than some of my parents' generation, all the people shown on the family trees were born in the Russian Empire).

Female relatives in my grandparents' and parents' generations are listed with their married names only, as their maiden names are clear from the linkages to their parents.

The dotted line is used to indicate a sister of my great-grandfather's on my father's maternal side. She and her daughter are listed, whereas other siblings and cousins in these two generations are not, because Anna (Voeikoff) has an important role in this family history.

Maternal Ancestors

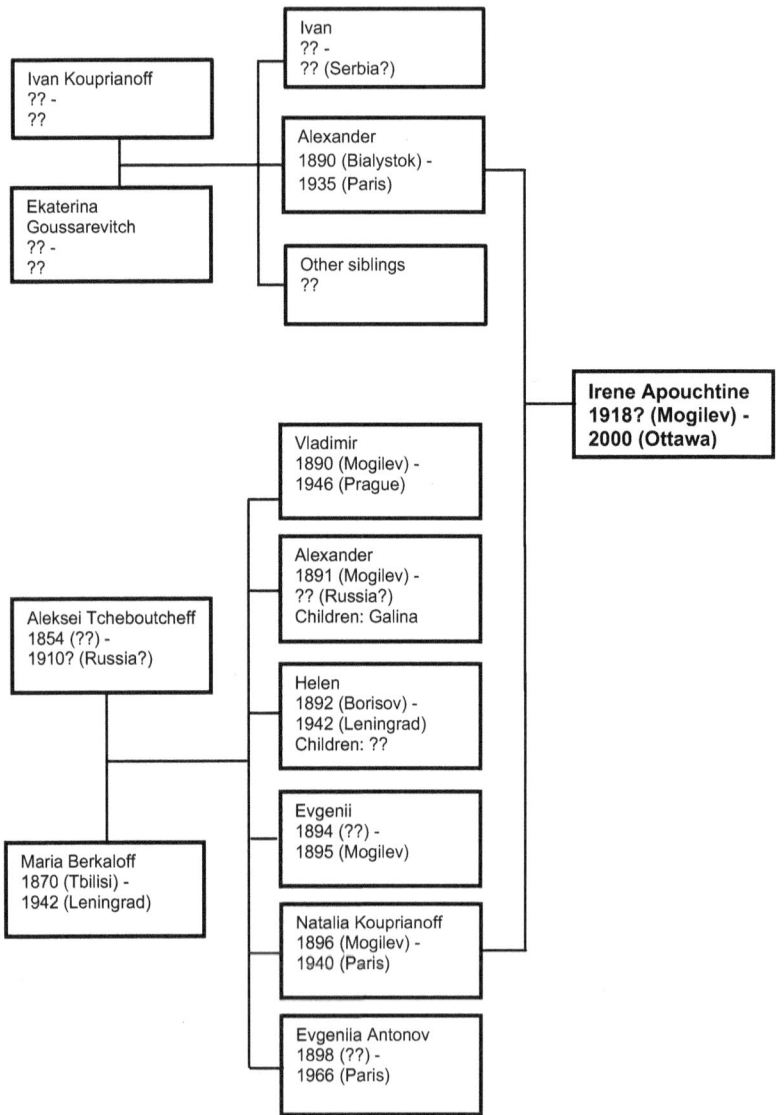

Paternal Ancestors

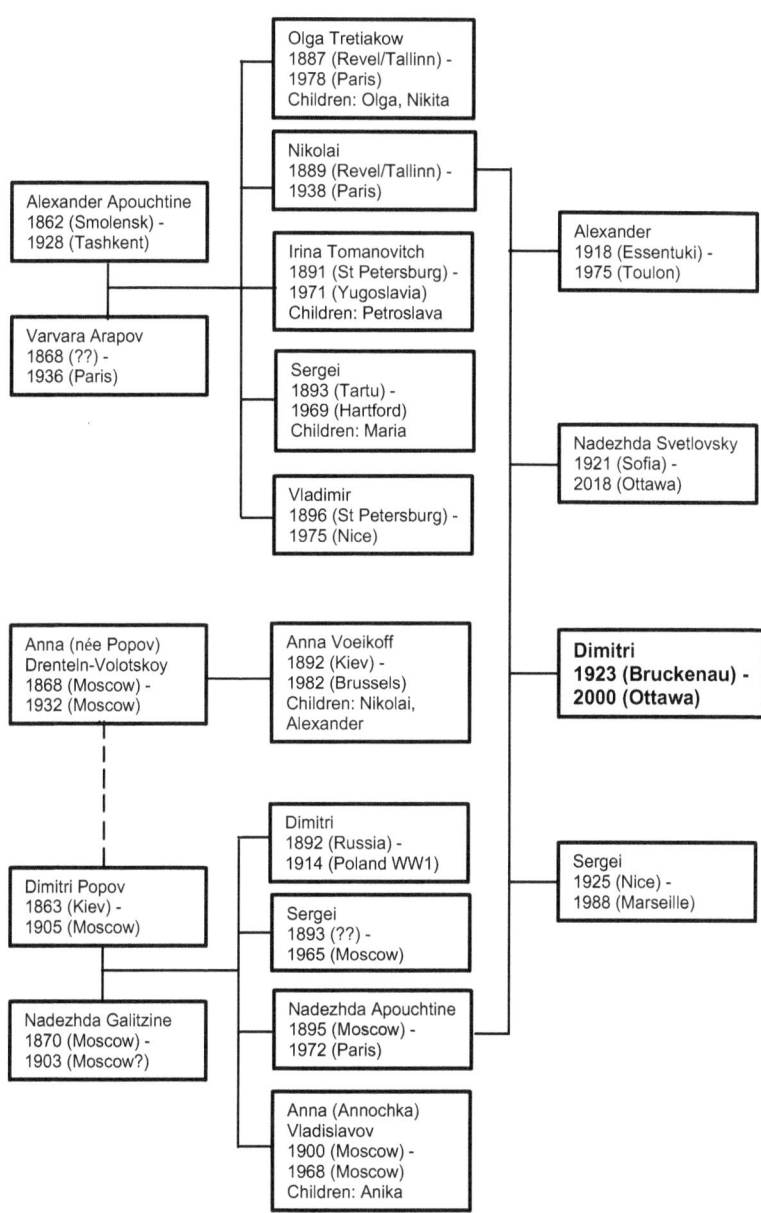

Prologue
Traces of the Past

In my family home in Canada, over the years, our lounge room came to increasingly look like an art gallery. My father was an artist and a craftsman and the shelves and walls became filled with his works and those of friends and fellow exhibitors.

Jostling for space on one wall was a rather plain item: a small brown picture frame, under the glass a black and white photocopy of a coat of arms. It consisted of a crown with tall thick feathers atop a collection of disparate elements, these garlanded by the words *nihil me retardet* – nothing stops me. Next to the coat of arms hung a military medal, in the shape of a Maltese Cross, enamelled white and with a tiny depiction in the centre of St George killing the dragon.

The shelves in the room were equally crowded: behind sculptures and craftworks – encyclopedias, art books, the Russian classics, and much else. Tucked away in a corner were two thin booklets. Dating back to the early 1900s, written in the pre-revolutionary Russian alphabet, these were frayed and fragile. They told about two estates; photos in them showed expansive buildings with columned entrances, vast gardens with statues and pavilions, huge rooms with grandiose furniture and chandeliers, and elaborate chapels.

We were descendants of the wave of Russians who had left their homeland in the 1920s. But my parents did not frequent the sorts of émigré groups where members greeted each other with obsolete titles and lamented the tsarist past, when most of them had not yet been born. Yet the coat of arms, the estates, the medal, all pointed to a similar history in my family. Our household spoke Russian, we celebrated and valued Russian traditions and culture. But there was little nostalgia for a world long gone in the stories we were told about our family's past in Russia. Recounted memories more often revolved around the experiences of our parents' families in pre-war France, the Second World War, and emigration to Canada.

Like many children of immigrants, away from home I had lived in a parallel universe, at times seemingly as remote from my home life as that fabled Russia of the tsars. But when school or playmates left me disgruntled, I would escape into daydreams about the grand houses on the estates. I would wonder what life would have been like if there had been no Revolution in 1917, with no real understanding of what that meant. When years later I set out to find out what it did mean, what I discovered was a host of stories and experiences, far more extraordinary than anything I had been able to dream up.

The families into which my grandparents were born, while not uniformly wealthy, had been privileged in a way that their later descendants would barely be able to grasp. But as with so many family histories, when I started to dig into the past, the stereotypes that seemed to go with the evidence in my parents' lounge room, did not always fit. There were knots and twists, which I set out to unravel, in my quest to understand how my parents and grandparents had experienced their unsettled lives.

As I explored what was known about my grandparents' predecessors, I found numerous clues on my father's side of the family – though I had to try to sort out what was myth and what had some basis in reality. On my mother's side, even myths were few and far between.

My father's father Nikolai descended from an old family; registers of the Russian nobility list the name from the sixteenth century onwards. There are two legends about the origin of the family before that, each tracing it back to a Frenchman who travelled east and settled on land that he acquired on the River Opukhta – hence the eventual surname Apouchtine (pronounced A-pukh-teen in Russian).

One of these stories dates to the eleventh century. The Frenchman is said to have been a knight who came with a delegation to Kiev, then the capital of the medieval state of Rus'. Their mission was to collect Anna, daughter of the ruler Prince Iaroslav the Wise, to escort her back to France to marry King Henry the First. This assignment completed, the man is said to have returned and settled on the river.

The other story places the arrival of the Frenchman in the fourteenth century. He is thought to have been a member of the French court. What is known of this tale is rather dry compared to one about fetching a bride for a king; it gives no motive for his relocation, but has him being accepted at the Russian court, being knighted, and using his wealth to buy vast lands on the River Opukhta.

Perhaps somewhere, deep in obscure archives, there is evidence to back one or the other version. The presence of two *fleur de lys*, the symbol of the royal family of France, on our coat of arms suggests that the French link, at least, has some basis. In having been passed down over the generations, these legends have no doubt added to the sense of deep connection to Russia's past among my relatives, something that was perhaps comforting during the most unsettled years of migration. It is unlikely however that those who ended up in

France after fleeing Russia found any consolation in the symmetry of this return to a legendary ancestor's homeland.

Among more recent notable ancestors on that side of the family was the late nineteenth century poet Aleksei Apouchtine, a great-great-great-uncle of mine. He died more than twenty years before the Revolution, yet his work continued to be reissued during the Soviet era, even though it was considered overly sentimental and not critical enough of social conditions. His close friendship with Peter Tchaikovsky gave him an additional toehold on posterity; the two collaborated, the composer having frequently put my ancestor's verse to music, the resulting romances still performed today.

There is an imposing monument at Aleksei Apouchtine's gravesite in St Petersburg, located among those of other writers and composers. For a family with many members both past and present who have put much energy into writing of one kind or another, this relative with a place in Russian literature would seem to be a fitting role model. But another aspect of this poet has been seen as more problematic: he was a known homosexual, something some of his descendants have found difficult to acknowledge, never mind accept. As in other families, the nature of ancestor memory is sometimes selective, with descendants "editing" the legacy they take from the past.

My father's mother Nadezhda came from an old family as well, though her maiden name Popov suggests another type of background. In Russian "pop" is one of several words for priest. Indeed, there had been clergy in my grandmother's family for generations – over some two hundred years. It was her grandfather who broke with the tradition, choosing law instead.

PROLOGUE

On her mother's side, my grandmother was related to the Galitzines, a family with close links to a succession of rulers over the centuries. Her grandfather, Prince Sergei Mikhailovich Galitzine, was one of the wealthiest men of pre-revolutionary Russia. My father used to joke that the Prince was so rich, he would lend the Tsar money. My father's discomfort with the notion of such great wealth no doubt fuelled this exaggeration – but it was probably not too far off the mark. Galitzine owned large estates in Russia, and properties in Western Europe. He was instrumental in the construction of the still imposing Russian Orthodox cathedral in Nice, in France, which was consecrated in 1912, three years before his death.

Photos of Prince Galitzine in his later years portray a solid dignified man, sporting a large white moustache, with an array of medals pinned to his uniformed chest. A different side to this formidable figure is that he was married four times. His first wife was a gypsy singer, Alexandra Gladkov, said to have been an extraordinarily talented artist. He is thought to have met her when she was performing at a social function. They had five children, including my great-grandmother. When they divorced, he is said to have split their children between them and to have denied her access to those who stayed with him. My grandmother later told about only meeting Alexandra, her own grandmother, when she was nearly an adult and about how upset she had been when she learned of the cruelty of her grandfather in keeping his ex-wife from some of her children.

His actions did not prevent his gypsy wife leaving a legacy, perceived as influential by the family to this day. Olive skin and dark hair, a moody or impetuous personality, a singing voice with inflections of deep emotion, or the urge to travel: when any of these aspects is evident in her descendants, it is said the gypsy blood is showing itself. Questionable stereotypes and the number of generations that has passed aside, there seems to be some sort of justice that a relatively obscure, lower class woman cast aside by a glittering prince left her mark, still cited more than a century after her death.

The chronicling of events by my father's large family in the West has been extensive: a number wrote or recorded memoirs and there are numerous descendants around the world who were able to share their recollections with me and provide old documents and photographs. As for my mother, very few of her relatives left Russia, and even among those who did, the links were lost: piecing together the past on her side has been much more difficult.

The Revolution and Civil War resulted in her family being scattered across the old Empire and beyond. Both my mother's parents died when she was still young, so the opportunity for her to seek more information from them disappeared. Under the circumstances, it is surprising how much she did ask her mother. Some of her knowledge about her forebears is also likely to have come from her aunt – her mother's sister – the only close relative with whom she was still in contact after the Second World War. She also retained a connection with a friend of her father's, whose closeness to the family was such that she thought of him as an uncle. But further emigration complicated these final links and they were later broken altogether, through death, lack of descendants in the West and return to the Soviet Union.

I have relied on stories recounted to her by her mother and aunt and "uncle", her own memories, and some old photographs, letters and documents – all that remained from her antecedents.

The families of my mother's parents did not – as far as she knew and as far as I have been able to discover – have high profile members, like some of those on my father's side and I have found no mention of them in published texts. My mother told me both her mother's and her father's families were in the nobility and were very comfortably off. They owned lands in the Russian Empire and abroad. The men of both families – at least in the years leading up to the Revolution – had military careers, as well as running estates.

My mother always regretted the missing knowledge about her ancestors. It seems the keen interest she often took in seeking more information on my father's family may have been part of an effort to compensate for the gaps in her own story.

Whatever had come before, like my father's, my mother's parents were young people finding their way in the world, when that world changed dramatically and completely – for them, their families and their country.

1
Foundation Stories

Although there are many family photographs of my father's father, the image that often comes to mind when I think of him is from a yellowed French newspaper clipping. It shows an officer speaking to a rally in what was then Petrograd. He is not identified in the description of the photo but the family has always believed it is my grandfather. The man has his right arm raised; where his other arm should be, hangs an empty sleeve. This page from *Le Miroir* of June 17, 1917 is titled "Une manifestation Russe en faveur des Alliés" ("A Russian demonstration in support of the Allies"). The caption says the officer is calling on gathered soldiers to support a new Russian offensive in the First World War. This was the period between the two Revolutions of 1917. The Bolsheviks were moving towards overthrowing the more moderate Provisional Government, which had been set up when the Tsar was ousted; their campaign for a withdrawal from the war was gaining momentum among a population tired of bloodshed.

The man's face in the clipping is in shadow. But the empty sleeve supports the belief that this is my grandfather, as he had by then lost his left arm in fighting at the front. This tangible evidence of his place as a participant amid turbulent historical events caught my imagination from the first time I saw the newspaper – leaving aside any niggling doubts as to the definite identity of the officer.

My grandfather Nikolai (1889-1938) died at the age of 48, before the

CHAPTER ONE

Second World War. For a long time, I had believed that he was not among those in the family inclined to writing, but later I discovered that he had in fact kept a diary about some of the events in Russia. After the death of his youngest son in Paris in 1988, with most remaining close family settled in North America, it fell to others to clean out an apartment that had been rented by various members of the family for over fifty years. They found Nikolai's diary, but decided its condition was too poor for it to be kept. When I learned this, it was as though a door had been slammed in my face; an avenue to a relative who had died before my birth had existed, and yet now was irretrievably lost. His brother Sergei and his sister Olga left extensive memoirs, written decades after they had fled Russia; through their stories and memories I could piece together some sense of the childhood and youth he had shared with them. These are precious sources. Yet I am tormented by the thought of the destroyed diary.

The memoirs, along with documents which confirm some of the key dates and other information, give some picture of the family into which Nikolai was born. His father Alexander was a senior military officer, who had a very successful career, receiving many promotions and decorations during the tsarist years. But he had had a less promising start to life. His mother had died giving birth to him, in Smolensk in 1862, and his father had died a few years later, leaving him to be brought up by a distant relative. When Alexander was old enough to take over his own affairs, he discovered that his inheritance had been stolen, even a church where generations of Apouchtines were buried. It is believed he sued his guardian to try to recover the family lands, but his own lawyer was said to have been bought off and he lost the case. It was his military career which allowed him to regain a level of affluence he may not have had otherwise.

In 1887, Alexander married a descendant of another prominent Russian family – Varvara Arapov, who had also been orphaned at a young age. His military postings took them to different parts of the Empire, as the family grew. There were five children: first Olga, then Nikolai, who was born in 1889 in Revel (now Tallinn) in Estonia. Then followed Irina, Sergei and Vladimir.

My great-grandfather fought in Russia's war against Japan in 1905, and was left with a badly damaged leg. But in spite of a permanent limp, he continued his officer duties, as well as teaching at a military academy and writing for military publications. One of the regiments to which he was attached often travelled with the Tsar and the court. This meant the family spent time in the various areas where the Tsar had palaces, among them Peterhof (or Petrodvorets) on the Gulf of Finland. There, according to Olga, her father dined with the Tsar and his family on Sundays. By 1914 Alexander had been promoted to lieutenant general.

It appears my grandfather and his siblings had a happy home life; from all accounts the children were close to their parents and to each other. In her memoir Olga described a time when the family was living in a country setting in Iouriev (now Tartu) in Estonia, recalling walks she and her little brother Nikolai were taken on by their governess in woods on estates belonging to local noble families:

> *All these forests were very well maintained, there were tables and benches of rustic wood, and one could be served milk there, and excellent black bread. It was in these forests that we learned mushroom gathering, which allowed us, later on, to distinguish the good ones from the bad ones; we also found*

CHAPTER ONE

large quantities of berries, wild strawberries and raspberries. These outings have remained for me one of the best memories of our childhood pastimes.

The many moves because of their father's work seem not to have caused the children distress. For the household was in many ways self-contained; they took with them servants, nannies, and other staff (even a seamstress who sewed all the children's clothes). Nikolai's brother Sergei described one such move with his other brother Vladimir, in the dead of winter, as something of an adventure. It was 1903 and Sergei was ten years old. While their parents had gone ahead to prepare the new home, a large sleigh pulled by a *troika* – a team of three horses – came for the boys:

...they loaded us, along with nanny and a maid, into the sleigh under a huge rug. It was already getting dark and it was very cold. The road, straight as an arrow, went through a dense forest, and with horror I listened to the conversation between nanny and the sleigh driver about wolves sometimes coming out onto the road. To cross the Volkhov River, we travelled right on the ice, for which the driver later got into big trouble; he should have gone on the ferry which crossed close by through a canal that had been chopped in the ice... [When we arrived] it was already very late... We awoke early, jumped out of bed and rushed to the window. Before us spread a boundless plain, the Volkhov, and beyond it flood plains, all merging into one endless sea of white... Far off against the white we could glimpse black dots moving around. We later found out that these were wolves.

These recollections of Sergei and Olga echo quintessential, traditional images of Russia. While this raises the question over whether their descriptions may have been coloured by other writings and memories, the actual events recounted have the ring of experience to them, along with nostalgia for what was left behind, and a flavour of time and place.

My grandfather Nikolai followed in his father's footsteps, embarking on a military education. He was sent to a cadet academy in St Petersburg, returning home only for holidays. Sergei remembered the admiration with which he and his younger brother greeted him on these visits:

> *In summer, Kolia (Nikolai) would come home from the cadet corps. To us younger boys he represented incontestable authority. When we went fishing, Kolia would arrange his rods along the bank and sit in the shade, and Volodia (Vladimir) and I had to watch the floats. If there was a bite we had to call him; we did not dare pull the line ourselves.*

Some aspects of Nikolai's life as a cadet can be guessed at through Sergei's descriptions when he himself later joined a similar institution. In his memoir, he wrote that his academy was "luxurious" in every way, it had its own chapel, a swimming pool and sauna, a tailor's workshop, and a huge dining room where the food was "tasty and plentiful." Each cadet was furnished with everything he required: clothing, books and other study needs. And – Sergei noted – it was all financed by the government: nothing was spared to educate the future officers.

Nikolai went on to the Corps of Pages, an exclusive military-educational institution which prepared young men for service in the court and the army. Students had to be from the upper nobility and to pass a difficult set of examinations; there were only forty new admissions each year.

Besides military courses, the students studied languages, history, mathematics, a range of science subjects, even dancing and drawing. An excerpt from the 1900 code of conduct stipulated that, to be assigned to imperial service, the Pages had to be:

> *...highly diligent, tactful, serene, mature, impeccably polite, respectful, obliging, prompt and orderly in executing their duties. But the Pages may not be officious or bothersome, and must remain clear headed in any crisis.*

My grandfather graduated from the Corps of Pages in 1908 and was accepted into the Fourth Imperial Family Rifle Guards Regiment as a second lieutenant. The Imperial Guards regiments were known for their active involvement in the vigorous social life of St Petersburg high society – indeed it was expected of them. Nikolai found this enticing, his brother Sergei remembered:

> *...all his time free from service he spent in high society amusements. He was very handsome and elegant in his distinctive and striking uniform; he was very popular and was constantly being invited somewhere for dinners, receptions and balls.*

Nikolai's sister Olga also wrote of her brother's presence at balls at the institute she attended, which were followed by grand dinners, where "the young men were seated on one side and the young women on the other, but where we had a good time nevertheless."

But the extravagance of this lifestyle caught up with Nikolai: his salary was not enough to maintain it and his father could not keep subsiding him. Sergei wrote about the outcome:

I found out that my brother Kolia wanted to abandon military service and switch to civilian life. Why did Kolia, such a brilliant officer, decide to take off his uniform? My whole being protested against this.
In my soul I blamed him for a reckless attitude to his duty... Kolia could not cut down on expenses, could not deny himself any pleasure. The main reason for his departure from the regiment was the too large demands with which father could not keep up. And I condemned Kolia and the Guards and all St Petersburg society for their meaningless pastimes...

According to Sergei, their father cleared Nikolai's debts and suggested his son move to a military unit less caught up in social events, preferably away from the capital and its temptations. But instead my grandfather left active duty in 1911 and took a job at the ministry of finance.

Sergei's condemnation of his brother seems severe, but it is no doubt partly due to his disappointment in someone he had so highly regarded. Also, as often happens in families when younger children are made to pay for their older siblings' mistakes, it resulted in his own education being stricter. His father kept a tighter rein on him, at one point threatening that he would end up as a sales clerk in a grocery store if he repeated some high jinks which got him into trouble at his academy. Sergei's own devotion to the military clearly also coloured his feelings.

Nikolai's life as a civil servant did not last long; he would soon be back in uniform and off to war.

CHAPTER ONE

I remember my father's mother as a small, stooped woman, dressed in black and cloaked in sadness. Nadezhda (1895-1972) was born into a very wealthy family, and her childhood and youth were spent in luxury. But even before her later life brought exile and poverty, she suffered a series of tragic losses. Nadezhda means hope in Russian. Whatever her hopes were for her life when she was young – I'm sure they were nothing like the events she was to see and experience.

My grandmother's mother – Nadezhda Popov (*née* Galitzine) – is said to have been good-hearted and beautiful. There is an extraordinary photograph of her, where she is a vision of feathers, ruffles and lace. There is no context to the photo; maybe this was normal attire for her, maybe she was about to attend a sumptuous social event.

My great-grandmother married Dimitri Popov, a marshal of the nobility in Kaluga province, south of Moscow. This position, held by members of the landed gentry, carried with it wide administrative powers and responsibilities in a country district, representing authority in the name of the tsar. The family divided its time between his estate and their home in Moscow.

In one family memoir Dimitri is said to have been involved in charity work, but there is no explanation of what that would have meant in practical terms. A story about him that has been passed down tells how when he was walking in a village one day he was approached by a barefoot beggar woman. He took pity on her because it was a cold day, but not having any money with him, he removed his shoes and gave them to her. It is hard to know how much to read into just one anecdote about a life when there is a dearth of other information. But clearly this incident was told to demonstrate the characteristic that relatives wanted to remember him by: his spontaneous generosity. On a wider scale, the story was a symbol of the perception they would have held of the largesse of the nobility. Another indication of the sort of person Dimitri may have been comes from the belief that he died of a broken heart after his wife's untimely death. In a couple of photos that I have of him, he looks very dapper. His face appears gentle, with expressive eyes, but then my impression may be influenced by the stories told about him.

My great-grandmother's health was never very good. She spent summers in the Crimea, on the Black Sea – considered to have a healthy climate. But at some point, she contracted tuberculosis. In spite of a number of trips to Italy for treatment, she died in 1903, some ten years after the photo in ruffles and lace was taken. She was in her 30s. She left behind four young children: Dimitri, Sergei, my grandmother Nadezhda – who had been born in 1895 in Moscow, and Annochka (Anna). Their father died a year or two later.

The children's care and upbringing were taken over by their paternal grandfather, Alexander Popov, a widower. He had worked as a judge in Kiev and Moscow and later became a senator. He is said to have been strict, but fair, in his judicial work, and to have been well liked and respected. But again, this description focuses on aspects his descendants found appealing and were happy to pass down the generations.

When my grandmother Nadezhda died in 1972, she – alone among my grandparents – left behind a personal account that was not lost, about the years of war and revolution in Russia and migration to the West. She was the only one of them who was still alive when I was born, the only one to have seen grandchildren, to have been a *babushka* to them. But she lived in France, which I left as a three year old for Canada; she came to visit us there only once, when I was too young to get to know her. By the time I first went to France, she had passed away.

Her diaries, written over nearly half-a-century, have provided a window into my grandmother's experiences. But they are somewhat impressionistic and sporadic, which is not surprising considering her unsettled and turbulent life. Thus memoirs tape-recorded by her first cousin Anna are also very valuable. The cousins were very close, both in Russia and later in emigration. Anna's memories help to shed light on Nadezhda and her family, and the times generally for families such as theirs. They are fresh and vivid. For although they were taped in her old age, after she had lived away from Russia for decades, they were apparently based on written diaries which she had kept as events were unfolding.

Nadezhda's grandfather may have brought the strictness he exercised in his judicial work to his role in bringing up his son's children, but they were very fond of him. The children were close, helping care for each other then and throughout their lives, as much as separation would allow. But while there seemed to have been no lack of warmth in the family, those close to my grandmother say she never got over the loss, at the age of eight, of her mother, and soon after – her father too. Her cousin Anna remembered Nadezhda speaking of suicide when they were both young girls:

> *Nadia's (Nadezhda's) character was very tormented. She sometimes would call me on the phone and say: "I am going to the riding school and I will take the most fiery horse because I do not want to live anymore." Of course, the horse would turn out to be not*

so fiery and nothing would happen, but I,
at home, prayed and worried terribly.

Anna and others also attributed her sometimes dark personality to her part-gypsy heritage, which was given as an explanation for Nadezhda's great sensitivity and her ability to feel emotions deeply.

One thing is certain, the children lacked nothing materially. Their grandfather hired tutors and governesses for them. Later the boys were sent to the best Moscow schools, while teachers were brought in to educate the girls. My grandmother learned to speak French, English and some German – very useful skills in her later life abroad. Besides languages, judging by Anna's education, she would probably have studied a large range of subjects: ancient history, physics, maths, chemistry, geography, literature, music and more. Beyond lessons in activities like sewing and embroidery, there was likely less focus on household skills – which would have been helpful later. After all, there were plenty of servants to care for the family's daily needs.

Life in Moscow seemed to have plenty of attractions for those who could afford them. My grandmother would have gone to art exhibitions, theatre, ballet and opera, and to a new phenomenon – something Anna called "electro-theatre". These were probably newsreels, because she described someone playing piano, and events shown, for instance, the Tsar's family or the military going through its paces, all "very fast and staccato". She mentioned films too, but said they were all American and English. They were "very primitive" and always ended happily, but "the acting was good".

There was always music in their lives. The Popov children were reputedly all talented in this respect, their gypsy heritage again believed to be expressing itself. Dimitri played violin, Sergei piano, and they both played guitar. My grandmother also played piano and was said to have a good voice, able to sing gypsy romances in an authentic way, "rolling her eyes" and hitting "real gypsy notes".

Anna found her cousins' home life very attractive, whether in Moscow or in the countryside. In her own family, English was spoken most often and there seemed to be a striving to emulate Western European ways. At the Popovs on the other hand, only Russian was spoken (though all the children knew French and English), amid a family steeped in Russian ways. Anna told of visiting their country estate, Piatnitskoe:

> *This was a real Russian landowner's house, with all the Russian customs. The garden was very large, there were lanes of shady linden trees, an endless quantity of apple trees... There were horses, there were little carriages... and we were allowed to ride in them.*

Photos of Piatnitskoe show the children – the girls in long pale dresses, the boys in their cadet uniforms: white belted tunic jackets with high collars – gathered on a wooden verandah with carved railings or in the yard surrounded by lush trees. Sometimes someone is plucking a guitar, or they are sitting on wicker chairs around a table, perhaps having just taken tea.

In the late 1980s, a cousin of mine from Moscow found out where the old estate was located in the Kaluga area and went to see what was left of it. The only building she found still standing was the stable. She was enchanted by the surrounding beauty of hills and forests.

My grandmother and her siblings would also have been guests at the estates belonging to their grandfather, Prince Galitzine. Anna told of visiting one of these, Dubrovitsy, with Nadezhda, when they were both adolescents. She spoke of lilacs blooming in profusion, of boat rides on the river, and walks in the park.

Another of his estates, Kuzminki, has been engulfed by the suburbs of Moscow. On a visit in the late 1990s, I found that several of the remaining buildings of the estate were closed to visitors behind a high fence. But the grounds were accessible, including a small lake with a couple of old pavilions still on its shores. Since then the estate has become a historic site, and some of the old buildings house exhibitions. When I visited, the banks of the lake were crowded with groups, lunches spread out on blankets and children splashing in the water. Amid the nearly naked sunbaking bodies, plastic dishes and packaged food, it was hard to imagine my grandmother, in a long dress and ribbons, walking the same banks, or paddling on the lake chatting with her cousin.

My grandmother would have attended services in the estate church, which is also now open to all. It had been badly damaged during the Soviet era, but its restoration was well advanced. The gleaming repainted white eighteenth century building with two towers was packed with worshippers for a church holiday when I visited. They were gathered reverently before the ornate gilded iconostasis (altar screen), which shimmered in the rays of sun pouring through the windows.

The rambling wooden family home at Piatnitskoe – from what I can judge from the photographs – seems more appealing than the more formal stone structures at Kuzminki. Visions of idle summer days on the balcony are tantalising. There are no photos from winter – the family would have been in the city then; freezing temperatures and an icy vista would be less inviting. The social context, which is hinted at in one photograph in which several men with huge sickles over their shoulders walk past the house, would have also been less appealing to my twenty-first century sensibilities: many servants in the house and peasants in the fields labouring to maintain the leisured lifestyle of their masters.

It is hard to know how much thought my grandmother and the rest of her family gave to these social disparities. She was still very young, yet her daughter, my Aunt Nadia, believed she was already highly conscious of the gap between her life and that of others around her, and that this was an added reason for her gloomy moods. Anna backed this up, saying Nadezhda had first made her aware of issues of which she herself had been oblivious – for instance questions of fairness and world affairs. Both these observations were made many years later, in hindsight. However much my grandmother may have been aware of these issues then, in later years she would certainly have understood, in a very concrete way, what living with constant material difficulty was like. As incongruous as that would have seemed amid the spreading hectares of Piatnitskoe, this is what awaited her.

There are only two photographs that have survived in my direct family of my mother's parents together. Both are believed to have been taken in Serbia, after they had left Russia. Their marriage consisted of separations: war, flight by different routes, and serious illness – all stepping between them. It is not surprising they had only one child – my mother, and that there were so many gaps in her knowledge of her antecedents.

My mother's mother Natalia was only 43 years old when she died (1896-1940), at the start of the Second World War. The full impact of what that meant was only brought home to me when I visited her grave in Paris more than sixty years after her death. Her husband, my grandfather, buried with her, had only been 45 at his death and my other grandfather had also not lived to fifty. And yet her dates on the sad simple headstone jumped out at me with particular force. Perhaps it was because I had inherited my name from her and thus felt more of a link. Perhaps it was because her memory had been kept alive for me more than that of my other grandparents by my mother frequently speaking about her over the years. It also came from the knowledge that the relatively few years she had been given contained much pain and difficulty.

Although Natalia was not from as prominent a family as my other grandmother, she certainly would have had a comfortable childhood. She hailed from the landed gentry, her father's family owning an estate near Mogilev – now in Belarus. Further evidence of the family's position in society comes from the fact that Natalia and her younger sister were sent to be educated at the St Petersburg school of choice for young noblewomen, the Smolny Institute.

My mother knew little about Natalia's father, Aleksei Tcheboutcheff. He inherited his parents' estate and he was a military officer, rising in rank over time to lieutenant colonel. She believed that his career had kept him too occupied to start a family, so he married late, at almost forty years of age.

My mother knew a bit more about Natalia's mother, Maria Berkaloff. In an interview I recorded with my mother, she said her grandmother came from a more city-oriented family:

> *The Berkaloffs were a wealthy family, they often travelled, they had a big social life; they were*

CHAPTER ONE

*from St. Petersburg, from an elegant line.
My great-grandfather was married several times,
the family was huge – my mother tried to list it all out
for me at one point, but got totally confused by it all.*

Critical for the family in later years was the fact that the Berkaloffs owned property outside Russia, which was to help support them when they migrated to France. My mother would get to know her grandmother's brother Sergei, who had been a general in Russia, when she would live with his family in southern France for a year or two as a young schoolgirl.

Maria's life must have changed radically when she married Aleksei and left the city to live on his family's estate in Mogilev. She married very young, at about seventeen, yet was often left to run the place, when her husband's military work took him away. My mother was a baby when she and Natalia later fled from there, and had no memories of her own of it. But from her mother's stories, she had learned that it was one of the largest estates in the Mogilev area, and had been in the family for many generations. It was pretty much self-sufficient in terms of the food grown on it. Maria and a manager administered it and its staff during Aleksei's absences. At the same time she raised a family of five children (a sixth died of scarlet fever before his second birthday): Vladimir, Elena, my grandmother Natalia, Evgeniia, and another son whose name my mother could not remember. (Much later I learned it was Alexander.)

In running the estate, my great-grandmother was said to have been tough but kind towards her workers. In the few photos of her that remain in my family she does indeed appear to be a no-nonsense person. Her solid frame is enclosed in dark simple clothing, but she is an attractive woman, luxuriant hair and large dark eyes softening an otherwise austere image. Her estate workers would repay her good treatment of them during the Civil War, trying to defend her when the Red Army arrived. But she ended up leaving, going back to live in St Petersburg.

My great-grandfather did not live to see the dramatic political changes. While my mother was not sure when he died, she believed Maria had already been widowed before the time of the Revolution (probably even before the First World War).

Natalia was born on the estate in 1896. She was probably cared for and educated by governesses and teachers brought there. She later went away to study in St Petersburg. Like many of her class and gender, she attended the elite Smolny Institute, as did her younger sister Evgeniia. In the imposing three-storey classical palace, still standing in St Petersburg today on the banks of the Neva River, my mother said her mother was taught many subjects. Some would often come in handy in later years in emigration, such as languages – including French and German, sewing, embroidery and cooking. My mother said the level of teaching was high, for instance Natalia was able to "work off a picture to sew: she would be brought a magazine say, and shown a dress, and she would go ahead and make it, without patterns or anything".

Outside several special rooms, the institute has been described as having been somewhat gloomy, with long, dimly lit corridors with wooden floors. Historian Orlando Figes describes classrooms like barracks:

> *Like most girls' academies of the nineteenth century, it was austere and practical, more like a prison than a place to broaden the mind and uplift the spirit.*

CHAPTER ONE

My paternal grandfather's sisters also attended Smolny, and one of them, Olga, later wrote in her memoirs that occasionally family were invited for concerts, after which the students could dance with each others' brothers or cousins. Otherwise visitors were allowed four hours a week. Her brother Sergei, in his memoirs, recalled going to see his sisters there:

> *A grand reception was always held in a large hall.*
> *I never enjoyed these visits. Whatever sweets or*
> *presents we brought had to be inspected by the teachers.*
> *They circulated among the visitors and interrupted*
> *conversations. The atmosphere was strained and*
> *nobody was at ease. I pitied my two spirited sisters,*
> *for the discipline and strictness in their institute*
> *was much tougher than in the cadet academy...*
> *The "institutki" were not allowed to leave the grounds,*
> *were given no personal freedom and were severely*
> *reprimanded for insubordination.*

For Natalia, with her family in faraway Mogilev, there was not the opportunity for the four-hour weekly reunion, though she had relatives in St Petersburg who likely came to visit. The strictness of the institute does not seem to have been enough to block out external influences and events. Olga wrote that leaflets of Bolshevik propaganda appeared on the girls' desks one day. They reacted with outrage, immediately handing in the fliers.

While the institute may have been somewhat austere and strict, there is no question the girls were well looked after. And there were distractions. Besides learning practical skills, the letters and sciences, Olga wrote there were also lessons in "society dancing, especially the gavotte, the minuet and the polonaise... music and singing – both secular and sacred."

In one photo from the time of the main room of the school – the lavish grand ballroom – the girls are shown putting into practice their dance lessons. Lines of them in flowing dresses gracefully point their toes and create patterns with long scarves in their hands, accompanied by a grand piano. The scene is dwarfed by the huge, grandiose features in the room. American journalist John Reed, later witnessing revolutionary meetings in this ballroom, described it:

> *A lofty white room lighted by glazed white chandeliers holding hundreds of ornate electric bulbs, and divided by two rows of massive columns; at one end a dais, flanked by two tall many-branched light standards... Here on festal occasions had been banked brilliant military and ecclesiastical uniforms, a setting for Grand Duchesses...*

And while the students may not have been allowed to leave the grounds unescorted, there were plenty of group outings, according to Olga: theatre, opera, and – for final year girls – a sail in the imperial yacht along the Neva and on the Gulf of Finland.

Natalia was younger than my paternal grandfather's sisters Olga and Irina, though it is possible her time there would have overlapped with Irina's stay; it is intriguing to imagine they may have met there.

In 1917 the institute was to become a communist icon; the October Revolution would be directed from the same rooms where just months earlier aristocratic girls in long white aprons over severe dresses had recited declensions of French verbs, or had watched demonstrations of the latest sewing techniques. As Figes points out, the contrast could hardly be greater: the girls would be replaced by crowded meetings of revolutionaries, exhaling clouds of strong-smelling tobacco smoke, spitting sunflower seed husks everywhere and shouting "obscenities which the young gentlewomen of the Smolny school could not even have imagined."

But by then Natalia was long gone from Smolny.

My mother knew even less about her father Alexander's predecessors than she did of Natalia's. His family seems to have been from the nobility also. My mother believed that her paternal grandfather Ivan Kouprianoff had been a career officer, and that he had been posted at some point to the Mogilev headquarters of the Russian military as commander. She thought he died later at the hands of the Bolsheviks. As is the case for my mother's other grandfather, no photos of Ivan have survived in the western branch of our family.

Of his wife, Ekaterina Goussarevitch there was only one small trait my mother recalled being told about: her grandmother, she said, was very tiny, and had to bring a chair to stand on to embrace or kiss her relatives, something over which she was constantly teased.

Alexander (1890-1935) was born in Bialystok (now in Poland). He had siblings but my mother did not know how many or what later happened to most of them. The only one about whom she had some recollection was a brother, for she and her parents would take refuge with him for a time in Serbia, after they fled Russia. She also remembered hearing about a sister, who seems to have ended up in China.

Beyond that, my maternal grandfather's family is a blank.

Alexander attended high school in Bialystok and Mogilev. At some point he took courses in economics, documented in a 1914 certificate from the Moscow Commercial Institute. Eventually he followed his father's lead and trained for the military, becoming an ensign in an aeronautic detachment. Whether he was one of those who went up in observation balloons to carry out surveillance, I do not know.

Alexander, like his wife, died relatively young. Preceding his death, he spent many years in hospital. Thus most of the photographs my mother had of her father were of him in his officer role during the First World War, as a young, still healthy man. He wears a uniform and is often with other officers, or with military nurses. But to me he always seems out of place, usually the smallest-built of the men in the pictures. A pince-nez perches on his nose, and he looks as though a desk or a classroom would have been a more appropriate setting for him than the business of war.

Yet the war which engulfed Russia, along with much of Europe and beyond, would have a huge impact on all my grandparents – whether in uniform or not – as it did indeed on most of their generation, east and west. Political developments, which were building as my grandparents were growing into adulthood, ultimately had even more dramatic consequences for them and their country.

2

Protest and Patriotism

Palace Square is the focal point of St Petersburg: a large open expanse with the ornate Winter Palace and the Hermitage on one side, the curved General Staff building with its imposing arch complete with chariot and horses on top on the other. And overlooking all this, the nearly fifty-metre tall Alexander Column.

When I first saw the square in the 1970s, my appreciation of the stunning beauty of the eighteenth and nineteenth century buildings was perturbed by a feeling that I was surrounded by ghosts. I thought I could sense lurking shadows, I could almost see blood stains on the smooth cobblestones. I could picture chanting crowds advancing towards the Winter Palace waving banners and flags: ragtag collections of men, women, and children full of demands – and hope, and troops waiting in neat lines, guns at the ready. I could hear the volleys of bullets that abruptly silenced the chants. I could imagine the crowd running in panic, leaving dead and injured strewn across the square.

Yet as I looked around, the only groups of people to be seen were tourists being led by individuals holding not banners, but signs on poles with the word "Intourist" in Russian and Latin letters. The only shooting was from cameras, and the sounds were conversation and laughter as visitors speaking a variety of languages posed and took each other's photographs. A queue of buses waited at the edge of the square, their drivers in a huddle, perhaps sharing thoughts on the foibles of their latest load of foreigners, or grumbling about the constant shortages in the shops.

While my imaginings in Palace Square owed much to film reconstructions of the early twentieth century, the real events that happened there had been a fundamental yet undeciphered part of who I was for as long as I could remember. When I was growing up, the past was seen in two phases: Before the Revolution and After the Revolution. And while I had become aware early on of other such events – the French and the American Revolutions, for instance – THE Revolution was the one that happened in Russia in 1917. Later I realised THE Revolution was actually made up of two major events in 1917. The first was the February Revolution – though on the calendar in use in the rest of Europe, it happened in March – just as the October Revolution happened in November (Russia's calendar at the time was 13 days different to the one used in the West).

And there was yet another revolution leading up to these two – that of 1905.

From all the available information, it seems my ancestors were for the most part faithful supporters of the Tsar. But this did not mean they opposed political and social reform. Those who were working for change before and during 1917 were very often from the educated and upper classes, though many remained loyal to the monarchy; indeed a large part of Russia across the classes realised reform was both inevitable and necessary. What was in dispute were the extent and pace of change.

The memoirs of family members in my grandparents' generation all unanimously decry what happened to Russia after 1917. As a fuller picture of the repression and terror that occurred when the Bolsheviks took complete power has come out over the years since, there are few who would argue with their dismay over the ultimate course of events. There are hints in the memoirs on the views of various of my relatives on attempts at reform, through actions they took or choices they made, but few actual statements of their beliefs or hopes for the future.

An exception is in the memoir of my great-uncle Sergei, the brother of my paternal grandfather. He wrote that his father – my great-grandfather Alexander – expressed to him the need for change, sometime around 1906:

> *Papa was convinced that the only salvation for the old order was for Russia to convert to a constitutional monarchy along the lines of Great Britain. He also believed that the Tsar, dedicated to the idea of totalitarianism ordained by God, would never allow this to happen. Papa was very fearful for the future of our country.*

When he recorded his memories of that time many years later, Sergei's knowledge of what would happen may have sharpened his perception of his father's concerns. Yet such worries would not have been surprising. The future had looked uncertain for some time, with dissent and agitation for change, in one form or another, having grown over the second half of the nineteenth century. Indeed my great-grandfather had returned wounded from the Japanese war just a few weeks after the first major explosion of discontent in the twentieth: the 1905 Revolution.

The Russo-Japanese war over the nations' conflicting imperial ambitions in the east was a factor in this unrest. Dissatisfaction over the way it was being waged and criticism of lives being wasted, had bolstered opposition activity in late 1904. Other factors included the rapid industrialisation of Russia, which had sped the growth of an urban working class, mostly made up of peasants from the country. They often lived and worked in dreadful conditions, and the stories they told when they visited their villages added to discontent brewing there over the desire for land. Incipient politicians tried to wrest agreement for reforms from a reluctant Tsar. Those impatient for change organised strikes and protests.

In January 1905 Palace Square witnessed what came to be known as Bloody Sunday. A huge crowd, led by a priest holding aloft a cross, marched on the Winter Palace with a list of wide-ranging demands, from improved working conditions to political reforms. Among the demonstrators were children, and some in the crowd carried portraits of the Tsar. They were met by gunfire from troops guarding the palace. Other confrontations around the city brought further bloodshed: at the end of the day, scores were dead and hundreds injured.

This incident is seen as a major turning point: disbelief over the way a peaceful demonstration became a bloodbath, turned to anger, and historian Orlando Figes argues "in that one vital moment the popular myth of a Good Tsar which had sustained the regime through the centuries was suddenly destroyed."

Continuing unrest over the subsequent months led to the Tsar agreeing to some fundamental reforms. But these would prove to be too little too late.

In the meantime, the war with Japan ended in disaster for Russia: for the first time, a major European nation was defeated by an Asian one. Sergei recorded in his memoir that my great-grandfather was appointed to head a committee given the task of reorganising the armed forces. Other important changes were initiated, but the disturbing events of 1905 – both at home and on the international stage – would not have been reassuring for many Russians. Well might my great-grandfather have been concerned for the future.

In 1905, the oldest of my grandparents, Nikolai, was fifteen and the youngest, Natalia, was eight. The whereabouts of my maternal grandparents is unclear, though it is likely that Natalia was living on her parents' estate in Mogilev, in Belarus, still being educated at home. Her future husband, Alexander, was possibly also by then living in Mogilev. My paternal grandmother Nadezhda was ten. Her mother had died two years earlier, and it seems her father died sometime that year. For her and her siblings, grief and the adjustments to their new situation, living with their grandfather in Moscow, would have been the notable concerns of that year. Nikolai was perhaps the only one of the four in St Petersburg during the 1905 Revolution, studying in a military academy. But I have no record of what he witnessed and thought of what was going on.

In spite of their young years and their sheltered environments, my grandparents were likely somewhat aware, if not of the events, then at least of their echoes, judging by the recollections of some of those close to them. My great-uncle Sergei was eleven at the time, yet decades later, in his memoirs, he remembered something of the incidents that year. Not surprisingly, his most notable recollections were of those developments which had a direct impact on his life or of events which he himself witnessed. An encounter with a protest on the main street of St Petersburg, which leads to Palace Square, left a strong impression, even if he did not understand its import:

I remember Nevskii Prospekt in the evening – a vast movement of people... Suddenly... out of nowhere,

> *Cossacks appeared, they flew into the crowd, they broke it up, and then on the empty avenue there were scattered only hats and galoshes. Ambulance carriages quickly took away the crushed and the hurt. I was not afraid, everything interested me, I did not understand anything that was happening – but it was terrible.*
>
> *Often there was no electricity and we used candles, fresh bread was not always available. For there was a general strike and the railroads were not working. My preparations for exams went badly. My tutor often did not turn up, or he was distracted and not very interested in me. I think he was more occupied by some sort of revolutionary work and student meetings, though he never spoke to me about this.*

My paternal grandmother's cousin Anna also mentioned the events of 1905 in her memoir. She was thirteen and staying in the country at the time, and was aware that politics were being discussed all around her. The anxiety expressed by the adults was exacerbated for her by divisions and arguments among members of the household, especially between her parents over their views:

> *Miserable politics was at the time at the centre of everyone's attention... there were disturbances in Russia, the trains stopped, there was no mail, and discussions at the table became intensely unpleasant... I remember I prayed before the icon in my room: "Lord, please help, so there are no scenes", before I went to have breakfast or lunch.*

In the wake of the 1905 Revolution, Anna's stepfather decided to give part of his estate to the Peasant Land Bank. It helped those wanting to set up their own farms, outside the village communal system commonly in place, with reforms after 1905 encouraging the process. Anna said her stepfather

> ...*was, for that time, of liberal views. He felt that landowners did not have the right to have too much land, while the peasants did not have enough... [He] consulted my mother and she completely agreed with him that land had to be given to the peasants. Which was quickly done. Some land surveyors were brought in, some sort of papers were drawn up, I don't know the details of how it was all done. But in short, it was considered that this was handed over to the Peasant Bank... Nikolai Mikhailovich got no benefit from this, but the peasants of course all grew rich over it and were grateful to him to the very end. We only kept four cows, and of course horses – a troika, and I think two or three working horses. We no longer had pastureland, just flood plains and the grove that was closest to the house. Everything else was given to the peasants.*

Anna said her stepfather's neighbours – although they too advocated land reform – were not very happy with the example he set, especially as concessions had emboldened peasants in some areas to attack gentry homes and seize their land; "...soon liberal landowners stopped coming to see us," she said.

But if Anna's stepfather found himself somewhat isolated in the country, in the city he became part of the political changes that followed the 1905 Revolution. Among concessions wrung from the Tsar were the creation of the first parliament in Russia – the Duma –

and the legalisation of political parties. Anna's stepfather joined one of these – the Constitutional Democrats, or Kadets for short – and was elected to the new legislature. Made up of nobles, intelligentsia and professionals, the party supported retaining the monarchy, but it called for greatly reducing the power of the Tsar and for other major political reforms.

The Duma had little real power to change things – several of them were elected and then dissolved by the Tsar – nor were the cumbersome procedures and inexperience of such a new institution for Russia conducive to effective operation. Yet after 1905, Russian society had turned a corner. The Duma and other, limited reforms – such as more freedom in the media and various changes to assist peasant land ownership – brought heightened expectations. The desire and necessity for more change were evident both to the politicians and on the streets, which now and then erupted into strikes or protests.

It was again my grandfather's brother Sergei who wrote about a brush with street unrest. It was 1910, he was sixteen and studying at a military academy in Moscow. He was still politically naïve, yet his description gives a sense of the type of volatility that was often evident in these years. Sergei, dressed in his uniform, came across a rally marking the death of the author Leo Tolstoy, a hero to some activists because of his rejection in his later years of authority and his determination to give up his property and to live like a peasant:

> *Once I found myself in a student demonstration at the time when Leo Tolstoy died. The students were gathering in small groups, trying to walk in the middle of the street, disrupting traffic, creating disorder and yelling "eternal memory" in frenzied voices. The police*

CHAPTER TWO

> *were... restoring order, pushing groups of students into side streets. I ended up in one of the side streets, in the general crowd, but a policeman saw me and said: "Go to the Corps, there is nothing for you to do here." And it was true, I had no business there, I had found myself in the thick of the crowd by chance and I could in no way understand why the memory of the great Russian writer was being honoured in this fashion.*

1905 and its aftermath laid the groundwork for the events of 1917. My sources do not reveal how much my young grandparents knew about everything that happened, how they felt about it, or how it contributed to their attitudes leading up to 1917. Yet the bits of family evidence from people close to them provide hints of how they may have learned about the start of a series of developments that would turn their lives upside down, and whose ripple effects would continue to be felt many decades later, into my generation.

The looming world war would further complicate the political situation and eventually bring it to a head. By the time it began, my grandparents were no longer watching the events from the distance of childhood; they were all young adults.

On the 19th of July (August first on the Western European calendar) 1914 Germany declared war on Russia. Events in preceding years, which had pitted Austria-Hungary and Germany against Russia's fellow Slavs in the Balkans, had aroused strong pan-Slavist feelings. There had been anti-German agitation and demonstrations in

Russia, in spite of tight connections between the German and Russian courts. But the Tsar and his government had hesitated to get involved in conflict. The army was seen as being unprepared and there was a fear – at least among some – that a military campaign could fuel the growing social unrest. On the other side, there were those who felt that facing a common enemy would unite the Russian people and stave off political discontent. Before the government could decide what to do, Germany's declaration of war left Russia no choice.

At first there was indeed a patriotic show of support for the regime. My paternal grandmother's cousin Anna told of witnessing an outburst of anti-German feeling in Moscow, a few months into the war:

> *...we saw a terribly big, noisy crowd, they were carrying pictures of the Tsar and Tsarina, and... with those same pictures they were breaking shop windows, and throwing out all sorts of products. This was an anti-German demonstration... Pianos were flying and were crashing on the pavement, dishes, materials, ribbons, writing paper, and goodness knows what else was landing in the middle of the street. One woman rushed over to pick up some fabric and someone ran to her and said: "Aren't you ashamed, you want to take German junk," and she of course immediately backed away. The tramways were running wrapped in lace... it was as if there was some sort of carnival. It was both terrifying and worrying.*

Anna's feelings would have been shared by others: approval for the patriotism and wonder at such displays, combined with nervousness over the destruction and the frenzy of the crowd. The increasing incidents of street unrest had emboldened many ordinary Russians; there was a growing understanding among people like Anna that such discontent could be turned to other, less desirable ends. Patriotism on a broad scale would be short-lived. Discontent, on the other hand, would be fuelled by events at the front, which brought much grief as the casualty count grew.

In Moscow, ten minutes' walk from the Kremlin, there is a pair of creamy-yellow coloured buildings, a couple of storeys high. The condition of these buildings when I first saw them in 1997 was somewhat less decrepit than many of Moscow's other pre-revolutionary structures. Still, the plaster was stained or peeling here and there, and the grimy windowpanes matched the scrappiness of the yard in exuding an atmosphere of neglect. Amid the shady trees in the yard sat an imposing statue of the nineteenth century writer Nikolai Gogol, who spent his last years living here.

During the Soviet era, according to academic of Slavic literature Svetlana Boym, the statue of Gogol was moved here from a major intersection. This was because the authorities felt it too "mystical and gloomy for cheerful Socialist Realist Soviet life" to be in such a public location. She wrote that a more upbeat version of him was placed where this statue had been. A library and museum devoted to Gogol now occupy the buildings. But the rooms in them had been *kommunalkas* during part of the Soviet era: several families would have been crammed in communal apartments, into spaces that might have been used as parlours, studies, or dressing rooms before the Revolution.

This was the family home of my paternal grandmother's

first husband; she had lived here, on the lower floor of one of the buildings at the start of the First World War. But while her living conditions were unimaginably luxurious to those who came later, her time here could not have been more unhappy. As I wandered around the buildings, encircled by an old black iron fence and hemmed in by busy traffic, I wondered which corner might have contained Nadezhda's rooms, which windows would have looked in on a young woman trying to come to terms with the terrible news that came from the front.

Sometime in the year or two before the war began, my grandmother met Andrei Katkov, a member of a prominent Moscow family, who was completing the Moscow Lyceum. They fell in love and became engaged to be married. In her memoirs, Nadezhda's cousin Anna remembered Andrei as a pleasant man, tall and slim, but not very handsome. She spoke of the pair coming to her place and of their happiness together. She had married about a year earlier, and from the vantage point of her established household, she envied them their young love and the excitement with which they anticipated their life together. Nadezhda and Andrei were married in May 1914. They were both just nineteen years old. They spent a few weeks at his family's *dacha* in the Caucasus, then settled in St Petersburg.

When war was declared, Andrei and his brother Mikhail were among the first to volunteer. They joined a cavalry regiment and were soon sent to the front. Among others who were quickly sent into battle was Nadezhda's oldest brother, Dimitri. Many years later, Anna recalled the painful send-off for the group that included Dimitri and her own husband. She clearly remembered the terrible tension, the fear that separations would be long and maybe permanent.

CHAPTER TWO

Anna said all the officers went to church for confession and communion. Afterwards couples exchanged small gold medallions containing their photographs. She remembered talk of dying for a glorious cause (but also one warning from a mother to an officer and his wife not to cheat on each other during their separation, something the woman saw as more terrible than death). There was a parade. A relative of the Tsar's was there to bless the men with an icon the ruler had sent.

The commander prohibited families coming to the train station to see off the military trains, but the wives rebelled, saying he could order his men around but not them. So families gathered on the platform as evening fell, amid great enthusiasm and patriotic songs. Emotions ran high, but Anna said not one person on the platform cried before the trains pulled out, holding their tears so those leaving would not see them. When her husband's train set off, as the lights faded down the track, she heard a voice call out "pray for us!"

Her cousin Dimitri's train was one of the last to leave. Anna said he was in a terribly distraught state as she made the sign of the cross over him and said good-bye.

Some days later, Anna went to see her cousin Nadezhda. She found my grandmother disconsolate and pessimistic over her husband's fate:

> *She was as if made of stone, my poor Nadia, only her eyes burned – with a frightful terrible glitter. She said to me "I know he will die, I know what will he. It's terrible, terrible." No matter how much I tried to convince her, no matter how much I assured her that nothing would happen, she constantly repeated, "no, no, I know that this will be."*

Nadezhda sometimes saw things from the dark side, but her pessimism in this case was well-founded. In one of the earliest encounters of the war, Andrei was killed, as she had predicted, along with his brother. He died in the first week of August, less than three months after his wedding. The brothers were killed on Russia's northwestern front, near Kaushen, an east Prussian village. They were part of an offensive that aimed to force Germany to move troops east and thus relieve the French in the west. Though it was successful in this, it resulted in a heavy human toll.

Nadezhda joined her parents-in-law in the grim task of going to claim the two bodies, to bring them back for burial. My Aunt Nadia said that her mother conveyed to her the dreadful memories of her trip to the front many years later: the fields strewn with dead horses and battle debris, frightening sounds of nearby conflict, her mother-in-law's advice to start smoking to mask the smells of death.

The brothers were buried on their family's estate. The memorial services held by the family were echoed across the country. The mourning from the very first weeks of the war was repeated many times over as the death toll multiplied. For while the army had been more prepared than the Germans had anticipated – a great deal of effort had been put into the military after Russia's defeat in its war with Japan – lack of transport infrastructure and shortages of supplies soon became problems. The political instability at home also had an impact, reflected in some erratic decision-making and questioning of authority in the conduct of the war.

Nadezhda settled with her in-laws in Moscow in the buildings near the Kremlin. It was a house of mourning; there were constant *panikhidas* – religious services for the dead. She was extremely miserable and shaken. She would go for walks and forget where she was.

Soon there was more bad news. Her grandfather, who had raised Nadezhda and her siblings after the deaths of their parents, died not long after the start of the war. He was 74 years old. The separation from his favourite grandson Dimitri and all the events surrounding the war and the deaths of so many young sons of families he knew, were said to have hastened his death.

My great-uncle Dimitri, as the eldest sibling, was given leave from the front to come to Moscow to settle the family's affairs. Anna said that when she saw Dimitri she feared the worst for him. His eyes had changed completely. She said it was hard to describe, but his was the type of look that suddenly seemed to fix on something not there, to become focused and concentrated, the look of "all those who have seen so much horror and death".

Later when Dimitri returned once more on leave, he asked Anna whether she thought he would survive. She reassured him, but she herself did not believe her own words, and she felt that he too knew he would be killed. A month after that second leave, in November 1914, my great-uncle Dimitri died at the front.

I have no record of how my grandmother accepted the news about her oldest brother – the third loss in four months. I can barely begin to imagine her grief and incomprehension, feelings shared by so many in Russia and all over Europe as the Great War continued.

Amid her grief, my grandmother knew she had to find a way to move on. She and her younger sister, whom she had brought to live with her, had their own suite of rooms in the Katkov house, they had their own carriage with a driver and a pair of horses so they could move around independently, her sister had a governess to continue her education. There was never a shortage of money for anything that was required or desired.

Nadezhda's mother-in-law, having lost both her sons, turned her affection towards her daughter-in-law and became increasingly attached to her. My grandmother felt somewhat constrained by this affection. Anna said she felt a need to break free from it and from the atmosphere of mourning in the house. So Nadezhda decided to become a nurse.

As the war continued, women on the home front increasingly sought to contribute, many by taking up nursing. Aristocratic homes had sections converted into hospitals, and the women volunteered their services in them.

My maternal grandmother Natalia was among these hastily trained nurses. A couple of certificates from late 1914 state that she took a wartime nursing course in Mogilev and then worked there for several months, helping with bandaging, attending operations, and caring for the wounded. It is unclear whether she continued this work after that, for there is also a document saying she successfully completed a teaching certificate at the Imperial Women's Pedagogical Institute in Petrograd in March 1917 (the name St Petersburg had been Russianised to Petrograd at the start of the war). Perhaps she studied and put in nursing shifts simultaneously.

There are a couple of photos of Natalia in nurse's uniform. One is dated January 1915, when she was eighteen years old. In the other photo, which is not clearly dated, she is part of a group of five young nurses with an older woman in the middle. Natalia is looking at the camera with large, vulnerable eyes. Behind the group are bits of hospital equipment: large bottles with tubes coming out of them, the end of a bed, the corner of a sink. These women seem very young to be facing the tasks that must have been placed before them.

My other grandmother's cousin Anna also joined the many women helping in medical facilities. She said that some did it because it was fashionable, and well-seen as a demonstration of patriotism:

> *In Tsarskoe Selo, in Petrograd, in Moscow, in all the cities of Russia, many new infirmaries started to appear, like mushrooms after rain. They were opened everywhere, by whoever could do so, and on the street there started to appear an endless number of white kerchiefs. Everyone who could – young and middle-aged women – went into nursing. For some it was like a vocation – the majority of course. But there were those who got into it because of the triangular headscarves. They were named after them – "sestry dlia kosinki" (sisters of the headscarf). Though this type dropped out quite quickly because in the end they weren't that interested. But others were incredibly self-sacrificing, and from them came wonderful nurses.*

While Natalia and Anna pursued nursing, Nadezhda – in spite of her best intentions – found she could not work with the war wounded as the sight of blood made her feel faint. So she put her energies into visiting patients.

Through Anna, she met the man who would become her second husband and my paternal grandfather. Nikolai had dropped his finance ministry job when the war had begun, and rejoined his regiment, quickly going off to the front. Nadezhda met him when he was home on leave after being injured. This was probably in late

1915, the second time he was wounded, when, according to his military record, he needed nearly six months to recover.

By all accounts, Nikolai was immediately taken with Nadezhda. But Anna said that her cousin was still a long way from thinking about another marriage:

> *...he had unusually good looks. I wouldn't say he was likeable, he was very cold rather. But he fell madly in love with Nadia and passed the whole evening next to her. He even made her a proposal a few days later, but she refused him, saying she would never marry. She could not even think about marriage, she was pining for Andrei so much.*

From everything I know about my grandfather, it is hard to imagine him as cold. Other family stories portray him as having a warm, gentle sense of humour, a great tolerance for people, and dogged persistence in the face of hardship. He was still a very young man; whatever he may have been like then, he may have changed over time, the difficult events of the coming years no doubt leaving deep marks.

Nikolai went back into action in December 1915. Seven months later, he was among a force of imperial guards sent into battle near the Stokhod River in what is now Ukraine. This was part of Russia's southwestern front in an offensive against the Germans to draw away forces from battlefronts where the French and Italians were struggling. At Stokhod, the Russians succeeded in breaking through enemy lines, but this came at a high price.

The Russian attack began in the afternoon of July 15th (July 28) 1916 through swampy country. On the fiftieth anniversary of the battle, an émigré publication in Paris carried an article by one of those who also took part. V. Timchenko-Ruban' wrote that the first units to advance came under heavy machine-gun and rifle fire from enemy forces and that "above their heads burst a whole rainstorm of shrapnel".

A document on the awarding of a medal to Nikolai for his actions in this battle states that my grandfather's company, under his leadership, was at the front of the attack, and that although already injured in the shoulder, he was the first to reach and start cutting what was described as the enemy's "strongly fortified" wire barrier. Eyewitness accounts quoted in the document include that of another officer in the company, Mikhail Parovchenko:

...when the regiment was ordered to advance, the tenth company went in the first line, so that it was we who had to surmount the [enemy's] wire entanglement. In spite of a hurricane of gunfire from the enemy the company, carried along by the commander... Lieutenant Apouchtine – quickly moved to the trenches of the enemy; just before the wire entanglement... Lieutenant Apouchtine was wounded, but in spite of the wound he continued to command... Bursting into the trenches of the enemy, our company took prisoner seven officers and 170 of lower rank, many were killed, while the rest threw themselves into flight... Having gone another few steps Lieutenant Apouchtine received two more heavy wounds to his left hand...

Timchenko-Ruban' was in a unit which moved in later in the day and he recalled the sight that greeted them:

The wounded floundered in the water, they were drowning in deep canals and ditches full of water.

What was happening was so horrible, that it is difficult, impossible to describe... We continually stumbled on the corpses of those killed and on wounded who had crawled away, we heard groans and cries for help, our feet sank into the swamp... [In the morning] The rising sun quickly dispersed the fog over the swamp and lit up a picture, unforgettable because of its horror. The whole swamp was sown with the dead.

The document about Nikolai's decoration summarises the losses in his company in the fighting at the Stokhod as 135 dead, while his regiment suffered 1200 deaths and injuries.

Criticisms at the time of what were seen as tactics bringing unnecessarily high casualty tolls throughout the Russian war effort came not only from internal opponents of the regime. One of the critics was the British liaison officer with the Russian forces. In his published dairies, Sir Alfred Knox bemoaned overall Russian problems of shortages of military equipment and even clothing, and poor and slow transport facilities. While admiring some of the senior commanders at the front, he had strong criticism for others and for those in headquarters. He wrote that their ineptitude ranged from frequent changes of commanding officers at various levels, to poor planning and coordination, and discouragement of initiative (which he blamed partly on fears among military superiors that too much independence among lower ranks could be dangerous). Knox described the senior commanders of the section of the front at the Stokhod as operating in "an atmosphere of failure and mistrust", and he wondered scathingly why "The Russian Command for some unknown reason seems always to choose a bog to drown in." The issue of ineffective leadership and decision-making is often cited by historians. Many agree with Knox's assessment, but others temper the criticism by pointing out that the Russians fought well in spite of such handicaps and taking into account many logistical difficulties.

Florence Farmborough, a British nurse working with a Russian medical outfit at the front, wrote in her memoir that she was impressed by the attitude of the fighting men, whatever the failings of their superiors:

> *The patience, the sustained endurance of the heavily-wounded is heart-rending... If anyone should ask me what I consider the outstanding qualities of the Russian soldier, I would have no hesitation in replying: patience and endurance.*

My grandfather was lucky to survive the fighting at the Stokhod. But he was very seriously wounded: he was hit in the head by a bullet, in the left side by another, and by many more in the left arm. His sister Olga wrote in her memoirs that he was left for dead, but his assistant went in search of him:

> *His batman, a boy of nineteen, found him unconscious, placed him in a wheelbarrow, and lugged him to the field hospitals. But after the nurses took his pulse, they would say there was nothing to be done, that he would die. But the brave little soldier continued his round to save his officer and thus he finally arrived at an English hospital seconded to Russia. The English surgeon became interested in this absolutely impossible case, amputated Nikolai's injured arm, and to stop the hemorrhaging, injected him with a serum that did not exist among the Russians. Thus operated on, he was to have been taken below into a shelter, as German*

planes were shelling hospitals, in spite of big red crosses on them. But Nikolai refused to be moved down and not a single bullet touched him, even though the tent ended up full of bullet holes.

Nikolai's brother Vladimir, who fought in the same battle, was also injured but not as seriously. Their other brother Sergei was allowed leave from his unit and said he would take Nikolai home. But the doctors believed he was dying and could not be moved. Years later, on Nikolai's death in France, Sergei told how he had felt that his brother would certainly not have survived if he had remained at the front. Against instructions, he got Nikolai onto a train and spent three days continually by his side, fighting off efforts to have him removed every time the train stopped. Sergei's defiance paid off. Once home, Nikolai slowly regained his health. After a period of convalescence in the Crimea, he returned to the reserve of his regiment, at Tsarskoe Selo, just outside Petrograd. There he took on the training of recruits. For his role at Stokhod, Nikolai received the Order of St George, Russia's highest military award at the time (as did his brother Vladimir).

Nikolai felt that his disability meant he could not impose himself on a wife and gave up the idea of marriage. Meanwhile Nadezhda, having found she was unable to give her life a purpose through nursing, had decided she would seek to have a family and dedicate herself to it. In response to Anna's encouragement, Nikolai proposed to Nadezhda again. This time she agreed to marry him, though Anna said she accepted mostly out of compassion for his condition for she still felt she could not duplicate the strong affection she retained for her first husband.

They were married in January 1917 and went to Crimea for a honeymoon. By the time they returned, Anna said Nadezhda had

found a measure of happiness:
> *I was surprised to find her calm, satisfied, even happy, as I had almost never seen her. Apouchtine was just radiant. Truly, he was a hero, awarded the Order of St George, and married to the woman he loved, who was of course both beautiful and very rich. But I think in this sense he was completely disinterested – he loved her not for her money, something he would prove by the actions of his whole life, including later when they were completely brought to ruin.*

They were to go through much together, and by all accounts, it was a successful and close marriage. From my grandmother's own diaries, when she described his death about twenty years later, it is clear she had grown to love him deeply.

The movements of my other grandfather during the First World War are more of a mystery. An initial search in military archives in Moscow did not locate his full record, coming up with just two documents from 1916 and 1917. The latter document states that he had been in action from the start of the war, at least some of the time operating in the north of the Russian front, in Estonia. He was part of the aeronautical detachment of the Sixth Siberian Corps. In November 1916 Alexander was awarded the Order of St Stanislaus for military valour. There is no information about which specific action won him the medal, but his commander noted that he was "courageous" and showed much "fervour" at all times, wanting "to be closer to the military operations" of his unit. The document states that he was married; his and Natalia's wedding had taken place in early 1915, presumably during leave Alexander had from the front.

He was badly wounded at some point, with shrapnel lodging in his spine, but it is likely that this occurred during the Civil War. Several photos of him in uniform and apparently in good health, with other military men, dating up to late 1917 back that supposition.

As the war dragged on, Russia's growing death toll – and the perceptions of blunders by the government and military leadership – fuelled those who opposed the regime. War weariness, bolstered by anti-government agitation, resulted in increasing numbers of desertions from the front. At home, food and other shortages soured things further. Even conservative politicians – among them patriotic nobles and members of the royal family – began to question some of the Tsar's actions and to press for him to conduct meaningful consultations on decisions, to little avail. Anna said that in her circle of relatives and friends too, she heard grumbles, for instance over government ministers being constantly changed.

This was possibly in 1916, when the Tsar was at the front, and the Tsarina was making many of the decisions on domestic matters, including the naming of ministers. Behind many of her actions was Grigorii Rasputin. A controversial 'holy man', he held great sway over the Tsarina due to his seeming ability to help her son Aleksei, the heir to the throne, overcome the hemophiliac attacks that he often suffered. Anna only saw Rasputin once:

> *It was a bad season for slush, the road was terrible; a carriage came towards me, and it turned out Rasputin was travelling in it. As we were moving very slowly, our eyes met. He was by the window of his carriage, I was travelling in a cab. All evening I wanted to wash out my eyes, to not see this face,*

> *so sharp was his look, so piercing as though penetrating into my very soul, and most unpleasant.*

Others who met Rasputin often also later remembered his eyes and what they saw as the evil in them. Perceptions of his power at the time and thus over the course of events likely influenced these recollections. Anna would have been aware of other such descriptions of a person with remarkable eyes, by any account. Their significance no doubt increased as he came to represent for many one of the causes behind the Revolution.

As the months went on, Anna said, whispered attacks on the Tsar and his family began to be spoken out loud, often along with Rasputin's name. And then, one night in December 1916, she was helping to sell drinks at a fund-raising concert for the war wounded, when some members of the audience circulated astonishing information:

> *They brought such news – it amazed everyone – that Rasputin had been killed. What – Rasputin killed? By whom was he killed?... I have to say, particularly a lot of champagne was drunk, because all hopes were pinned on the thought that now Rasputin was gone, everything should go back to normal.*

It later emerged that he had been assassinated by a group of prominent aristocrats. While some members of high society had been entranced by Rasputin, others – including members of the Tsar's closest circle – had become increasingly wary of his role. Indeed Anna's father had lost his position as an aide-de-camp to the ruler on suspicion he was linked to a report criticising Rasputin, which had originated from a highly placed official. Such reports indicated an understanding of his negative influence on the country's affairs, but perceptions of the extent of the holy man's power likely evolved further in later years in the thinking of those who supported the monarchy. Anna and many others in her social group were reluctant to place the blame for the problems in Russia and the subsequent events on the Tsar. In hindsight, the tendency to demonise Rasputin as the source of many questionable decisions would provide a more acceptable way of making sense of developments. Historians too believe Rasputin's role, in influencing the Tsarina and through her the Tsar, was a factor in Russia's slide into growing crisis. But it was one among many that helped pave the way for revolution.

Hopes that things would improve after Rasputin's assassination did not eventuate. There was little good news from the war, and the economic situation continued to deteriorate. Shortages were compounded by increasing resistance by the peasants to give up their production for the cities. Anna spoke of long queues at bread shops in Petrograd, of strikes becoming more frequent, of some newspapers starting to openly call for revolution. Morale was so low and the atmosphere so tense, that officers she knew who came home on leave were keen to get back to the battle front as they felt the "…panic situation in Petrograd was unbearable for the nerves". Anna herself experienced growing feelings of fear without quite being able to define exactly what she was afraid of.

At about this time, my grandfather's brother Sergei was called back from the front. He was seconded to a special Combined Regiment made up of officers and soldiers from a range of units, whose main function was the protection of the Tsar and his family. He was sent to the section of this regiment that had the task of guarding the Tsarina and her children, who were staying at Tsarskoe Selo, just outside the capital. In his memoirs, he too noted the growing atmosphere of disquiet in Petrograd: there were rumours and gossip all over town, including inferences he found highly distasteful, about the relationship Rasputin had had with the Tsarina, and about her true loyalties, in view of her German origins.

In spite of his firm allegiance to the regime, Sergei had had occasion, during his time at the front, to note the arrogance of some generals. He felt they often had too little close contact with the soldiers and thus were sometimes unaware of the consequences of their decisions or just too inflexible to adjust them to match the circumstances. But in view of the atmosphere of discontent, he was more concerned about disloyalty in all ranks. He questioned the lack of any political vetting of officers placed in responsible positions, even those entrusted with protecting the royal family:

> *...never – either in peacetime, or at the front – was there either a question or the shadow of a question about political trustworthiness. I don't know and I don't think that any section of the police made inquiries about regimental officers. Maybe it should have been done, but somehow, the thought never entered one's head that an officer could be politically suspect and not loyal when it came to the royal family.*

Sergei wrote this many years after the events, perhaps influenced by hindsight – and other later writings about possible sabotage within the military. But already in January 1917, he had reason for concern. A soldier who had also been in the Combined Regiment came to warn him to leave it for his own safety, after an uncle of his who was in the Duma hinted of trouble to come for anyone too close to the Tsar. Sergei was appalled by the implications of this tip-off, which to him demonstrated "that even in our exclusive circle of people, guarding the Tsar's family, all sorts of undesirable propaganda could penetrate."

While in the Combined Regiment, Sergei often travelled to nearby Petrograd. During his visits there in early 1917, he found that the imprint of the war was increasingly evident everywhere, that more necessities were in short supply and that the mood was ever more ominous:

> *...I visited my relatives and friends. Everywhere I was bombarded with questions about life in Tsarskoe Selo, and I found myself often surprised and outraged at how many falsehoods and how much unfairness there were in these questions in relation to the Tsar's family. Petrograd was seething... Of course, the main role was played by the malicious propaganda of the bitter enemies of the Tsar's regime, but also by society's complete lack of information about life in Tsarskoe Selo... My soul was pained, seeing and hearing all this. I strived to return home more quickly to Tsarskoe Selo, quiet and buried in snow.*

This quiet would not last long, for when the February Revolution began, it very quickly found its way to the little town.

"Some sort of new life was beginning..."

Tsarskoe Selo – now called Pushkin – is virtually a suburb of St Petersburg, just 25 kilometres south. The two were linked in 1837 by the first rail service in Russia, built primarily to transport the royal family to its palaces in Tsarskoe Selo and nearby Pavlovsk. What was the imperial waiting room still exists in St Petersburg's Vitebsk Station, a grandiose hall with chandeliers, carved wooden panelling and paintings of other old train stations.

When I travelled on the line with my sister and father, 160 years after it opened, the service was more unreliable than during probably most of its long history. There were frequent and abrupt train cancellations for budgetary and maintenance reasons, part of the overall disorganisation of early post-Soviet times.

Delayed by half a day in our investigation of venues connected to our family's past because of this, we had plenty of opportunity to look around the area adjacent to the Vitebsk Station. The pavements were crowded with stalls selling food and clothing. There was also a bright yellow mini-tanker with a tap, from which a woman was dispensing *kvas* – a traditional slightly fizzy drink, which can be mildly alcoholic. Like so much in post-communist Russia, this tradition was giving ground to the onslaught of western influences. The availability of brand name soft drinks and bottled, overly sweet and bubbly versions of *kvas* itself, were making the once ubiquitous mini-tankers an endangered sight.

But the most distressing sellers at railway stations were people in two rows forming a reception line for passengers. These were mostly elderly women. They held up two or three items, sometimes only one. Some sold bottles of vodka or loaves of bread, presumably for a tiny profit over what they paid for them. Others offered homemade *pirozhki*, little deep-fried pockets of dough filled with meat or cabbage or eggs. Occasionally a woman would hold out a pathetic bunch of half-wilted wild flowers, picked somewhere on a rare patch of earth not crowded with people and buildings.

The saddest ones were those who held up a second-hand jacket, a pair of shoes, or a dress. Clearly they had nothing left to resort to, other than their own wardrobes, to try to fetch a few desperately needed roubles. Unlike street vendors in many parts of the world who cajole and harass passersby, these salespeople – women with kerchiefs tied under their chins and lined, defeated faces – did not tout, as they stood there for hours or days, silently holding out their wares. Above them towered flashing neon signs or huge billboards advertising luxury goods with foreign logos, luring a different sort of Russian – the newly-rich, beneficiaries, and some would say looters, of former state enterprises that were broken up when the Soviet Union collapsed. These overnight converts from communism to capitalism zoomed past the lines of *babushkas* in late-model western cars.

Trying to understand 1917 in 1997, for me there was something terribly poignant in this glaring gap between the poor and the rich. So much blood had been spilt, so much misery endured for so long, and yet things seemed to have come full circle: the players were different, but yet again, this was a society of great wealth and great poverty. Nearly three decades on, one has to hope that the disadvantaged of Russia are now faring better.

CHAPTER THREE

When we finally boarded a train and travelled to Pushkin, we also found plenty of evidence of flaunted wealth there, this time from the past. Tsarskoe Selo means Tsar's Village. In the Soviet era it was renamed Pushkin in honour of Russia's favourite poet Alexander Pushkin, who lived and studied there for a time in the nineteenth century. While the original name is gone (though creeping back into usage), two eighteenth century tsarist palaces remain.

The bigger and more opulent of the two, the Catherine Palace, was severely damaged during the Second World War by German bombardment. In spite of its very tsarist stamp, the Soviet government went to great pains to restore a large part of the building to its original splendour. It was after all a popular tourist destination, a magnet for much-needed foreign currency. Perhaps it was also seen as a useful example of the outrageous extravagance of the old regime.

And extravagant it is. The intense blue exterior of the building is smothered in icing-like white and gold trim, columns and statues. At one end, on the roof above the chapel, are glistening golden onion domes. Inside, there is one lavish room after another, all richly adorned – from wooden marquetry floors with complicated inlaid designs to ornately painted ceilings with huge cascading chandeliers, and in-between: walls decorated with valuable paintings, gilded woodcarving, patterned silk, or mosaics of semi-precious stones.

The smaller, more understated Alexander Palace was where the family of Nicholas the Second spent the years of the First World War and the first part of 1917. A museum in the 1920s and 30s, the building was not as severely damaged as the Catherine Palace during the Second World War – but nor was it as completely refurbished. For many years, it served in various government capacities. More recently it has undergone extensive restoration work. Much of it was reopened to the public in late 2021. In 1997, it was all locked up.

Between and around the palaces are extensive parklands, with ponds, bridges and a scattering of small buildings: former tearooms, bathhouses, performance spaces and such, in eclectic architectural styles. Wandering in the palace precinct, I imagined that this enclave of the tsarist era might have looked quite similar in 1917, when a number of my relatives were living close by, as the February Revolution approached from nearby Petrograd.

There were some military units based at Tsarskoe Selo, where training was done and reserves were housed. This is where my paternal grandfather Nikolai brought his bride Nadezhda after their honeymoon. Her cousin Anna, and Nikolai's sister Olga also had homes here while their officer husbands served at the front. Walking in the residential area between the palaces and the train station, it was intriguing to speculate where exactly these relatives had lived. Olga's daughter, on a visit in 1970, had managed to find her mother's old address, even though the street name had been changed, only to discover the building was gone. But might Nikolai and Nadezhda's or Anna's former homes still exist among the newer, Soviet-era apartment blocks? My grandfather's brother Sergei was also in Tsarskoe Selo then, based at the Alexander Palace, serving in the Combined Regiment guarding the Tsarina and her children.

As for my grandparents on my mother's side, I have only a few clues on their whereabouts during the events about to unfold. I can only wonder what they witnessed and experienced, and the impact the turmoil had on them. In early 1917 they were already married but it is likely that Alexander was at the front. Natalia's Petrograd teaching certificate is dated about a month after the February coup. So she may have been a witness to the start of the Revolution. Did

CHAPTER THREE

she see out many more events in the city? It seems that some time that year she returned to her parents' estate. Were the disturbances part of the reason she left the capital? Or perhaps, with Mogilev closer to the front, she went there in the hope of having more opportunities to see her husband.

It is unlikely I will ever know the answers to these questions. I can only rely on the memoirs of my father's relatives for a sense of how at least that side of the family experienced the February Revolution. Being in Tsarskoe Selo, just that short distance from Petrograd, in their recollections there is a sense of their being part of the drama, yet on the edge of it, at least at first, until events engulfed the town as well.

Towards the end of February 1917, Nikolai and Nadezhda arrived in Tsarskoe Selo from a month's honeymoon in Crimea. Since his left arm had been amputated at the battlefront, my grandfather had been working with the reserve of his regiment in the town. His mother and his sister Olga had prepared his apartment for the newly-weds. On February 25th there was a housewarming in the young couple's home, as Olga described in her memoir:

> ...the famous chef I have already mentioned prepared a dinner no less notable; I remember there was "ukha" (fish soup)... particularly creamy and tasty. After dinner the regimental band gave our ears a treat. And this was taking place [just]... before the Revolution erupted, but who could have known it!...
> Life should then have been quiet for them; Nikolai, an invalid, no longer had to return to the front.

Nadezhda's cousin Anna remembered the atmosphere differently:
There were singers, it all seemed cheerful, but in fact there was anxiety in our hearts. Friends of Nikolai's who had come from Petrograd said that there, disturbances were beginning... They spoke about strikes, shooting at policemen. We continued to drink wine and to listen to the singers, but... within us there was a lot of nervousness.

The discrepancy in these memories may have been due to Olga's thoughts having been taken up with getting the apartment ready in time. She was also occupied with her first child, a daughter born just four months earlier. Anna's first son, by contrast, was already three years old. Perhaps too, her personal connections to recent happenings in Petrograd – her father's transfer away from the Tsar's side, and also the dismissal of an uncle from the ministry – had made her more aware of the situation.

At the same time as my grandparents and their friends were enjoying the housewarming, crucial developments were occurring in Petrograd. There had been street protests during the preceding days over growing food shortages. The Tsar, at military headquarters near the front, was kept informed of events in the capital, but was apparently misled as to their seriousness. That evening Petrograd's military commander received a telegram from Nicholas, with directions to restore order. The next day, February 26th, police and soldiers fired on demonstrators. Dozens were killed or wounded. The bloodshed set off more angry protests, and mutinies in the military, and a political crisis that had been growing for months, if not years, came to a head.

As the unrest in Petrograd grew, the residents of Tsarskoe Selo struggled to keep up with what was happening. In the family memoirs a common thread is the difficulty of getting clear, consistent information: all mention hearsay and contradictory reports. But there was similar confusion in the thick of the events, for phone calls and arrivals from the city provided little overall clarity. A sense of unreality, yet inevitability, at first pervaded the town, Sergei noted:

> *...Tsarskoe Selo, so close to Petrograd, lived somehow on its own. About that which was happening in the capital, there were only rumours. Officers arriving from Petrograd... told about the disorders, about the start of the rebellion, but all this was perceived as something happening far away, not having any connection to us... in Tsarskoe Selo, covered in snow, everything was quiet and calm.*

Over the next couple of days, among the disturbing rumours that my relatives heard, there were some that would prove to be true – while others would turn out to be exaggerations, distortions or figments of someone's imagination.

Among the truthful information, they learned that the Tsar had ordered the Duma be dissolved. Instead, members of the parliament created an executive committee which soon proclaimed itself in authority. To Sergei the significance of this was profound: "...it became clear, that this was not only a soldiers' revolt and street unrest, but revolution..." Other rumours that would eventually be confirmed included reports that ministers of the Tsar's government were being arrested and that increasing numbers of military units were declaring their loyalty to the new leaders, all of which upset Sergei and those around him:

...some sort of disquiet over the situation in the capital seized all the officers. None of the officers who were off duty went to Petrograd. Now and again they phoned their relatives and friends and these shared with them increasingly terrible news. In the capital everywhere shooting was heard, fires were visible, it was said police stations had been set alight. On the streets cars and trucks rushed about, crammed with armed people and red flags. Police... were nowhere to be seen.

Amid the false information reaching Tsarskoe Selo was that an army of factory workers from a nearby town was marching over to storm the Alexander Palace. Sergei wrote that the numbers involved grew with each retelling, and as telephone links with that town were cut, there was no way to check.

While the crowd of protestors allegedly advancing on the town did not materialise, a reserve regiment did march there from Petrograd. But it did not support the revolt – indeed that is why it had left the capital. What disturbed Sergei was that along the way it had not been challenged by anyone about its intentions. This indicated to him that the military leadership was in disarray or had gone over to the Revolution. It also concerned him that such a military unit, but with hostile intentions, could just as easily march to the quarters of the Tsarina and her children.

Upon reporting at the Alexander Palace, the newly arrived troops yelled in unison the traditional *ura!* (hurrah) for the Tsar. Sergei, looking back, lamented that this was probably the last time that the ruler was thus cheered.

Anna too heard the rumours about the crowd of strikers approaching the town to attack the palace, and told of the impact of

such stories:
> *In Tsarskoe Selo all was calm, I remember activities involving the soldiers continued as usual. But of course everyone was in a keyed-up, anxious state, all were waiting to hear what was happening in Petrograd – no-one knew exactly very well, it was even said there were some policemen killed, that disturbances were happening at the queues at the shops. I remember I went out and bought all that I could in the way of provisions – afterwards, all that I had left in my pocket was exactly fifty kopeks, that is all the money I had left.*

On the evening of February 28th, unrest spilled over into Tsarskoe Selo. Officers at the palace heard shots in the part of town where reserve forces were housed, the start of a soldiers' uprising. Patrols were sent out – Sergei remembered their reports:
> *The soldiers, who had left their barracks, had gathered in groups on the streets, they were building campfires, bawling songs, yelling "ura" and now and then, shooting into the air. The soldiers had immediately looted a big wine shop and warehouse. Many got completely drunk but many others were returning to barracks. There were attempts to break into private homes, but it had not reached violence. It seemed, in spite of everything, that someone was still in charge of the rebellious crowd and was not allowing bloodshed.*

But the threat of violence was certainly there. Sergei heard that a number of big guns from the nearby artillery school had been trained on the palace, and would be used if there was any attempt to stop the revolt. He never believed this particular rumour, but it did have the effect of damaging the morale of the palace defenders and raising the escalating tensions.

The heightened tensions were not confined to the palace, as military rebellion spread. During the night fear grew as the dark hid the sources of threatening sounds. Olga sat up with her mother and her baby daughter (also named Olga) listening to noises of rebellious soldiers outside, after an afternoon of muddled and contradictory reports:

> *A mad anguish seized me, a very oppressive feeling, difficult to describe. When night fell (at that time of year about four o'clock), I gave the order not to turn on the lights and, illuminated by the flame of a single candle placed on the floor, we remained with mother racked by dark thoughts. And all of a sudden, I heard noise as if the man who took care of the heating was splitting wood near the house and was preparing a supply of logs and I was surprised that he would do this when it was already dark. I opened a little windowpane... and I clearly heard gunshots, the bullets lodging in our wooden house, and the yelling of the crowd...*
>
> *Then I telephoned the Fourth Riflemen (the Fourth Imperial Family Rifle Guards Regiment) to consult my brother Nikolai. To my request to speak to Colonel [sic] Apouchtine (*) I received the answer that there were no longer any colonels,*

that all that was finished!...
Then the feeling of oppression turned into a dreadful anxiety. We instructed the servants... to remain dressed, like us, in coats and felt boots in case we were forced to flee. We wrapped Olga warmly and stayed this way waiting. Outside, the sounds of bullets hitting the house and the yelling of the crowd continued. We stayed there not knowing what to do. And then towards five o'clock in the morning the front door bell sounded shrilly. After a few solid minutes of agonising my mother and I decided to open up... we thought it might perhaps be one of my brothers seeking refuge... While we were stealthily going down the interior staircase from the first floor, and when we had arrived almost at the last step... a violent blow shook the door... fortunately without breaking it... it made us freeze... it was clearly not my brothers! We stayed there I don't know how long without moving, waiting. And day came, and the light... In the early morning, we saw tanks passing in the street with revolutionary slogans on them...

When it was safe to investigate, Olga learned that a group of soldiers had taken shelter from the winter cold in the doorway of her house. There they had spent the night drinking looted alcohol, smashing bottles and, as they became more drunk, crashing about and leaning on the doorbell.

For Anna also the anxiety of not knowing what was going on, was amplified at night. When other senses could not penetrate the dark, all she could do was listen to the sounds of the newly unfamiliar, menacing landscape outside. What they signalled dominated her memory of a night – probably the same night described by Olga – when in spite of her and her small son being joined by a neighbouring family, the hours till daylight were long and fearful:

> *We carefully closed the shutters and suddenly we heard from the distance, like a wave of battle from afar, like a roar passing by. Then unexpectedly, along the roof, we heard bullets... The mob and its roar passed by on the pavement, in the direction of the palace. Goodness, what a terrifying night. We sat, not moving, listening to every rustle.*
>
> *Finally all went quiet, it started to get light, I partly opened the curtain in the drawing room and I saw walking along the street, soldiers of our regiment from the reserve battalion. They had on their arms, on their sleeves, white handkerchiefs. It turned out that these handkerchiefs meant they had surrendered to the Revolution.*

Later that morning Anna ventured out to see her cousin Nadezhda.

> *I ran to the regiment to see Nadia. She was confused, she was standing in the yard waiting. Her husband was not there – he had been speaking with the soldiers who had already rebelled. All night long, Nadia told me, he had been trying to persuade them to change their minds.*

While Nikolai had been employing his persuasive powers on the troops, his brother Sergei had been called upon for his calming abilities. He had spent the night trying to comfort the Tsarina in the Alexander Palace, his sister Olga remembered (though strangely this is not mentioned in Sergei's own memoirs). The distraught Tsarina, leaning on Sergei's arm, wandered from room to room among her children, who were sick with measles, crying and worrying about her husband's safety. She afterwards gave him her tear-filled handkerchief and an ashtray from the imperial porcelain factory. Nearly nine decades later, I saw and held the delicate ashtray in the Connecticut home of Sergei's daughter – a relic of another era and another world that had survived to travel halfway around the globe and into the twenty-first century.

Amid the uncertainty and the tensions, and worry over the next act in this unfathomable drama, there were lighter moments. Anna remembered witnessing an incident of looting which turned into a farce:

> *...in the shop which was on the opposite side of the small street from us... a soldier had broken through the window of the dairy. He had fallen into a barrel of sour cream and was climbing out of the broken window like a ghost. A collection of cooks and soldiers stood all around, chewing seeds, and laughing boisterously and loudly.*

She also remembered the visit of the son of a manager at her parents' estate, whom she had known since her childhood. The young man, who was now a soldier, arrived wearing a red bow on his arm. Anna queried him over it:

> *"Well, because it's lots of fun for me to travel on the train" [he said]. "Now, if you wear a red ribbon, you can travel free of charge. I arrive in Petrograd in first class, then I come back. And then I go there again, and back again. That's how we ride – it is very enjoyable, very entertaining for me."*

While Anna's memoir details what must have seemed a surreal atmosphere, as the town balanced between extraordinary events and a semblance of practical day-to-day life, Sergei was witnessing attempts to reverse the political developments. He told of the Tsarina meeting with other members of the royal family who lived nearby to discuss options on how to deal with the Duma members in the Tsar's absence, unaware that things had moved too far for her intervention. He said forces arrived in town from the front, in order to put down the Petrograd rebellion; but their advance was stopped by the military leadership and they were ordered back to their former positions.

Soon Sergei heard that in Petrograd "...some sort of soldiers' and workers' committee was formed...". Indeed, as the Duma was setting up its executive committee, the Petrograd Soviet of Workers' and Soldiers' Deputies was created by the socialist parties. Negotiations between the two bodies resulted in a Duma-based Provisional Government being named. The Soviet agreed to work with the Duma, but in effect, in the coming months, it would often act as a rival power base.

Their disagreement on important issues had already been evident when the Duma committee had tried to get rebellious solders back to barracks. In response the Soviet had produced Order Number One. It provided for soldiers' committees to counterbalance their officers' authority. The Order also took away many of the hated practices which enforced hierarchical relationships in the military, for example, the use of honorific titles and the requirement that off-duty soldiers salute their superiors. In Sergei's words, this decree "destroyed the army". It was certainly to have a huge impact on the armed forces, and thus, on the progress of the Revolution and the war.

CHAPTER THREE

The measures were popular, and increasing numbers of military units pledged their support to the new authorities. The leaders of Sergei's regiment guarding the Tsarina at Tsarskoe Selo were not about to follow suit, but they could see that in any confrontation, their forces would be no match numerically against the rebels. So a delegation was sent to Petrograd to declare the regiment's neutrality to the new government. It would pledge not to act against rebel forces as long as they did not attack the palace. The group returned having failed to meet the military commander of Petrograd. But their trip satisfied local rebel soldiers that those guarding the palace were no threat.

While the delegation had been unable to carry out its primary intention, they brought back their impressions of what they had seen. These stunned Sergei and his colleagues:

> *[They told us] we would not recognise our dear Petrograd. The whole capital is draped in red flags, which have turned into dirty, wet rags, since a thaw has set in, and wet snow is falling. On the streets, trucks and private cars rush by, filled with armed soldiers and students with flags. Everywhere, there are lots of people, as if no-one ever sleeps. On street corners are groups, animatedly yelling something and trying to prove something to each other. In the Duma it is impossible to push one's way through. Soldiers and crowds have filled the huge building, no-one knows anything, and amid these crowds appear some rumpled people – dirty, exhausted, dazed, unshaven... These are the members of the Duma, the plotters, who have seized power, in vain urging the crowds to disperse and go home.*

On the way back, the delegation had overheard talk about the abdication of the Tsar. Again, no-one knew what was true and what was fabrication. But soon the "bitter truth" was confirmed at the palace: the Tsar had abdicated on March 2nd for himself and for his twelve-year-old son Aleksei, weak and sickly with haemophilia. The new tsar was to be Nicholas' brother, the Grand Duke Mikhail Aleksandrovich. Sergei noted with contempt that even some of the officers at the palace were quick to cut off the insignia of Nicholas the Second from their uniforms.

There was more shocking news to come; so many developments tumbled one after the other, Sergei said, that there was barely time to react to them. A day after the Tsar's abdication, in a meeting with ministers of the Provisional Government, the Grand Duke declined the crown. While the Tsar had basically been left with no choice but to leave the throne, the action of his brother – to people like Sergei – was unforgivable:

> *The Grand Duke did not show any desire to fight for his rights, not understanding his responsibility before Russia and the Russian people. In a weak-willed way he agreed to everything the members of the Provisional Government proposed, without negotiating any provisos either for himself or for his brother and his family... With his signature the Grand Duke ended the three-hundred-year existence of the Romanov Dynasty.*

The historical record indicates that Grand Duke Mikhail was not impressed by his brother's decision to hand him the throne without prior consultation. With crowds celebrating the Tsar's abdication and tearing down tsarist symbols in Petrograd, the Grand

Duke requested a guarantee for his safety. This was something the new government could not – or would not – give him, and he refused the position. Some believe he rejected the throne for other reasons, feeling it was too late for change that should have been brought in earlier, and that the new government would now not cooperate. In Sergei's words, "Russia was left deprived of a leader, having a government, but having no head of government."

For those of my relatives who had had personal contact with Nicholas and his family these developments were devastating on levels beyond the political. Anna had had encounters with the ruling family through her father when he had occupied a senior role at the palace, and through her own brief time as a lady-in-waiting at the court. On hearing the news of the abdication she felt empathy for them as individuals. She also feared what their removal meant more broadly, sensing that it indicated the world around her was changing utterly and irrevocably:

> *The cup [of tea] in my hand was shaking so much that I could not drink... I understood that everything was finished, everything, literally everything. Some sort of new life was beginning which was immeasurably frightening... in the Provisional Government sat people who were decent... but actually something else was operating, something frightening, something sinister – the Soviet of Soldiers' and Workers' Deputies.*

Nicholas the Second has been represented as a weak tsar, as someone who – had he been different – could have changed the course of Russian history. A combination of an unshakeable belief in his God-given role as autocratic ruler, and a reputedly irresolute personality, contributed to him underestimating the forces for change. Yet clearly the abrupt end to his rule, along with the lack of a framework to replace the tsarist system, was a momentous development. Historian Richard Pipes writes that:

> *In the context of the time, Nicholas's abdication was something of an anticlimax, since he had been effectively deposed four days earlier by the Duma and the Petrograd Soviet. But in a broader context, it was an event of the greatest significance. The Tsar was the linchpin of the country's political structure... His removal left a vacuum: the state vanished.*

Soon after his abdication, Nicholas returned to Tsarskoe Selo, to house arrest with his family in the Alexander Palace. Both his supporters and his detractors were keenly aware of his presence. Anna was never to see the former Tsar again, but on an outing to run some errands soon after his return, she passed close to the palace. Before leaving the house, she had been reminded of its irrelevance in any ability to provide protection for people like herself and of the importance of acknowledging the symbolism of the new circumstances. A family friend who had come to accompany her picked up a toy of her son's:

> *Just in case, he took from Gulinka's little rabbit a red ribbon that was tied onto it and put it into his pocket and said "If it becomes necessary, I will put it on.... who knows whether there might be any sort of trouble..."*

The memory of this trivial, almost absurd detail of a toy's trim seems somehow incongruous in the wider context of the times. Yet this link in Anna's recollection between what should have been an intimate, insignificant element, and the larger picture of developments, indicates the way they were increasingly seeping into small details of everyday life. It seems the red ribbon was not needed. However on her way home, Anna was chilled by a gathering she passed:

> ... I saw a huge crowd, standing around the garden of the Alexander Palace. This crowd was hooting and yelling and it seemed as if it was looking at someone – probably it was the sovereign in the park, digging snow. I of course did not see him, but this crowd made a horrific impression on me..

When newspapers resumed publishing after a break due to the unrest, Anna noted that their tone had changed:

> ...we were amazed at how much these newspapers, which had sung the praises of the Tsar's family, the Russian Army, and so on, were delirious, just delirious with joy over the Revolution.

The Tsar was gone, but the Provisional Government's subsequent delays and ultimate failure to hold elections for a Constituent Assembly would mean continuing crises and instability. The men who would eventually fill the vacuum – Vladimir Lenin and his successors – though seen as representing an extreme opposite to the tsars, would in fact, in many ways, have much in common with their despised predecessors, in their autocratic style of ruling. But much else would change along the way.

(*) Nikolai was not yet a Colonel at this point – he was only promoted in July.

4

"We've taken power and we won't give it up…"

The Peter and Paul Fortress is the oldest structure in St Petersburg. It was built in 1703 on the Neva River by Peter the Great on land coveted by Sweden – and for a time occupied by it. As conflict continued with the Scandinavian foe, the Fortress was raised as a defence. In the end, it was never needed against the Swedes. It led the way to the construction by Peter of the city that still bears his name (though for nearly seventy years its name was given to Lenin).

The Fortress is the venue of my grandfather Nikolai's surprising involvement in the new Provisional Government which took over after the February Revolution. He did not last long in the position he was given there, but the fact he accepted it seems to indicate his desire to give the new regime a chance.

The star-shaped Fortress is on an island across the water from the Winter Palace and the central part of St Petersburg, its thick stone walls enclosing a scattering of buildings. Amid them towers the 123 metre tall golden spire of the Fortress' cathedral. Within the huge elaborate church are buried many of Russia's tsars. But the Fortress was notorious through much of its history for another reason: its use as a political prison. The cells are within its walls, under the towers at each star point.

I went there as a tourist. But I was also seeking evidence of that unlikely connection to my grandfather. In the cathedral, I joined visitors from Russia and abroad filing past huge marble slabs covering the tsars' graves. Some of the dungeons in the walls were also open to visitors: small cells with heavy iron doors and potted histories of various former inmates. The Fortress is Russia's Bastille; like its French counterpart it is laden with symbolism and an evil reputation, though in retrospect some historians believe the conditions there were not as bad as many perceptions suggest. Yet I found the thick stone walls and dank corridors still intimidating; they exuded a sense of menace and claustrophobia.

Other buildings inside the Fortress house museums and exhibition rooms. The commandant's house contains the central exhibition of the Museum of the History of St Petersburg. When I visited, the first room off the entrance lobby was the only one devoted to its former usage. In the list of commanders over the years, near the bottom, there it was – my grandfather's name: "Captain Apouchtine, June 1st to July 15th 1917". This is the only information I found about Nikolai's tenure here, not even his first name was noted. Perhaps he would have liked it this way, to have left little mark on the place. The commander's position in tsarist times was described as an honorary appointment. It is unclear whether this had changed under the Provisional Government.

There was disappointingly little left to help visualise Nikolai's life in the commandant's house, with the inside of the building modernised to accommodate displays. Whatever his role, the brevity of his time there suggests it was not a pleasant posting for him.

Nikolai's brief attempt at being part of the new regime came amid a whirlwind of events between the February and October Revolutions. After the Tsar's abdication, there was talk of troops rebelling and deserting at the front, and about killings of officers. When a group of soldiers arrived at my grandmother's cousin's door in Tsarskoe Selo seeking to arrest officers who might be hiding there, Anna responded with anger. Taken aback, they apologised and left. The defiance concealed growing fear among families like hers.

The Tsar's abdication document had called on the military to obey the new rulers. So Nikolai and his brother Sergei continued to do their work as best they could amid the changes. Their sister Olga believed their good leadership resulted in them retaining the respect of their men. This seemed to be borne out, at least initially, when their units carried out Order Number One by choosing soldiers' committees. In Sergei's regiment, the committee gave its leadership a vote of confidence. In the case of my grandfather, Olga wrote that Nikolai "had organised his battalion so well that after the revolutionary days, he was unanimously chosen by his men to command them…"

But before long, any respect their men did have for Sergei and Nikolai was eroded by the general atmosphere. For soon they both found it increasingly difficult to work with their soldiers, as Olga noted:

> *Despite the efforts of numerous officers to maintain a certain discipline in the army as the war was continuing, there was nothing to be done, there was complete disarray… My brothers… tried to rein in their soldiers, but the more time passed, the more impossible this became. The soldiers rejected all training, walked en masse in the palace park to look at the elephant which had been given to Nicholas the Second by the Shah of Persia and which was kept in a charming little house in the middle of the park. They also came*

> *to watch the Tsar saw wood behind the palisade of the private garden of the imperial family.*

Documents in my grandfather's military record indicate he requested retirement a few weeks after the February Revolution, on the basis of his previous injuries, and there is a letter from late May granting him a service pension. But it seems that Nikolai had not yet taken up his approval to retire, when – according to Olga – the Minister of War visited his regiment.

> *...my brother Nikolai, a one-hundred-percent invalid, having the right to be freed of military functions, had decided it was important not to resign himself to the revolutionary situation which had established itself... Towards the month of May, I think, the Minister of War, [Alexander] Kerensky, reviewed all the reserve battalions and was impressed by the order that ruled in my brother's; on the spot he named him commander of the Saint Peter and Saint Paul Fortress... they thus moved, Nadia and he, into the Fortress.*

His daughter, my aunt Nadia, believed that Nikolai agreed to accept the posting in St Petersburg rather than retiring because he was optimistic about the new regime:

> *Perhaps he hoped that Kerensky would do something [positive]... Because I think on the whole, like many others, he was probably taken with the idea of the Provisional Government, with the hope that there would be changes for the better in Russia – very many believed this. Unfortunately it did not turn out that way.*

My aunt believed that her mother, unlike many others of her class, keenly felt the unfairness of the disparities between rich and poor in Russian society. Perhaps then my grandmother too, was open to the possibilities that the new government presented.

My grandparents left Tsarskoe Selo and moved into the Fortress not long before a series of events which was to provide a new batch of prisoners for its cells.

The Provisional Government was planning a major offensive in the war, hoping this would help unite Russians through patriotism, after the upheaval of the preceding months. The new regime also wanted to secure legitimacy in the eyes of its Western European allies, which were pressuring Russia to act. Thus coverage of a pro-offensive demonstration in Petrograd in the June 17th 1917 (June 4th in Russia) issue of the French newspaper *Le Miroir* was in line with western priorities. This is the item that contains the photograph of a man who my family believed was my grandfather. Under the headline "A Russian Demonstration in Support of the Allies" is a wide shot of a crowd in St Isaac's Square: a sea of heads massed between a building draped with flags and banners and the huge, grandiose St Isaac's Cathedral. Another photo, the close up of a thin man with a pointed beard, thought to be Nikolai, is labelled: "A disabled officer speaking in the open air". The gathering is described as "patriotic, extremely moving". Among appeals to support the offensive, the "vibrant speech of a one-armed officer secured considerable approval."

Countering such support for the offensive was the push by the opposition Bolsheviks for an end to Russian involvement in the war. This was gaining support amid demoralised and fatigued forces at the front. Patriotism was negated by the growing feeling among many soldiers that the war was being fought for imperial interests, not for any benefit to people like themselves. The offensive went ahead on June 16th, but within days Russian forces were on the run.

Attempts to send reinforcements from the Petrograd garrison sparked demonstrations which swelled into a revolt. On July 3rd, the streets filled with crowds; there were bloody confrontations. Among those protesting were armed sailors from the Kronstadt Naval Base. On the night of July 4th a large group of them took over the Peter and Paul Fortress. But it seems they were not quite sure what to do with their prize. Historian Orlando Figes writes that "it was just a symbol of the old regime which it seemed a good idea to capture as a final hostage of the uprising." They left the next day after they were allowed to keep their weapons and return to their base.

One would assume that my grandfather, as commander, must have been caught up in this incident, perhaps being held hostage along with the Fortress. Yet there is no mention of these events in any family memoirs. Perhaps Nikolai happened to be away from the Fortress when the sailors arrived.

The Bolsheviks had quickly taken the leadership in the uprising. They were one of the parties in the Petrograd Soviet. But contrary to other socialist groups in this council vying for power with the Provisional Government, they had refused to take part in a recently formed coalition ministry with it. While this may have strengthened their claim that they were the only real opposition, the Bolsheviks were divided over how to channel the anger in the streets. To this vacillation was added the spreading by the government of allegations that the Bolsheviks were acting as German agents. Whatever people felt about Russia's continuation in the war, cooperating with the enemy was going too far. The accusations triggered an angry reaction and the revolt fell apart.

There was a crackdown on the Bolsheviks, with many arrests. Some of these were incarcerated at the Fortress. Again, I have not found any information on my grandfather's possible role in the administration of this influx. According to Olga, the prison aspect of his job was one he never relished, though she linked his discomfort to the presence of highly placed people from the tsarist regime in the cells, some of whom he had known in previous times. Whatever his part in all this, just days after the revolt was quelled, Nikolai quit his post. Olga wrote that Nikolai "...called on his rights to retire and had himself relieved from his functions. Nadia and he then fled, literally, to Moscow where all of Nadia's relatives lived."

It was the end of any involvement by him with the new regime.

By the time of the so-called July Days, my other relatives in Tsarskoe Selo had all gradually left the town.

Anna's husband was still at the front at the time of the February Revolution, and amid the ongoing political instability, her mother in Moscow had suggested she might be safer there. Anna had packed up "...all my silver, all my jewellery, some linen, some dresses, all that could be taken along..." and travelled with her small son to the home of her mother and stepfather. The trip had been uneventful, though she was disturbed by the story of an officer she met, who told her he was fleeing his men because they had tried to kill him. On arrival in Moscow, she had been amazed at how changed it was:

> *Petrograd was tragic, but all of Moscow was like a continuous fair – everywhere there were red flags, everywhere you could hear cheerful songs, people*

> *walked in crowds as if it was a... bazaar. They were just about kissing in the street – "freedom, freedom, freedom" is all that could be heard. At the big monuments, meetings gathered, which of course also yelled about freedom. At this early stage there was still no malicious attitude to the bourgeois... which developed with time. Then, it was total rejoicing. It was all somehow strange. In my soul there was such sorrow.*

Anna's feelings obviously left her out of step with many others. The sense of the growing exclusion of people like her in the developing scheme of things and fears of hostility would have contributed to her reaction to these scenes. In the face of continuing uncertainty, and the somewhat threatening situation, she would soon move again, with others of her family, to their country estate.

Olga had also left Tsarskoe Selo – for a time, or so she thought. She travelled with her baby daughter to the home of an aunt in Kiev, in Ukraine, to be closer to the sector of the front where her husband was based. Her preparations before the trip reflected contradictory feelings:

> *I packed a full trunk with... the portrait of [my husband], my jewellery, some icons, and a dozen table settings of silver cutlery made by Fabergé that I had received as dowry, all this even though the thought that I was leaving forever did not even cross my mind for a moment; now I regret I left behind my photo album which went back to my childhood and the documents that I had placed in the safe.*

To her surprise, someone had wanted to rent her apartment, so she and her mother had quickly sewn covers to protect the silk upholstery on some of her chairs. Clearly Olga had every hope of returning, strengthened no doubt by her unwillingness to believe that the situation would not stabilise. While she may not have been very keen on the changes, it seems that she – like others among my relatives – probably felt she would be able to adapt to what had already occurred, once things settled down. In the meantime, it was a matter of finding the best practical ways to get by, whatever the future held. A Bolshevik seizure of power is not likely to have been a possibility in her mind.

Sergei's time in Tsarskoe Selo, at the Alexander Palace, also ended. The Combined Regiment was replaced by other forces there, and then was disbanded altogether a few months later. He wrote that offers were made to the officers to join Allied forces in France. Or they could go back to their regiments of origin. Sergei's was at the front, and he had to decide whether to return there:

> *There was fear – how would the regiments and regimental committees treat officers who had served and protected the Tsar's family. Among us officers, there were many discussions on how to deal with this situation. I took the view that to abandon my homeland at the moment of its greatest devastation was impossible, that each of us could and must make a sacrifice, and according to his strength, help in the renewal of the army. Some agreed with me, others objected that we could not help in any way and took advantage of the opportunity to leave the country.*

So while my grandfather gave up on a military role under the new regime in July, his brother stayed in the army several more months. Sergei went back to the front, where in spite of his misgivings, he was well received. His regiment, the St Petersburg Guards, was in what is now western Ukraine. It was operating smoothly and relations between soldiers and officers were good. Elsewhere, calls for Russia to pull out of the war and the political changes were having big impacts:

> *The army was going through the revolutionary illness with difficulty. All sorts of excesses... and constant meetings turned the army into an armed throng without discipline and order. Often all the efforts of the officers to maintain at least the semblance of a military unit were unsuccessful.*

In one incident, Sergei came across a group of about eight hundred soldiers waiting to surrender to the Austrian army. When he tried to convince them that captivity would not be pleasant, they mocked him. However when he suggested they would have to give up their weapons, they changed their minds and returned to their unit. But their commanders did not punish them, evidence Sergei believed, of nervousness over how the men might apply their new rights under Order Number One if the officers were too strict.

Later Sergei was chosen to travel to headquarters with two other officers to convey the difficulties of conducting the war amid the chaos at the front. Like Olga, Sergei could not yet believe that it was impossible to get things back on track, in ways that he could accept, in spite of his disturbing experiences:

> *Farewelling my friends, I did not think that I would never again return to my regiment, and that the regiment would end its glorious two-hundred-year existence.*
>
> *These three months of my stay at the front*

*were the hardest in my life. I often remembered my
friends from the Combined Regiment, who had left
for France... [but] I thought that the route, chosen
by me, was right; all of us officers had to serve
in our regiments to the last opportunity.*

En route, travelling on trains packed with deserters fleeing the war, Sergei said the leader of the delegation prepared a request for order to be restored:

*...[he] put together something like an appeal –
addressing both officers and public opinion, and
most of all, our senior leadership. In it he mentioned
loyalty to the Allies, the necessity of continuing the
war till final victory... the readiness [of the officers] to
continue... but it asked and demanded understanding
of this sacrifice, support for it. We demanded the
end to all meetings in the battle zone at the front,
the prohibition of speeches by irresponsible agitators,
who showed up at the front goodness knows how,
who advocated fraternisation [with the enemy],
the ending of the war and departure from the front...
everything written by him was a cry from the
tormented soul of the Russian officer.*

At headquarters in Mogilev they found more chaos, and senior commanders who were also powerless. They were being directed "by lawyers and former terrorists" in the Provisional Government, they said, and Sergei's group would have to go directly to them in Petrograd to plead their case.

The delegation arrived in the capital on October 15th, ten days before the Bolshevik Revolution. The weather was gloomy and wet, matching the feelings Sergei found among his colleagues there:

In our regimental reserve the mood was one of melancholy. The officers had no doubt of the inevitability of the Bolsheviks moving to grab power; [yet they also] hated Kerensky and his band which had taken the leadership of the government...

Among the soldiers there was unrestrained agitation by the Bolsheviks. Daily meetings, the airing of proposals to quickly conclude peace, return home and divide the landowners' land could not help but tempt the tired mass of soldiers. And there was no agitation to counterbalance this – good, organised agitation, with people dedicated to their ideas.

Sergei and his travelling companions finally achieved a meeting with now Prime Minister Kerensky in the Winter Palace. Sergei found his residing in the Tsar's former quarters distasteful, but Kerensky received the trio sympathetically. He told them something would be done to restore order at the front, though he also suggested they publish their appeal in the newspapers. To Sergei and the others, this was the sad proof that the Provisional Government had lost its grip:

We left. And that was all. And for this we had made our way with such difficulty to the capital, in order to see this figure, helpless and powerless, kept in power only by inertia.

Sergei went to stay with his father, who had a room in a hotel. According to Olga, their father had left the front only once during the first part of the war, believing his place was with his men. But after the February Revolution, my great-grandfather had felt he could not work effectively under Order Number One, so he returned to the capital. Sergei wrote that he was appointed to a commission of the War Ministry, tasked with writing new service regulations; they were never to be completed.

During Sergei's time at the front, the Prime Minister had indeed lost much of his power. After the July uprising, the Provisional Government, with Kerensky at the helm, had responded by moving to roll back some of the freedoms gained since February. This had done nothing to stem discontent over the desire for peace, and labour and land reform. There were strikes, increasing crime, attacks by peasants on gentry in the country, and moves toward independence by non-Russian sections of the Empire. Bolsheviks who had been jailed at the Peter and Paul Fortress were gradually released and resumed their campaigning in civilian, as well as military sectors.

As crisis followed crisis the Prime Minister became increasingly indecisive, the Provisional Government more paralysed, and society more polarised. At the same time the socialist parties, among them the Bolsheviks, had been bolstering their parallel organisations, setting up Soviets all over the country. With their inclusion of worker and peasant representation, these councils were popular. The growing impatience with an ineffectual government, and its delaying of elections, helped them gain support. In spite of the Bolsheviks initially being a small part of this movement, the party was able to take advantage of the circumstances to advance its agenda, pushing the country relentlessly towards the October Revolution.

I only once witnessed the anniversary of the October Revolution in the Soviet Union. This was the most important date on the country's calendar during communist rule and simultaneously symbolised everything my forebears had fought against. Where I was staying, in the city of Sukhumi in Georgia, as elsewhere, factories, schools and other organisations were preparing to take part in a celebratory parade. In spite of niggling thoughts of disloyalty to my family's past, my curiosity triumphed and I decided to go along. I discovered that while many people were required to march, no matter how they felt about the regime, unconnected spectators were not encouraged. Presumably the authorities were nervous of any gatherings not directed by them. But the family which was hosting me managed – with a bit of bribery I suspect – to get me a ticket. Cameras, however, were not permitted.

The parade was predictable, a smaller scale version of the familiar scenes from Moscow beamed each year to the West: rows of uniformed children and adults waving red flags, banners and flowers, and slogan-covered floats proclaiming industrial achievements. There was some weaponry – hardly enough, it seemed, to warrant the ban on photographs, especially considering the rows upon rows of missiles, tanks, guns, and troops seen in the Kremlin broadcasts. There were the usual enormous pictures of Karl Marx, Friedrich Engels and Vladimir Lenin, of the then leader Leonid Brezhnev, and even of Josef Stalin. With much of the Soviet Union having quietly, and with relief, put Stalin's portraits away after Nikita Khrushchev's denunciation of him, this seemed strange. The speech by Stalin's successor in 1956 accused him of abuses of power and condemned the purges which saw many innocent people punished or executed. But Georgia was Stalin's homeland and his native son status still retained him some following there – at least among those who had not been victims of his regime. Seeing his picture carried aloft was disturbing; the wide, moustachioed face was an unpleasant reminder of the extremes of the outcomes of the October Revolution.

The woodenness and painted smiles on many faces around made me wonder how many others were secretly harbouring negative thoughts about this cheerful show so at odds with daily reality. But perhaps I read too much into what I thought I saw, perhaps it was a way of appeasing my guilt that I was somehow betraying my family, for clearly some of the enthusiasm on display was real. October 1917 too, was greeted by many at the time – if not with enthusiasm after all the upheaval already experienced – at least with equanimity and hope for the future.

For my relatives though, it closed the door on their past.

My great-uncle Sergei found himself in the middle of the drama of the Bolshevik Revolution in Petrograd. During the last days before the overthrow of the Provisional Government, Sergei had stayed with his father but had reported daily to his regiment. On the evening of October 24th he and other officers were asked to stay close by, because of rumours about impending events. He slept on a couch in the regiment's billiard room, but was awoken in the early hours and told to attend a meeting. He set off in a car that had come for him, but soon realised it was not heading towards the War Minister's residence. Instead the driver was taking him to the Smolny Institute, the headquarters of the Petrograd Soviet. As the car sped through deserted streets, Sergei learned that the Bolsheviks had taken over key points in the city:

> *[The driver told me] "This night there was a coup.*
> *The Bolsheviks seized power, and the new government*
> *is at the Smolny Institute... they sent me for you.*
> *I have instructions to bring you alive or dead.*

CHAPTER FOUR

> *Don't try to run or resist. I am not yet a Bolshevik, but I am sympathetic to the coup. It is no longer possible to tolerate the idiotic Provisional Government and the crazy fool Kerensky." I understood that I had landed in an unpleasant mess. I had nowhere to run...*
> *"Today is an amazing day," the ensign continued.*
> *"If the Bolsheviks take power, for each one of us a wide road opens up to the most incredible possibilities. I envy you, captain. You're a combatant officer, I see this by your decorations, and in Smolny there are no officers at all, only ensigns. Yet the Bolsheviks now need officers... If you want, this very day you will be a commander of the army."*

That was the last thing Sergei wanted. As they approached Smolny, he remembered his visits to his sisters when they were students at the former academy for girls. Its appearance now was rather different:

> *At the entrance gates to the park a bonfire burned, and some sloppily unkempt soldiers stopped our car. My ensign showed them some certificate, and they let us pass. In the yard in front of the main doorway languished workers and sailors. From a truck rifles and cartridges were being given out to them. Here also a large bonfire burned, it was cold and damp. On the stairs stood two machine guns, and sailors wearing crossed cartridge belts were cleaning them. Many cars stood to the side, right on the lawn. Crowds of people were entering the doorway or coming out.*

Inside, Sergei met several other officers who had been summoned.

His driver had been right: the Bolsheviks wanted someone to lead soldiers against troops resisting them. The officers had a few moments to decide on a strategy to divert the newly installed Commissar for War (War Minister), Nikolai Krylenko. They came up with the name of an officer whose politics they knew to be different from their own and unanimously recommended him. Sergei said they then quickly slipped away:

> *Taking a wrong turn, I found myself in the main hall of Smolny. It was right here – in this huge two storey high colonnaded hall – that I used to meet with my sisters, when I came to see them during visiting hours. But what had it become? A solid wall of grey greatcoats filled it. Several speakers were simultaneously yelling something, to which no-one was listening. Clouds of tobacco smoke drifted across the hall. The densely standing soldiers were yelling: "Give us peace! We don't agree to fight any longer!" I barely managed to get out of the hall, and again jostling along the corridor, went out onto the staircase of the main doorway.*

Sergei found the car and the man who had brought him and they drove off.

A century later, the building where these events took place remains a grand, beautiful structure. It is a pastel yellow-beige, with white columns and trim. A large two-headed eagle spreads its wings at the top of the building. Seeing the stately architecture with the winged symbol of the tsars and the peaceful trees and lawns around it on a summer visit in the late 1990s, I tried to picture the scene described by Sergei: the cold, the crowds, the weapons, the rushing about.

The building houses municipal offices and was closed to the public (now it is accessible through pre-arranged tours). When I was there only the odd civil servant sauntered in or out. Instead of frenzied activity, a sleepy atmosphere prevailed. Peering into the foyer, I could see gloomy corridors with dark walls and doors. Looking up from the pavement to the second floor with its rows of large windows, I wondered whether they looked in on the colonnaded hall. When my maternal grandmother and three of my great-aunts were students here, music and young female voices would have resonated behind those windows. When the Bolsheviks directed the October Revolution from here, the sounds would have been those of excited debate and argument. The contrast could not have been more vivid. How much more so it would have been for Sergei, arriving on that fateful night to find a revolution underway.

From Smolny, Sergei returned to his regiment. He found it had voted to remain neutral. But he wrote that the new War Commissar himself, with "superhuman energy", went around that day addressing those troops who did not yet support the Bolsheviks. And Sergei's regiment did soon join the tide, while he wondered what had happened to his superiors: no orders came from them.

The hotel where he was staying with his father was gripped in panic. There were rumours that the Winter Palace would be stormed. There, members of the Provisional Government were holed up, guarded by the remnant troops still loyal to them, though Kerensky had managed to steal away.

My great-grandfather had a copy of a notice issued by the Bolsheviks declaring themselves the new government, with Lenin as leader and Leon Trotsky as Commissar for Foreign Affairs. Sergei conveyed his father's scorn: " 'They're condemning themselves to failure... The Allies will never recognise such a government and will not negotiate with some [character called] Trotsky.' "

But after what he had witnessed, Sergei was not so sure:

...I remembered... the words of Krylenko [at Smolny]:
"We've taken power and we won't give it up to anyone.
We will fight for every house, for each stone," and
I thought that these fanatics were capable of destroying
the city and would indeed fight for every stone.

In the morning, they learned that the Winter Palace had indeed been taken over, and the ministers of the Provisional Government arrested. A Congress of Soviets, with delegates from around the country, that had been due to start a few days earlier, had finally begun during the night at Smolny. The Bolsheviks, with more than their fair share of seats, had gained approval for their coup.

Sergei was called to his regiment, but he got away again quickly:

I said goodbye to my friends and returned to the hotel.
From that day, my service finished... I was under
orders of the commander of the regiment; but in the
regiment, in the coming days, there were going to be
elections for the commanding officers, and strictly
speaking all of us – the officers of the regiment – found
ourselves in an uncertain situation. The majority of
the senior officers, and I among them, did not want
to be elected, nor as a matter of fact, to continue our
service and submit to the new power. From this time,
I stopped feeling like the former person I had been,
and soon went underground.

With this written many years later, it is hard to know how much

CHAPTER FOUR

Sergei realised at the time the finality of events and as such, that there was no longer a comfortable place for him in them. The fact that he would later join the White Forces to fight the Bolsheviks indicates he retained some hope things could be reversed. But whatever his understanding of it all at that time, the sense of loss is evident. It was not just the loss of a way of life, but a fundamental loss of identity. The Bolsheviks coined the term "former people" for those they believed did not belong in their society. The Russian phrase in Sergei's memoir is not exactly the same as the words the new rulers used but it echoes the same sentiment of alienation from the opposite side of the divide. (Later in 1917 the Bolsheviks would take the notion of "former people" further, decreeing obligatory registration for groups that fit their definition.)

In the country, where Anna and her family had sought refuge from the turbulence in the cities, the months leading up to the October Revolution had been quiet. Here physical separation combined with psychological isolation kept events happening elsewhere at bay – at least for a time. Violent seizures of estates were occurring more frequently in some areas, but not yet here. Daily life on Anna's family's estate – at least superficially – continued as normal:

...there was indeed complete peace. The peasants as before, when they met us, greeted us – you could think that no revolution had happened, none of them knew anything about it. All the servants were on hand, we ate as always, there were provisions as much as we wanted. There were no worries arriving, except in the newspapers, which of course upset us all very much each time they came. But life somehow takes its

course. In spite of the awful state of mind in which we found ourselves... the country air somehow calmed us all a little bit. Besides it turned out that we were not allowed to hire workers to harvest the hay, and so we had to do it ourselves, which was extremely healthy – the nerves of our men seemed to calm down and they started to eat and sleep much better.

    The reality of what was happening all around could not have failed to influence Anna's feelings, in spite of her best efforts to portray this as a period when things were much as they had always been. But perhaps she wanted to retain this image of this time as a way of holding on to her past, to a time and place which symbolised stability and happiness, in contrast to later difficult and unsettled years.

    The illusion of peace was not to last. One of the first decrees passed by the Soviet Congress meeting in Smolny dealt with taking over gentry land. Soon Anna's family would be subject to confiscations, and then threats, and they would have to leave the estate.

    The family of my paternal grandmother Nadezhda had left its estate behind more than a year before. A photograph dated August 1916 is identified as being the family's final departure from Piatnitskoe. Leaving for Moscow after having spent the summer there, as they did every year, those in the photo probably did not realise they would never return: the February Revolution would intervene before the next spring. The photo is small and not very sharp; it is difficult to identify the individuals. They are mostly women, with a few children. They are wearing capes and hats or scarves – it must have been a cool August. To one side of the group are a few bundles and cases. To the other, a bit apart, are a boy wearing knee-high boots and a cap, and a woman with her arms crossed over her apron, no doubt villagers who worked on the estate. The photo encapsulates a world about to disappear. Perhaps the people posing were lucky to be leaving the past behind unknowingly. For them – unlike for Anna – the recognition of the loss would come from afar.

Fourteen months after this photo was taken, Nadezhda travelled south with Nikolai. It seems they left Moscow right after the October Revolution, escaping bloody street battles. These continued for more than a week before the city finally came under Bolshevik control.

In November the much-delayed elections for a Constituent Assembly were held. The Bolsheviks failed to gain a majority. Unable to dominate proceedings, they dissolved it shortly after the start of its first session in January.

By then my paternal grandparents' journey had taken them to the Caucasus. Most of Nikolai's family had left before them. His mother, his sister Olga, and his brother Vladimir were in Kiev. Sergei was soon to follow. Of Nadezhda's two remaining siblings, her younger sister Annochka (Anna) also travelled to the Caucasus.

It seems my mother's parents were apart through this period; probably Alexander was still at the front and Natalia in Mogilev. She would also eventually join those fleeing south, with my mother as a baby. In Odessa Natalia would be reunited with two of her siblings who joined the stream of travellers: her sister Evgeniia and her brother Vladimir.

Departures were imminent for many other people. They were often thought to be temporary moves: some to places where opponents of the Bolsheviks gathered to prepare to try to oust the new regime, others to areas believed to be safer, in anticipation of future events. For many these trips would end up being staging posts on journeys much further afield – into exile.

5

Former People

When I was a child, I often heard the phrase "sitting on their suitcases" in reference to Russian refugees in France between the world wars. It was a strong image in my young mind: my relatives, most of whom I knew only from photos, and their Russian friends and acquaintances sitting on bulging cases, ready to jump up at a moment's notice and hurry back to the homeland they had fled after the 1917 Revolution.

As with much of what I heard – and often misunderstood – I thought this colourful turn of phrase was unique to my family's folklore. It was only much later that I discovered it was a shared vision of the belief that the collapse of communism was imminent in what had been Russia. For instance, historian Marc Raeff writes: "In a most literal sense they did not 'unpack' their suitcases; they sat on their trunks."

If ten and twenty years after the events of 1917, Russian refugees from the political changes found it hard to accept that the Communist regime was there to stay, how much more difficult it must have been in 1918. A wide range of opinion in Russia and outside, whatever their views of the new government, assumed it would be short-lived. So there was much agonising among many over whether to stay or leave. And when the decision to leave was made, questions over how long the absence might be.

My paternal grandparents Nikolai and Nadezhda, who had left

Moscow soon after the October Revolution, were no doubt among those initially hoping to soon go home. That they had not planned to be away long was confirmed by Nadezhda's cousin Anna, then still in Moscow. In her memoirs, she remembered the visit sometime in 1918 of an acquaintance who had came back to the city after spending time in the south. It seems this woman was able to travel relatively freely compared to many people because she had papers from an area no longer part of Russia, due to the war. She was planning to return south and asked Anna to gather some clothing of my grandparents to take to them there, because what they had packed was inadequate for their extended absence.

Nikolai and Nadezhda first went to the Caucasus in southern Russia, a multi-ethnic region between the Black and Caspian Seas. They travelled to Essentuki, in the central Caucasus, an area renowned to this day for its many mineral springs. From the late eighteenth century, health resorts, spas and sanatoria proliferated in the region. It became a popular holiday destination for both the ill and the well, with the upper classes transporting many of the activities of high society to towns set in the scenic Caucasus Mountains.

The locale may have been pleasant enough, but in the circumstances, it was hardly an agreeable stay: dictated by necessity, far from family and amid uncertainty over the future. In sporadic impressions in a diary of my grandmother's, she told of the boredom and idleness of their life in Essentuki, and of the distress in thinking about the home they had left behind. She found "the days of endless waiting" increasingly difficult:

> *My daydreams merged with my reminiscences and they seemed so hopeless that I felt I was in prison in my little Essentuki room. So physically far from my past*

> *life and previous people... From the window – there was always the same scene: a field, a roadway, an English garden. Sometimes the sky took on beautiful colours of sunset... But because this was happening in distant confinement, even nature became detestable to me – like the empty ornamentation of a hated life.*

Escalating civil war added to their concerns. The first battle between the Bolsheviks and their opponents had occurred just weeks after the October take-over, and as it spread in 1918, my grandparents became worried about being trapped by conflict. Returning north was at that point out of the question, but they also feared being cut off from Nikolai's family. Fighting was taking place to the west of Essentuki and some family members were further west still, to the north of the Black Sea in Ukraine.

In April 1918 my grandmother had her first child, Alexander. This added to the dilemma over what to do: both travelling on and staying presented dangers, especially for the baby, so small and also in weak health. While it was hard to find out exactly what was happening in the conflict, they heard reports of massacres in the Caucasus region. The fighting was fluid, with various groups skirmishing in many locales and wreaking violence on others over hatreds both spawned by the Revolution and dating back further. My grandparents pondered whether to risk trying to reach Kiev. Had Nikolai perhaps by then already resolved to join the forces opposing the Bolsheviks? If he had, another possible consideration was that it would be better to leave his wife and baby with his family while he went off to the White Army.

By early 1918 many Russians were sick of war. The World War was a horrific conflict for all the nations involved; for Russia too it was disastrous. Estimates of the death toll vary widely, ranging from one to two million, with millions more injured, taken prisoner-of-war or displaced. Yet there was still opinion backing the country's commitment to its allies in the conflict. At the same time others craved an end to the killing, and for them, the Bolshevik promise of peace was attractive.

But while the Bolsheviks wanted to sign a separate treaty with Germany and get out of that war, they had different views about conflict for their political aims. For them, civil war was part of the class struggle, a necessity to force the upper layers of society to give up their privileges. Indeed, many of them saw ordinary Germans as natural class allies, against whom they did not want to keep fighting – and who they hoped would soon join the revolutionary struggle. The real enemy was the upper classes, whether in Russia, Germany or elsewhere.

Some of the Bolsheviks' implacable enemies were prepared to take up the challenge in what had become a battle for their own future in their country, as my grandfather's brother Sergei wrote:

> *From the moment the new power came into existence there also sprang up a struggle against it... Opposition to the Bolsheviks was instinctual, their unacceptability obvious, and the fight against them – which would flood all Russia with blood... was conceded to be unavoidable.*

The new rulers signed the Brest-Litovsk Treaty with Germany to end Russia's participation in the World War in March 1918. The bloody hostilities of the Civil War now produced the victims. Whatever the political rhetoric, in civil wars the enemy is not clearly defined; who is seen as that enemy can often be tainted by desires for revenge or hatred which have little to do with the stated reasons for the conflict. Members of the same family, neighbours, friends can turn into enemies. The fighting was to continue for three years – and to add considerably to the casualty toll accumulating since 1914.

Sergei was among those who would join the anti-Bolshevik forces, as were his brothers: my grandfather Nikolai and Vladimir. My mother believed her father Alexander also fought in the army of those who became known as the Whites – trying to unseat the Reds.

Before Sergei travelled to the White forces in the south, he spent the first half of 1918 in Petrograd, observing changes there with alarm:

> *In Petrograd, a rather crazy life set in. The Bolsheviks increasingly felt more certain of their power. But in fact all authority was being challenged, in the city all sorts of gangs of crooks appeared, and no-one knew who was breaking into apartments – representatives of the authorities or thieves. But people disappeared, the "extraordinaries" [secret police] were at work, and arrests and executions became everyday occurrences... Stores which still had something to sell were open, and even the huge store of the Guards' Economic Society was trading, while a restaurant operated on the top floor. It is possible the authorities purposely did not close it, because many officers – like moths to a flame – gathered here, and here too arrests were carried out. Prices for everything became absurd...*

The lack of structures to replace the old abandoned system was unsettling. And there were questions as to whether this regime would prove to be transitory – like the preceding one. The retention, at first, of some familiar elements of the past may have provided comforting continuity, but as Sergei pointed out, even this could be deceptively – and dangerously – misleading. Hindsight would have accentuated his awareness of the dangers when he later wrote this, but there would have already been plenty of evidence around him of his vulnerability, and of those like him, in the evolving situation.

During most of this time Sergei lived with his father, my great-grandfather Alexander, in his hotel room. But he also managed to be admitted to hospital for treatment of his hands, which had been wounded in the war. In this, and in many other ways, he and his father were helped by his former batman. Iakov, a Latvian, had taken every opportunity to educate himself while he was with Sergei at war; he had mastered Russian and had devoured every book he could to better his knowledge. Now he was making quick progress in the new regime, acquiring a position which gave him access to valuable information. In spite of his new role, he remained loyal to Sergei and his family, warning them of impending measures that would affect them. He also provided practical help with the increasing difficulties of day-to-day survival. Sergei and Alexander took their ration cards to an aunt and shared meals with her, but as time went on, these bought ever less food, and of poorer quality. Iakov was their "guardian-angel" – he brought provisions and found good excuses to counter their attempts to refuse his charity. (In later years, the aunt's maid Dunia would become Iakov's wife.)

Sergei became involved in a secret organisation which helped officers travel south to join the White forces. His role was to solicit funds from business people still operating, or from nobles who retained property:

My task was not easy. After two coups people were frightened, extremely untrusting, and even close friends looked at me suspiciously, when I – knowing they had means – approached them for help. But then the secret hope that the officers could destroy this hated power opened wallets, and I collected considerable sums, which helped many officers make their way south.

In his memoirs Sergei realised that it was sad and absurd that the members of this organisation were naïve enough to think the government did not know about it. If anything, he later surmised, it was a convenient grouping for the authorities to infiltrate, to find out what the opposition was up to. This was confirmed when Iakov delivered a warning, though Sergei had never said anything to him about his activities. Iakov had told Sergei he understood that he could not support the new regime, and it seems there was a tacit agreement between them not to discuss politics more than necessary. In Iakov's warning now, nothing was spelled out, except that it was best to avoid a particular address as arrests would soon occur there, information passed on as Iakov looked at Sergei "sternly and meaningfully".

In the course of his secret role, Sergei was offered the opportunity to leave for Finland. But as before, he felt he should stay and work for what he believed was best for his country. In spite of doubts about what the White forces in the south could achieve, he increasingly felt his place was with them, that there was no other viable option for opposing the Bolsheviks; these forces provided "the only bright ray in the gloom, which had seized Russia." But he was torn because of Alexander:

CHAPTER FIVE

In the small [hotel] room, which seemed cosy to me, we spent whole evenings talking, my father and I. The light burned weakly, it was hard to read; I listened to my father's stories, and I could clearly picture the whole life of my family.

Yet for a long time now, there was no family here... my mother, brothers and sister were in the south... cut off from us, and only I remained with my father. I felt how much my father was afraid of losing me and yet he understood that for my own safety I would need to leave Petrograd...

...every day brought new arrests and executions. I was held back by anxiety over my father... Father often said that is was time for me to go, but right away he would add: "And I will remain alone. God will not grant that we will see each other again soon."

Sergei was offered a way of getting to the south, with Ukrainian members of his regiment going home. Ukraine was then occupied by the Germans and it provided a transit point to the White forces. He was tempted to go; he thought he could slip over the border with the troops who were being officially repatriated. But Iakov warned against it and Sergei trusted his former batman's advice. Later he would learn about the fate of many of the young officers he helped escape to the south by various routes: some managed to get through the train searches and checkpoints and reach the White Army safely, some had to hide away en route awaiting better circumstances, but many died at the hands of Red patrols.

In the spring, the new authorities ordered that all military officers put their names on a register. This was presumably in preparation for the mass conscription of tsarist officers that would be set in motion by Leon Trotsky in the summer. The War Commissar recognised the disorganisation of the army and the need for military professionals if the regime was to successfully wage war against its opponents. Sergei's father offered to go first, to test whether this was a ploy to carry out arrests. Sergei was moved by Alexander's willingness to jeopardise his own safety for his sake. He believed his father hoped to find evidence there was no danger in the sign-up so he could stay on.

Iakov told them there would be no risk for Alexander, but he recommended that Sergei avoid registering. He also said his ability to protect him was running out and that it was best for him to leave soon. Iakov set about organising his escape and told him to be ready at a moment's notice. Then the signal came.

> *[My father] would not even consider leaving Petrograd and always said that he had served his whole life in the Petrograd district and would never abandon it. His desire was to die in his favourite city. And I, knowing all the difficulties and dangers of the journey to the south, could not imagine how my father would have endured them...*
>
> *[Yet] To act differently than what Iakov suggested, we could not. With emotion I farewelled my father; he blessed me and said with calm certainty: "Spend the summer in Kiev, and in the autumn come back. By then everything will have settled down and again we will all be able to live together." Either my father was fooling himself or he was detached from reality.*

Sergei and his father were never to see each other again.

CHAPTER FIVE

Iakov was waiting at the appointed train station, with documents, money and food for the journey. He placed Sergei in the care of a trusted conductor and assured him that he would look after his father and his aunt:

> *[Iakov said] "I'm sorry that you are leaving, but it has to be this way... I cannot be with you. I already belong to the new regime and I cannot leave it... I know you will go to... [the White forces]. What of that, go ahead. You cannot do otherwise. Well, God bless you." Iakov made the sign of the cross over me. He had tears in his eyes. I was also emotional. My faithful Iakov! Batman and friend, sharing with me all the hardships and joys of life and service. A prominent Red commissar, but to the end a loyal person, thinking of and caring not only for me, but also for my father and aunt.*

Events in the cities began to be echoed in the country, as my grandmother's cousin Anna discovered during the first half of 1918. She, her husband (another Nikolai) and their small son were living with her mother and stepfather on his estate, to the northeast of Moscow, beyond Yaroslavl. Turbulent times sometimes brought together people in unusual ways: another resident on the estate at this time was Anna's father. Though he and Anna's mother had been divorced for some years, his loss of his position in the Tsar's household over the controversy surrounding Rasputin, and then his departure from the military altogether after the Revolution, had left him adrift. So he ended up staying with his ex-wife and her husband.

That is where a telegram from Trotsky found him, ordering him back to duty. He was adamant he would not provide his officer's experience to the Bolsheviks. So he travelled to a nearby psychiatric institution, where a doctor he knew was working. He told the doctor that he would commit suicide unless he was given a certificate that he was mentally incompetent to return to the military. The doctor coached him on symptoms to emphasise and then called in the hospital director, who was easily convinced he was unfit. The local military authorities accepted the certificate without question, surprising perhaps in view of his former role with the Tsar. Yet there was no further question of him returning to service.

Soon the family began to feel the effects of Lenin's Decree on Land, which called for the expropriation of properties belonging to the gentry, without compensation. Implementation was gradual and uneven at first. This was due in part to the sporadic communication of government decrees and information in the country, but was also influenced by variable local attitudes. The first signs of impending expropriation of Anna's stepfather's estate came with searches and the cataloguing of belongings. She described the first such search as frightening, but somewhat farcical. One of the search party came upon a wine bottle which was being used to store a chemical. He took a big swig and declared the wine disgusting. Anna was horrified, but believed he escaped being poisoned.

Gradually the searchers moved from listing property to taking it, though at this stage, again, there were different attitudes among different groups. This was demonstrated when some peasants came from a village a short distance away to ask Anna's stepfather for a disused barn:

> *They said: "We have heard that we are now in power and that everything is ours, so if possible we will take this building... and if later there is a law which says it*

is yours, then we will pay you. So if you could please sign this deed." He signed the deed, which he called a useless scrap of paper, and soon workers came with axes to break up the barn and to take away logs on sleds to their village... All of a sudden some peasants came from our nearest village... They said: "We heard that some people came to humiliate you over your building... just give the order and we will kill them all with our axes." ...they of course had all removed their hats and had very politely greeted us. Mama said "God save us! That barn has been given to them, through a special agreement and no-one is offending us or touching us" and she thanked them very much... And really, we felt that the [local peasants] had affection for us and wanted to help us should any sort of outrage be directed at us.*

Former workers of the nobility retaining esteem for their bosses, in spite of declarations that they were now the masters and could – and even should – turf out their former overseers, was not uncommon. There are plenty of stories of peasants supporting their local gentry in confrontations, especially initially, protecting them or their property, hiding them or helping them escape. People did not always fit into stereotypical categories – on both sides – and past relationships influenced attitudes. Besides many peasants in the country did not trust the Bolsheviks, and the feelings were somewhat mutual. At times fear came into the equation: there was no guarantee this government would survive, and who knew what would happen to those seizing property if new rulers took over.

The family may have been heartened by the protectiveness

of the locals at this stage – if horrified over the means proposed. But they knew it was only a matter of time before they would have to give up the estate.

Soon after the tussle over the barn, they learned that a nearby estate had been partially taken over by the village Soviet. Anna said the search parties, now directed by Soviet officials, became more frequent:

> *Some people came... and said we should make an inventory of the livestock and all the carriages, in a word, all the external... household. Which was done. And in a week they came to take everything away according to this list. It was a long procession: our cows were mooing – they left us one; the horses were neighing – they took the troika; the carriages – they left us a small springless carriage and one horse. All this stretched out along the road, this terrible parade... Then they came again, very courteous and very polite, to do an inventory of the house. They inventoried every room... they said the only things that did not interest them were foreign books and icons and also household linen... But all the cupboards, chairs, paintings, were written down. We knew what that meant. But at that point, they did not yet take them away. They made [my stepfather] the guardian responsible for this national property, in which we continued to live.*

There is a touch of irony in Anna observing that her stepfather, an "enemy of the people", was placed in charge of property to be nationalised. But this did little to mitigate what must have been a distressing sight: the dismantling of their home – and their way of life.

Anna gave birth to a second son in April, but the joyful occasion was soon overshadowed by startling news. In July, the Tsar and his family were executed in Siberia, in the house where they had been held prisoner. This devastated the family. Anna believed her stepfather, who had been active in opposition to the Tsar before the Revolution, was as distressed as the others, because the reform he had helped initiate had gone so wrong: "all his ideals were destroyed... all the meaning of his life... whereas the others had had a premonition that if there was revolution things would not go well..."

During this period, Anna's husband was earning some income as a travelling buyer of leather for the army, while her stepfather sold whatever still belonged to the family:

[My stepfather] travelled now and then to Moscow to sell my or Mama's jewellery because there was by now nothing left to live on. The banks were all closed. And they had written to us to say that all the silver, which we had foolishly put in the bank, thinking the government bank was the most stable that there could be – they sent us a paper to say that all our things, that is to say the silver and some jewellery... were now considered to be nationalised property.

As the household struggled, Nikolai began to seek a livelihood in Moscow. His brother's family was scraping a living by baking *pirozhki* to sell on the streets. Others peddled a variety of goods: sweets, knitwear, matches, and so on. Many shops had closed, but a new type was opening in increasing numbers: they bought antiques, artwork, silverware, and other valuables from the former upper classes. They then sold them to foreigners, such as diplomats, or to the evolving ruling class – those rising in the new regime's ranks. Anna's husband decided to open such a store. He found suitable premises and someone to help him paint and clean it. He rented a *dacha* on the outskirts of the city and sent for his family.

Anna left her parents in August with a heavy heart, wondering what would become of them; she knew their house could be taken at any moment. She, her sons, their nanny and a servant who had worked for her since before the Revolution, travelled by train, seeing occasional signs of unrest, smoke rising from areas of recent conflict. Arriving in Moscow after an absence of just over a year, Anna was shocked at the change:

> *Moscow was totally unrecognisable. All the stores were closed, many windows were broken by bullets... there were these people walking around in leather jackets, with revolvers in their belts. Some troops wandered about, half undressed. I cannot convey the horror of this empty and frightening Moscow.*

But as they travelled on, Anna was cheered by a beautiful moonlit night. She found the *dacha* Nikolai had rented charming. In spite of everything that was happening, she remembered the next while as relatively happy. It was brief, but one of the few times during a marriage interrupted by war and revolution that she and her husband had anything resembling a normal family life in their own home. He commuted to his shop in the city and to seek provisions. They supplemented their rations with vegetables from the garden and the many mushrooms growing there and in the woods beyond. When Anna visited relatives in Moscow, she realised her family was relatively well off. There, food shortages were getting worse, there was virtually no lighting, shooting could often be heard, and few people ventured out. She was always happy to return to the *dacha*.

But again, political events shattered their brief moment of tranquillity. An uncle of Anna's had been a Minister of the Interior under the Tsar, and in September she learned that he – along with about twenty other former ministers – had been executed. In deep shock she rushed to Moscow to be with her aunt. The widow, unable to comprehend her husband's fate, did understand one thing clearly: she had to leave the country with her children.

Anna also decided that Russia was now too dangerous for those who had had any role in the previous regime. She felt her husband, who had been a senior officer, would sooner or later be targeted and she determined he should leave. If he had any doubts about this, these were soon dispelled. He had grown a full beard, and changed his style of dress, and thought he was unrecognisable. But one day in Moscow, a soldier from his former regiment spotted him and immediately saw through his disguise. The man said it was courting disaster to be walking the streets openly. Now a train conductor on the Kiev run, he offered to smuggle Nikolai to the Ukraine border. Anna encouraged her husband to take up this offer, though this would mean another separation: travelling as a family was too dangerous. Anna was hopeful she and the children would soon be able to join him. She had been born in Ukraine; it was out of Russian control at this time, so if he could obtain Ukrainian papers for her, and somehow get them to her, she could cross the border freely.

About a week later the conductor gave them a day's warning. At the appointed time, Anna and her husband made their way to the small local station, where a train would make an unscheduled stop. She tried to remain optimistic that they would soon be reunited, but she held great fears that she would never see her husband again:

> *At the station we walked back and forth on the platform. We were unable to speak... there were still seven minutes, then five minutes – there was still time, we were still together. At last the train appeared, a long, long train. We heard a loud whistle and the whole train shuddered and stopped. Kolia [Nikolai] jumped on... I made the sign of the cross and stood there a long, long time until the small red light disappeared in the distance, around a curve. And then I went home. The sky was grey and torn clouds scudded across it, there was a strong wind, a wet one, leaves were being torn off trees and they slapped me in the face... I knew that before me stretched a difficult, enormous road – what it would be like, what the future held, I did not know... I just somehow felt it would be terrible.*

Anna had an agonising wait for news. After several days she got word that her husband had slipped across the border with the help of local villagers, narrowly escaping a military patrol. Soon there was more good news: an acquaintance arrived from Kiev with official documents that Nikolai had obtained for her. Anna prepared to join him.

For my mother's relatives too, there were difficult decisions to be made about whether to abandon their homes, and questions about where these departures would take them. My mother was born and spent the first months of her life in Mogilev, today in Belarus. Close to the western edge of the Empire, and thus to the front, the city had been used to headquarter the Russian Army through much of the First World War. After the Revolution there was fighting and political instability in the area; it saw Soviet leadership and German occupation. When the Bolsheviks moved in, their control was often patchy. For instance, in late 1918 there was a peasant uprising in Mogilev province against their policies.

My grandmother Natalia's deliberations on whether to leave Mogilev with her baby daughter would have been influenced by such unrest. But possibly her strongest reason for considering traveling south was to search for her husband, who was with the White forces, and whom she had not seen for many months.

In the absence of any diaries or memoirs, I have often tried to imagine my grandmother contemplating her future and pondering the best course of action. All I have to go on is the little that my mother remembered Natalia telling her in later years.

Basically she had two options. She could stay in the family home and take her chances. Information would have been hard to come by. But snatches of news along the grapevine would have brought reports and rumours of clashes, of terror tactics used against apparently innocent villagers, of attacks on estate families and the destruction of their homes and property, of shifting and unpredictable loyalties – all of which would have posed threats to her safety on the estate.

The other main option for Natalia was to join the flood of people trying to escape Bolshevik-controlled areas, probably with little idea of an ultimate destination, a time frame or any long-term goal. That meant traveling through areas in conflict, which changed hands between the Reds and their White opponents, and various other factions. Then there were the groups which seemed nothing more than bandits, whose main aim often was to take advantage of the chaos, and terrorise and steal.

My grandmother would have been pulled in different directions by considering those to whom she was closest. News from her husband would have been sporadic or non-existent. Alexander was thought to be with the White Army, and at some point was badly wounded, with shrapnel lodging in his spine. Did Natalia know this? As for Natalia's mother, she was convinced that Bolshevik rule was temporary, and that control would soon revert to a more palatable regime. Besides she felt responsible for the estate; it had been left in her care when her husband died – she was not budging. And there was my mother, an infant, who had no opinion on the matter, but whose future was the most fragile.

I visualise the estate house from photographs I have seen and descriptions I have read of similar places. My grandmother is on the wide balcony of a big wooden house. The windows and doors are framed by elaborate carvings – like fine lace edgings defining another world within. My mother is sleeping in a cot next to a trellis submerged in vines. My grandmother looks out over the garden. Further away are the fields and the village. Is she wondering if and when the villagers who have worked on the estate for generations will turn against her family? Is she thinking about the dangers she will face if she flees the place where she was born and grew up?

Photographs of my grandmother taken at about this time show a young woman with soft dark hair, pulled back, but always with a few curls or frizzy strands framing her face. Her eyes are large and expressive. Along with a half-smile, they negate the sternness and formality of many other family photos from this time, a gentle subversion of photographic convention. The openness and at times mischievousness of her glance seem to denote a lightness unsuited to what lies ahead for her. In later photos, taken when she was already in

CHAPTER FIVE

exile, her eyes still captivate the viewer, but they are sad, unfocussed, as though she does not want to see the sharp edges of her life.

My mother believed that in the end, what motivated Natalia's decision most strongly was the desire to find her husband. Unless the Whites started winning the Civil War, probably the only way to be reunited with him was to go to him. Then there was the opportunity presented by a convoy that was passing by on its way south.

It is not clear when Natalia set off with her daughter – it may have been in 1918 or sometime in 1919. She hated to leave her mother behind, but there was no convincing her to abandon the estate. My mother told me she learned afterwards that when the campaign against the landed gentry intensified, some of her grandmother's workers offered to help her escape, by dressing her in peasant clothes and accompanying her. Apparently even then she refused to flee and those workers who remained promised to try to defend her and the estate. When it was taken over by Soviet authorities, she continued to live there in a servant's room. But this arrangement was short-lived, and with the entire house confiscated, she left as well, travelling to Petrograd to live with the family of another of her daughters.

Natalia's parting with her mother must have been painful, though it is impossible to know whether mother and daughter realised they would never see each other again

The wrenching farewells multiplied as the flood of departures grew. The travellers found themselves moving further and further from home. But for many there was still hope of return, hope the Civil War would push out the hated Bolsheviks.

6

Reluctant Exiles

The flight of one of my great-aunts would eventually take her to Belgium. More than half a century after the Revolution, when I would visit her, she always reminded me that she had never taken out Belgian citizenship.

"I could never swear allegiance to any country other than Russia," she would say.

We would sit in her room in an old folks' home, every corner and wall space crammed with mementoes of a life long past: icons with glittering silver covers, delicate ornately-decorated Fabergé eggs, ancient leather bound volumes, photographs of her as a lady-in-waiting at the Tsar's court and of various relatives in uniforms trimmed with braid, epaulettes and medals.

Although my great-aunt lived many more years in Western Europe than in Russia, she never replaced her United Nations identity document. It and other international permits which preceded the establishment of the UN, allowed her to live and travel freely in the West.

Many of those who left Russia became reconciled to life in their adopted countries. But others, like her, never accepted their exile. Many decades later, they maintained a symbolic resistance to the idea that their Russia was no more. Regardless of how well settled they were in their new homes, to them, the life they had led before was more real... Everything that followed could never measure up.

CHAPTER SIX

Both my parents' families were among those to edge further from their past lives as events unfolded in 1918. As with many others, Ukraine became their first destination. Several of my father's family made their way to Kiev. My maternal grandmother Natalia headed to another part of Ukraine – Odessa, on the Black Sea – when she left Mogilev with my mother Irene.

Ukraine had long been part of the Russian Empire. In the wake of the October Revolution, the dream of many Ukrainians was fulfilled with a declaration of independence. But the nationalist government was weak and during 1918, there would be five changes of regime. One of these brought in a Soviet Republic in February, but it lasted less than a month. After the signing of the Brest-Litovsk treaty in March, which took Russia out of the war, the Germans occupied it, installing a puppet Ukrainian government. The Germans remained until December.

Throughout 1918, people fleeing the Bolsheviks flooded into Ukraine. Many found life under the rule of those who had been their enemies in the World War a humiliation. Yet it was seen as a lesser evil than being subject to the Reds.

For my mother, what she knew of the refugee exodus she was part of as a baby, was echoed by one she witnessed two decades later: the panicked flight of Parisians as the Germans marched into France during the Second World War, departures which took them to destinations only vaguely known and sometimes just as dangerous as the place they left behind. The first major refugee wave of the twentieth century – the one out of Russia – seems like a template for many more that century and this one. The scenes of people escaping conflict or persecution have become all too familiar, a broken record of broken homes and countries.

In Mogilev, Irene believed her mother carefully weighed up her options whether to stay or go. But in an interview I recorded with her, she said there was also the same element of alarm and confusion she would later experience in France:

> ...*I think my mother panicked too, leaving on a horse convoy led by Cossacks heading for Odessa. Some people had wagons, some were able to take things, others left with absolutely nothing. Some helped out – my mother found room for us on a wagon... All of Russia was in flux – parts shifted White to Red to White to Red again. And we would stop and get food, but how, I don't know – at times things were very bad... At times there was no water and very little food... but often others gave food to my mother for me because I was the youngest in the convoy.... Some of the villages along the way had run out of food... the Cossacks occasionally clashed [with the Reds, to get through]... My mother used to tell me that at times there was intense fighting... But she did not speak about all this much – she was very young, with a baby, and I think she maybe even later regretted fleeing and leaving everything behind.*

From Mogilev to Odessa is about nine hundred kilometres. Moving through fighting, and with the constant search for provisions, it must have been an arduous trip. But they made it safely. Because of the overcrowding due to the many other arrivals, an abandoned railway carriage with other refugees became home for Natalia and my mother at first. There was plenty of disease around; a group of people living in close quarters with insufficient heating and nutrition provided a good breeding ground for illness and Irene said Natalia caught whatever was passing through:

> I remember my mother was very sick at one time – she had typhus... We were living on the train then, and many were ill – she also got pneumonia and God knows what else... As for how we survived [financially] in Odessa, I have no idea, but I think my mother had taken jewellery with her and was selling it...

Eventually my grandmother made contact with her sister, Evgeniia; how and when she arrived in the city is not clear. Evgeniia moved into the railway carriage and was no doubt vital to my mother's survival during my grandmother's illnesses. They were later reunited with their brother, Vladimir. He was appalled at their conditions and helped his sisters and niece get better accommodation and obtain sufficient food.

While my mother and her relatives were struggling in Odessa, my father's family was gradually congregating in the Ukrainian capital Kiev. My grandfather's sister Olga and her baby daughter had been there since May 1917, staying with an aunt. In June, her husband had arrived without warning, exhausted and demoralised. After the military reforms of Order Number One, he had given up on his regiment, which was in disarray. Soon her mother and her brother Vladimir had appeared. The regiment in which he and my grandfather Nikolai had served – the Fourth Imperial Family Rifle Guards Regiment – had been disbanded.

Over the winter of 1917-1918, the Bolsheviks had bombarded

Kiev, to wrest it from the nationalist government; Olga wrote that the family often had to shelter in the basement. One time a bomb landed close by, but no-one in the building was hurt. After the twenty-day period of Soviet rule, Olga had witnessed the Germans marching in:

> *...it was grandiose: a formidable mass of men all dressed in the same uniform and round helmets... They were everywhere and made off with anything that was edible... The government of Hetman Skoropadskii, put into place by the occupiers, established order and the markets became well supplied with goods at reasonable prices.*

At Easter the aunt died, and they had to move. But with the inheritance that they received from her, they were able to buy a large apartment. It seems odd that Olga and her husband decided to buy a home. On the one hand, this indicates that they did not foresee going back north in a hurry. On the other, it implies that they expected continuing stability in the area, in spite of the Civil War not far away.

It was just as well the apartment was large, because soon there would be an influx of friends. Some stayed, others just came for meals. Olga said most were officers who had fled Petrograd. They would hold meetings in the apartment, organising to link up with the White forces. And more family members started trickling in too.

Among the arrivals was my great-uncle Sergei. He had farewelled his father and Iakov in Petrograd in June 1918. Kiev was his desired destination but first he had faced a risky journey.

As his train set off, he had much to ponder. Travelling through familiar areas, he wondered whether he would ever see them again. He worried about his father and aunt, left behind in a "hungry,

CHAPTER SIX

dying Petrograd", though he was comforted by Iakov's promise to take care of them. He thought of the events of the preceding two years: he questioned the dubious actions of some and their disastrous impact on Russia. And he was anxious about how he was going to cross the border into Ukraine. The weather was sunny, the fields were green, but both the farms and the stations they passed seemed empty, "as if the people had hidden somewhere."

When he arrived at the border, Sergei deliberated over how to continue. Without entry documents – Iakov had provided only exit papers from Russia – he felt the only way to get into Ukraine would be to sneak across, in the woods away from the rail line:

> *Now I had to look for a smuggler for crossing the border. I have to admit, I felt confused. Holding my small suitcase, I loitered anxiously on the platform. It was very dangerous to ask anyone – agents of the Bolsheviks also loitered here. Peasants, who provided transportation, watched for those arriving and inconspicuously offered their services.*

He met a nurse who was travelling with a group of Russian soldiers returning home from Ukraine. Some Ukrainian soldiers who had come from the north were waiting to switch to the train that had brought her and her charges to the border. She was allowed to cross freely to arrange the transfers. She offered that he go with her with the excuse that he was helping with luggage. But they were stopped and Sergei was directed into a booth. He felt the game was up, especially when the customs agent there instructed him to wait and left. These were words Sergei had learned to dread:

> *Back in Petrograd, when someone said to me "Wait a minute," I felt things were getting dangerous.*

> *My interlocutor could return with an agent of the Reds. So I would always try to leave quickly, and not wait. But here there was nowhere for me to go. I stayed in the booth, I felt as though I was in a cage.*

But to his amazement, the man returned and told him all was well for him to slip across. He had picked Sergei for an officer in spite of his civilian clothing and was more than sympathetic:

> *[He said] "My booth has a secret. This door here is to Soviet Russia, and this" – he pointed to a door on the opposite side of the booth – "to Ukraine. Go, nice young man, to Ukraine. Go straight to the train, the nurse will see you and approach. Go, don't look back. May God help you." I started to thank him. "There's no need to thank me. You are not the first, and you will not be the last. I myself am waiting for my son, also an officer. When he arrives we will leave for Ukraine together"... He opened the small door and pushed me. "Go"... The nurse, seeing me, quickly approached. I must have been pale. She looked at me with concern. "Don't worry, walk slowly."*

The nurse left Sergei in the care of a conductor. She too waved away his gratitude: " 'Think in what times we live,' [she said] 'if we don't help each other, then we will all perish.' "

There was still a tense moment ahead, as the commander overseeing the troops being repatriated had to give permission for Sergei to travel with them. It turned out that he was happy to do so; he too opposed the Bolsheviks and was not planning to return north. He said how foolish trying to cross the border with a smuggler would have been:

CHAPTER SIX

> *[The commander said] "You are a naive person. You have no idea what's going on here. [Between the Germans and the Reds]... a void has been created, a no man's land... and here bandits, deserters, and all sorts of riff raff from nearby villages are active. These bandits rob mercilessly those crossing the no man's land. At best, they release them in only their underwear to go to the Germans, but more often they just shoot them in the nearest ravine. Both the Germans and the Reds struggle against the bandits... but the ease of spoils tempts people, and there's no getting rid of them. This is the danger you faced, and this is what the nurse saved you from."*

These lucky meetings seem almost unbelievable, like coincidental encounters in fiction. Yet also they reflect the patchy control by the Bolsheviks and the many people who were less than convinced of their authority. Against the barbarity of the Civil War, on both sides, especially in the period ahead, evidence of human decency among strangers is heartening. Though even in these circumstances, the helpful links and connections of the old world are still evident. There was sympathy among many officers, and the nurse – Sergei would later learn – was from an aristocratic family. As a religious man, he himself believed that God had protected him.

After all the anxiety he had experienced, Sergei fell fast asleep. When he awoke the train was at a station. He could hardly believe what he saw:

> *I approached the window, and truly, it seemed to me that I was still dreaming. Along the platform stood counters, piled up with all sorts of food:*

fried fowl, dairy products, all sorts of vegetables, berries, and most important – bread: round breads, loaves, buns, rolls, in huge quantities. Rosy-cheeked friendly-looking women, yelling loudly, were persuasively inviting buyers.

How famished we had all become, those of us arriving from the north! The abundance of bread seemed miraculous – what if I suddenly woke up and all this disappeared? I drank my fill of milk and bought a huge loaf of bread...

The train travelled quickly, stopping rarely, but where it did stop, everywhere the scenes of indescribable abundance were repeated... [In one town] Along the platform of the station walked masses of youths, so happy, so cheerful. Everyone smiled and laughed, calling jokes to each other... it was so inexpressibly joyful to see the happy people living here.

On arrival in Kiev, Sergei continued to be amazed at the bright lights, bustling shops, and lively people on the streets as he walked to his family's apartment. They had not known he was coming and there was much joy at his appearance. But while the family celebrated, Sergei could not banish thoughts of the dismal, half-ruined cities of the north, and of his father left behind in "gloomy, dying, distant but beloved Petrograd".

My paternal grandparents Nadezhda and Nikolai decided to risk the difficult journey from the Caucasus to Kiev also in June 1918. They prepared to leave Essentuki with three-month-old Alexander and his nanny. In her diary Nadezhda wrote that on the evening before their departure, Nikolai brought home "a reasonably large sum of money" from selling a brooch of hers to pay for the trip. But there was still turmoil in her feelings over their plans, especially over the dangers to Musik – as they had nicknamed their son:

> ...*I must admit that in my soul I was uncertain whether we would carry out our decision or not, and I kept comforting myself with the thought that there was still a whole night to think about it. A terrible night!... Our little, modest apartment took on a chaotic appearance. All night we carried around clothing, filled bottles with boiled water for Musik, washed his diapers. I remember particularly well the open suitcases, soap, icons, all sorts of clothes, which I sadly packed.*

In the morning, dull weather deepened her apprehension. They left for the railway station in pouring rain. The first part of their trip, to the nearest town on the main line, was relatively comfortable. While they waited for their connection, Nadezhda was sorely tempted to abandon the journey.

When their train arrived, they found space in a crowded, dirty car, the conditions exacerbated by many wanting to flee. Fear over the fighting in the Civil War all around added to her grim impressions of this part of the trip:

> ...*the train started – there was no longer any going back. Considering the events, one could foresee being shot at or getting into the middle of a battle and being cut off at some small station... At night... Musik was unsettled, often awoke. More and more people jammed*

in – there were now people sitting at our feet and under our feet... the window was open, and so in spite of the stink and the crowd, the air stayed fairly fresh. But towards morning, at every station, yet more passengers started to get on, with baskets and luggage. By midday the heat became unbearable. Musik fretted, screamed terribly... We ourselves were so stressed that we could not calm him. The women all gave their advice, reproaching me over his hunger and accusing me of feeding him by the clock...

Finally my grandparents arrived in Novorossiisk on the northeastern shore of the Black Sea. Battles to the north and east of the city had brought defeats for the Whites in the early months of 1918. But local Cossacks, terrorised by the brief Bolshevik rule that had followed, bolstered the White effort in an uneasy alliance. By the time Nadezhda and Nikolai reached Novorossiisk, the anti-Bolshevik groups were in the ascendancy; in the coming months they would push the Red forces northwards.

It was a huge relief for my grandparents to have evaded fighting along the way and to now escape the crammed train in a town where there were doctors, chemists, hotels and other services. Hotels there were, but they were all overfull; even restaurants were being used for accommodation. In the women's washroom in the station, where Nadezhda and the nanny bathed the baby, they met a woman who had camped there for a week for lack of somewhere else to sleep. She had other information that upset my grandmother: a group of children with diphtheria had been there earlier that day. Nadezhda quickly fled the washroom with Alexander.

Without much hope, Nikolai went off to seek accommodation.

He made a lucky discovery: at one hotel he came across a family my grandparents knew. Nadezhda determined that she would plead with them to take in at least the baby for the night. But that was not necessary. In spite of occupying only a small room and a balcony, the family of four welcomed the extra lodgers.

The next day my grandparents learned that rooms were not the only commodity in short supply. They had hoped to quickly get a ship to Crimea. But there were only small boats, considered unsafe, making the crossing. A German transport ship was expected soon; it would repatriate German troops who had been imprisoned during the war, and would also take some paying passengers. But no-one knew exactly when it might arrive.

Again, luck and acquaintances combined to get them out of a difficult situation. Through friends of friends, they were able to get a room in the home of the German director of a cement factory across the bay from the town centre. Nadezhda found it strange to be in such a peaceful place amid all that had been happening – in a home that seemed already from another era: their hosts "...lived like kings and the Revolution had in no way touched their luxurious way of life."

A pram was found for Alexander, and Nadezhda spent her days walking him around the garden next to the house, which was perched high on a hill. She agonised over their future prospects. And again her awareness of natural beauty had almost the opposite effect to the one it might normally have had. Amid the volatile circumstances, it failed to soothe her. Perhaps it also served to underline her separation from home and familiar scenery, to remind her of her displacement:

[There was] a wonderful view of the sea. Because
of the sea and the high position, it was never hot.

> *Roses grew on the slope of the hill... Day after day I passed by them, constantly walking... and the possibility of getting to Kiev seemed infinitely distant and almost unachievable. These green mountains, the light of the sea, the fresh comforting wind – they were like a vice which gripped us and sternly whispered they would not let us go soon from their charming captivity... To remain in Novorossiisk... would have been in essence absurd, but to show how much fantasy there is in my nature, I admit I was already fabricating means of existence, was imagining that Kolia [Nikolai] could work in Novorossiisk, give lessons – that somehow we would survive... But when my moods were different, I cursed that we had left Essentuki to take a terrible voyage, and had got stuck in an alien town... At such times there descended on my soul a really inexpressible despair.*

She found a bit of consolation from the many friends they discovered also in the town, like them mostly in transit to somewhere else. It was as if a chunk of society had been transported en masse. Nadezhda's younger sister, still in her teens, was there too, with her governess. It is unclear how they had made their way to Novorossiisk; they would travel further on with Nadezhda and Nikolai. Their hosts at the cement factory also provided warm hospitality; these strangers would become friends by the time they parted company. They helped my grandparents in many practical ways, and also got them a promise of places on the much-anticipated transport ship.

Finally one day a plume of smoke became visible on the horizon, across the bay. Everyone in the household ran to the upper veranda, where there were telescopes. It was definitely the transport, and as it got closer, it seemed "very large and grand".

My grandfather rushed into town and was told his family should be on the dock the next morning to board the ship. My grandmother remembered feeling anxious and unwell all night, with headache and fever. It was bad preparation for the emotional roller coaster the next day would turn out to be.

In the morning my grandparents farewelled their hosts and headed for the waterfront. There they found a hectic scene: the German ex-prisoners had only just begun boarding, and a crowd of hopeful passengers had gathered. The dock was so congested that cabs bringing new arrivals piled their luggage on the nearby street. Guessing it would be a while before they could embark, Nadezhda took Alexander to the apartment of some friends nearby. It was already evening when Nikolai sent word that they come back:

...the prisoners had all been loaded. But it turned out there were so many of them and there was so little room left, that among the passengers, they were first going to load German citizens. Something inside me snapped when I learned this information but I still decided to go, though with weak fading hope... when we arrived at the dock I saw there the same scene as before, except that the load of things and the crowd of people had grown and you could now feel among them worry, tension, and anxiety. After waiting in the cab for a time, I saw Kolia with an almost desperate face and understood that we could hope for nothing.

Nadezhda returned to the apartment. When Nikolai eventually came to get her, he said that the cement factory director had spent the whole day on the dock trying to intercede on their behalf. Having failed, he had invited my grandparents back to his home:

...all that was left was to accept his offer... Riding past the transport, we stopped. For a moment hope flickered again. Somehow or other, a friend... had noticed that an ordinary German sailor had already accommodated several despairing passengers – seemingly it was just a matter of a simple bribe. (It had not entered into any of our heads that even Germans could be bought with bribes.) And so in just a few minutes in that way, [a family of our friends] got on to the transport. But... when we approached their benefactor with our pleas, it turned out he was already powerless to do anything. Night had arrived, calm, moon-filled, warm, but I now feared the effects of the damp on Musinka, and yearned only to put him to bed and to lie down myself... fatigue was taking over, deadening even the most intense feelings.

When they returned to the home of the cement factory director, in spite of the late hour they were greeted warmly and with sincere concern. This helped calm them and they settled in once again. The transport remained in port for another day, and at the last minute, they were offered space on it. But by then the price was so high Nikolai and Nadezhda could not consider it, so the ship sailed without them.

Over the next few days the search for a way out became more urgent when cases of cholera were reported. There was talk of an epidemic and of the lightning speed with which it could overwhelm the town. If that happened my grandparents might not be allowed to leave. So in spite of grave misgivings, they decided to buy passage on one of the small boats they had at first rejected as unsafe.

Two weeks after arriving in Novorossiisk, my grandparents again said their farewells and boarded a boat called The Raven. Nadezhda wrote that it took seventy passengers and when they settled onto the deck, it was hard to find room to walk among them. She thought the price exorbitant; no doubt such vessels took advantage of people's desperation. The only cabin was the captain's, and in spite of their diminishing funds, Nikolai paid extra for one of the three divans in it, so his wife and baby could shelter from the elements. Following a long, hot day in port, The Raven set sail, to Nadezhda's relief:

After the humidity of the day and the immobility...
a breeze blew in, the sea rocked slightly in the bay...
The sunset was wonderful: the sea became golden,
it shone like enamel, the mountains took on a purple
hue. Through the haze, from the shore, the lights
looked at us in a friendly way. On our departure from
the harbour, it started to rock slightly more, but we did
not pay attention, so happy with the realisation that
we had left Novorossiisk.

They did not travel far. As the waves continued to grow, suddenly the boat turned around. Even passengers who were seasick objected, but the captain said it would get too rough. They tied up again at the dock. As rain began to sprinkle on the people crammed on the deck, Nadezhda, her sister and baby Alexander squeezed into the cabin.

At three o'clock in the morning, the engines started up. As the sun rose they were again underway, with everything "cloaked in a blue and golden radiant mist... while the air was transparent and clean like crystal." Now sitting on their cases on the deck, my grandparents just had time for some tea before the big swell hit again. But this time, The Raven did not turn back.

It was a rough trip, with much seasickness. As huge waves increasingly washed over the huddled passengers, there was also alarm. When he went to fetch a bottle for Alexander, Nikolai found he could no longer get back to his wife and son because of the rolling of the boat. The bottle was passed along from hand to hand. For the rest of the trip he could only look at them across the deck, over the heads of others. Nadezhda was left to face the waves without him, her inexperience of the sea no doubt contributing to her fear:

> *It seemed to me that I went through a whole long lifetime in those hours!... We all felt that we – this little handful of people on a little shell amid the waves – were in the power of something mysterious, terrible and unavoidable... I hugged Musik to myself, looked at Kolia, who could not in these terrifying hours be next to me... I continually repeated the same prayer: have pity on us, save us Lord. And thus passed many hours... Suddenly [there was] barely perceptible calming... the rocking lessened... People... started to liven up. Everyone got into an extremely friendly mood...*

The sense of being helpless amid something huge and out of control seems a fitting metaphor for the whole situation my grandparents found themselves in. The Raven finally docked safely at Kerch, a town on the easternmost tip of the Crimean peninsula.

At this point, there is a gap in my grandmother's diary. Perhaps the rest of the trip was relatively uneventful; perhaps, on the contrary,

CHAPTER SIX

there were such hardships she preferred not to record them. They likely went by rail, arriving in the Ukrainian capital in late July or early August.

The family savoured their reunion, however brief, and getting to know the new generation: my grandparents' son Alexander and Olga's daughter Olga. But the three brothers had military expertise to offer and they aimed to join the forces trying to dislodge the Bolsheviks. Against that, Kiev offered many enticements, which multiplied as more and more escapees, many still with money to spend, poured into town. Sergei was 25 and single and his brother Vladimir was 23 and also unmarried. After four years of war and revolution the lively social scene around them was tempting, Sergei wrote:

> Kiev lived a stormy, feverish life. More and more new clubs, restaurants and nightspots opened, and everywhere was overcrowded. Tired of war, and deprivations under the Bolsheviks, people threw themselves into the whirlpool of life. Day and night the streets were full, and it seemed as if this city never slept and never rested. I too was drawn by this whirlpool. I was young, healthy, full of life and energy.

But life under German control had unpleasant aspects. Sergei had to stop himself tearing the medal from the chest of a former Russian officer, working as a waiter in a café and serving the occupiers with unseemly servility. Sergei understood the need to make a living. But after seeing them as the enemy over his years of war service, he resented the ever-present German officers, and what he saw as their victorious demeanour.

Soon Sergei and Vladimir left Kiev to join the Whites. He could not then know what the future would bring, but in his memoirs, my great-uncle lamented that "...I was leaving behind the remnants of our big family, never again to gather like this" (*). Nikolai did not leave with his brothers. With just one arm, he could not be a combatant. But he took on an administrative role with the forces. According to Olga, this involved liaison and propaganda. At times Nadezhda and Alexander travelled with him, at others they were separated for long periods.

Propaganda was important for both sides in the Civil War. Convincing people they would be better off under one administration or another was helpful for gaining cooperation when collecting supplies and fresh recruits. However to many, neither the Reds nor the Whites seemed relevant to their aspirations. People were not in a hurry to give up their crops or to get back into uniform. Thus both the Reds and the Whites would increasingly resort to terror to obtain supplies from reluctant local populations and to force submission to their leadership.

The implications of this would later become evident to Sergei. He and Vladimir arrived in Ekaterinodar, in the Caucasus, in September, about a month after it had been retaken from the Reds. The brothers enlisted in the Volunteer Army, the main White force in the south, and were billeted with Cossack civilians. The local population welcomed them, but Sergei wrote that it was a rich area and could afford to feed the troops; this would often not be the case later in the war. How much he himself would witness, or whether he would find himself required to take cruel actions, is unknown, as his memoirs end at the point just before he became directly involved in combat (**).

In commenting on the Whites' requisitioning activities

here, he was probably anticipating events later on. In so doing, he acknowledged that his side of the conflict would be guilty of violent coercion in conquered territory. In Ekaterinodar, upon showing surprise at the warm reception in his first billet, Sergei got this response from a colleague:

> *[He said to me] "To feed us does not cost them anything. We are protecting them from the Reds, and they are grateful to us. This is called a 'grateful population' ". This was the first time I heard this expression, which later became current and became one of the important reasons for the failure of the Volunteer Army. The army thoroughly bungled its supplying of itself... With the progress of the army to the north it came across a population suffering from shortages of foodstuffs and the plundering of the Reds. And we frequently had to resort to requisitions, often to the detriment of the population. The expression "grateful population" lost its original lofty meaning and became a synonym for all sorts of violence.*

There was soon another sign of things to come, with the slaughter in the first battle in their sector after the brothers arrived. The regiment they were in fought the Red Army to try to hold on to Armavir, east of Ekaterinodar, in late September. Sergei was not present during most of the fighting as he had been sent to another town on military business. But on his return, he was shaken by the outcome:

> *It is difficult for me to write about the battle... I arrived at the regiment when the retreat and the pursuit by the Red cavalry were already underway. The regiment took huge losses. The enthusiastic*

volunteers had gone on the attack armed only with rifles, without machine guns and artillery, but strong in spirit and enthusiasm.

All of us, who remained whole, deeply suffered this failure... on return to Ekaterinodar, I was summoned for the identification of the bodies, brought back from the battlefield. This was a ghastly sight. The Reds had savagely finished off the wounded, and the bodies of our comrades were chopped up and unrecognisable...

At the Ekaterinodar cemetery a long line of officers' tombs... appeared.

While the White forces did poorly in this battle, the following months would be more successful for them. The Volunteer Army would consolidate its hold on the southern Cossack region, then start to advance northwards. Other White armies were fighting inwards from the east and the northwest. The ultimate goal was for them to join up and move on Moscow, the capital of the new regime, which now called itself Communist.

Vladimir escaped with just slight wounds at Armavir. Now he and Sergei were given a different assignment which would take them away from the fighting for six months. A decision was made, partly on the prodding of Sergei and several colleagues, to set up a unit to echo the role of the Combined Regiment which had guarded the royal family in Tsarskoe Selo and of which he had been part. The killings of Nicholas and his family had left some feeling they had failed in their duty as imperial officers to protect them, even though the Tsar's fate had been taken out of their hands. Several members of his family were now holed up in German-occupied Crimea. There were fears that when the Germans left they would be exposed to Red attack. Among them were the Dowager-Empress Maria Fedorovna, Nicholas' mother, and the Grand Duke Nikolai Nikolaevich, the Tsar's uncle and former Commander-in-Chief of the Army. Sergei and Vladimir were among a small group of officers sent to defend the remnants of the dynasty.

In November, one month after the brothers went to Alupka, near Yalta in the southern Crimean peninsula, the First World War ended. This meant the end of German occupation of areas that were formerly part of Russia. A patchwork of different groups moved in to fill the vacuum.

In Crimea, the German departure did not, as anticipated, immediately usher in the Communists; on the contrary, the administration which took over opposed them. There were unexpected benefits for Sergei's small force as the occupiers pulled out: they unofficially passed on weapons and field telephones. Their exit also encouraged other officers in the area, who had been keeping a low profile since a period of Bolshevik domination in early 1918, to join his unit. He wrote that civilian life bounced back quickly too:

It was surprising that in spite of the terrible persecution and execution of officers, which the Bolsheviks had carried out during the time they were in power, on the southern shore of Crimea we now found ourselves rather numerous.

It was also surprising that in spite of... Red rule and German occupation, the population of the southern shore retained such spirit for life and activity.

> *Bazaars and shops immediately opened, goods that had been hidden away suddenly appeared: wine, fruit – [the locals] willingly sold all sorts of foodstuffs.*

This respite lasted until late March 1919. When southern Crimea came under threat from Red forces, evacuation plans were made. The British had controversially failed to rescue the Tsar, the cousin of their King, George the Fifth, from execution; now they prepared to whisk away other members of the imperial family.

Sergei escorted the Dowager-Empress and a companion to a beach where British officers were waiting. He led the "two old, small women... depressed and helpless" to the spot from which they would be ferried to a navy ship anchored nearby. The Empress thanked and farewelled each of the Russian officers, holding in check strong emotions with "a sort of majesty..." Before her ship sailed to Constantinople (now Istanbul), the transport which would take him and the other officers to the Caucasus to rejoin the White forces circled her ship:

> *On the very tip of the stern stood the Empress and the Grand Duke... The Grand Duke stood motionless saluting us, while the Empress waved to us with a handkerchief, now and then pressing it to her eyes. She was crying. We yelled with frenzy "ura" and... also cried.*

In spite of the attachment Sergei and his companions clearly felt for the royal family, they understood that this was the only possible outcome. Sergei said the officers had debated among themselves whether they were right in doing nothing to encourage the Grand Duke to take a leadership role in the White Army. But whatever varied opinions different leaders of the Whites held about the type of government they wanted for Russia, most did not support the restoration of the monarchy. The royals now safely on their journey away from Russia, the brothers returned to the Civil War.

While the brothers were in Crimea, their family left Kiev. There too, the Germans had pulled out after the armistice and had not been replaced by the Communists immediately. But in early February 1919, the Reds moved in. Olga wrote that on the eve of the take-over, she was among a family party of eleven who managed to get on a train, bursting with others fleeing. They were bound for Odessa. Nadezhda, her sister and baby Alexander were probably in the group. It is unclear whether Nikolai was with them at this time or away with the White forces.

Odessa, like Kiev, had seesawed among different factions holding power over the period since the October Revolution. The Germans had occupied the port city too. On their departure, there was a struggle for control among Communists, Whites, Ukrainian nationalists and others. French and other Allied troops landed into this chaos late in December 1918, restoring some order and naming a senior White officer military governor.

From the time of the armistice, those opposing the Communists had held high hopes that the Allies, freed from fighting the Germans, would provide substantial help in the Civil War. The arrival of the foreign troops in the south no doubt bolstered those hopes. But the French would not stay long. Whatever assistance the Allies had given the Whites before the end of the war had been tied in with their own aims of trying to restore a Russian role against the Germans, or at the very least of removing a supply line to them from occupied Russian territory. Now, with the devastating conflict ended, the countries of Western Europe were not keen to get involved in anymore fighting. With a few exceptions, help that was given was mainly in the form of military supplies, and by late 1919 even that would mostly end. Historians generally concur that the uncoordinated and often half-hearted Allied interventions were ultimately of little help to the Whites, perhaps at most delaying their defeat. Some say the assistance was even detrimental, engendering a degree of dependence on the anticipated help among the Whites and leading to poor planning. At the same time it gave the Reds ammunition in seeking popular support, through propaganda calling their opponents tools of Western capitalism.

But in early 1919, the Allied presence made Odessa a safe haven for opponents of the Communists. When the train carrying the family group arrived in the city, it was already swamped with refugees from the north; my mother and her relatives were likely still among them.

It is intriguing to wonder whether the paths of the two families crossed in the city. It seems the material means of my maternal grandmother were more limited than those of my paternal grandparents. And her family does not seem to have had the benefit of prominent friends from the past. Thus her circle in Odessa is likely to have been a different one to that of the Apouchtines.

Accommodation facilities in the city were overflowing. My father's family was lucky once again, finding friends who had a large apartment and took in all of the travellers for a few nights until they could find somewhere to rent. They crammed in together on the floor of a room, grateful to have found shelter.

Olga remembered that it was a very cold winter, with temperatures dropping to twenty degrees below zero, and that heating was close to non-existent. Fuel was hard to get. The acacias which adorned the streets were cut down and the wood quickly sold, but it was green and burned badly. The family group was somehow able to find space to rent – at first all together in one premises, later in two groups in different locations.

Throughout 1919 Odessa continued to live with instability. The Allies pulled out in the spring, and as Red forces moved in, some members of my father's family left. But both my grandmothers were probably in the city for at least some of the more than four months that the Communists controlled it. There is no record of how they coped. Natalia had still not been reunited with Alexander, while in Nadezhda's case, her husband was away somewhere with the White troops.

In August there was yet another change of rulers, when the White Army marched in for its last period of control of the city before being finally defeated in the Civil War. After a gap of more than a year, Nadezhda's diary recollections resumed with a description of the arrival of the Whites. It was rainy and windy, but the weather could not dampen her joy and excitement, as she went to celebrate at the home of some friends:

> *On the street everything was new. Every little corner of the road, so well known to us, seemed to have nothing in common with what had been before. Flags were already hung out, ours, real national flags, the symbol of our homeland... Only in childhood is the soul able to be so imbued with the love of life. I experienced this in childhood and now... We sat, we talked, we built plans for the future, as only*

those who are at the beginning of life build them.
At this instant, revived, we all were young again...
Our pockets were of course empty – but in our souls
what riches, I never before in life saw such festive
faces as every one of us had.

Nadezhda's joy grew further when she returned home to find that Nikolai had arrived with the White troops. Her boundless happiness at him being safe and their being together heightened her optimism that the future would now go their way.

Indeed in the coming weeks, the Whites would do well, defeating the Reds as they advanced ever further north towards Moscow. But Nadezhda's hopes, rekindled on that rainy day in Odessa, that these victories might herald a restoration of her past life would eventually be shattered.

By the end of 1919, the White forces would falter, and be pushed back south. More defeats in the coming months would bring another exodus. This time the masses of people escaping would not be going to other parts of the former Russian Empire, but to new and foreign lands – and they would be leaving for good.

Flight from the homeland and all that that implies, has dominated my image of my grandparents over the decades, but what it means has changed over time. Along with my perception of people like my relatives as victims who had suffered tragically at the hands of history, I became increasingly aware that they – by virtue of being from a particular social class – were also agents of that history. Yet eventually I also came to comprehend the limits which the context of the times placed on them. Through their memoirs and others' stories about these relatives, most of whom I had never

CHAPTER SIX

known, stereotypical ideas about their social definitions gave way to the discovery of them as more tangible and complicated human beings, with many layers to their identities. These various elements have pulled me in different directions in this family history. Yet sympathy for the position of my grandparents – perhaps inevitable given my link to them – reasserted itself the more I explored their lives so constrained by historical events. The fact that what resulted in Russia was a society no less unjust than the previous era provided only sad symmetry.

However much my relatives might have been complicit in past injustices over the centuries, those in my grandparents' generation paid for it more than amply for the rest of their lives. In the next phase awaiting both those who stayed and those who fled, everything they had been and known would be drastically – and sometimes brutally – altered.

(*) The family – including Sergei – did actually briefly reunite for a time in Sofia, probably in early 1921. Besides their father who remained in Petrograd, the other member of Sergei and Nikolai's direct family who was not in Kiev or Sofia was their sister Irina, who had married a Montenegrin and was living in Montenegro.

(**) The last chapter of Sergei's memoirs concludes with the words: "the following period of my life was filled with events, meetings and experiences" that would be described in a separate chapter. But he was unable to fulfil his intention to write more due to ill health, and not long afterwards he passed away.

7

Divergent Paths

The flight of anti-communist refugees from Russia at the time of the Civil War has always sparked an image in my mind of desperate crowds trying to push their way onto ships, overflowing with people, about to sail across the Black Sea to Constantinople (now Istanbul). A story that my mother told, though she could not remember its source, illustrates this perception: she had heard that crews on British ships helping in one frantic evacuation cut ropes to prevent more people, terrified of being left behind, from climbing on board. Other stories told of people being denied passage at the last minute by captains favouring those willing to pay more, or of overloaded or decrepit vessels nearly capsising.

Whether the details are accurate is not as pertinent as the atmosphere this story and many more evoke: the overall vision of a frightened exodus as the Red Army gradually pushed its opponents, trapping them in ever smaller areas on the edge of the sea.

The Black Sea crossing was one of a number of escape routes. Departures occurred, there and elsewhere, during an extended period of time – many left before the situation became quite so dire. So while there was usually urgency, not everyone sailed away in chaotic conditions. Yet the sense of desperation is certainly evident in many accounts. Even where the flight was more orderly and less risky – whether via land or water – the mingled feelings of confusion and fear for the future, and grief at having to abandon the homeland, built on anxiety over the actual logistics of various escapes.

CHAPTER SEVEN

In late 1919 and 1920, as the Civil War increasingly went the way of the Reds, many of those who had gathered in the south of the old empire to escape them, began to consider the unthinkable: going abroad. The only hint in family memoirs of participation in the mass departure at the time of the final defeat of the Whites in the south relates to the brothers of my paternal grandfather Nikolai, Sergei and Vladimir. It seems they stayed with the White Army to the end and escaped with the last big group to flee across the Black Sea. It is possible my maternal grandfather Alexander was also part of this evacuation. Most other family departures occurred earlier, avoiding some of the more panicked circumstances.

The port of Odessa was one of the major departure points. Among the first in my family to obtain boat tickets to leave was Nikolai's sister Olga. At this stage there was still a realistic possibility that the Whites might prevail in the Civil War, so Olga believed it would be just a brief absence: "we still had great hope that all this Bolshevik trouble would be quickly settled."

But in fact, "Bolshevik trouble" was once again just around the corner. Feeling cheered by the warm temperatures in the spring of 1919 after the icy winter, and pleased that her husband's duties with the White forces meant he could be with her for a time, Olga decided to delay her departure. One day in early April, she went to get her boat tickets refunded. On her way home she had a rude shock:

> *I was totally happy walking in the street lit up by sunshine when all of a sudden, I saw [my husband] coming towards me, all distraught, who told me between clenched teeth when we reached each other: "tomorrow, the Bolsheviks will enter Odessa!" My good humour crumbled instantly; I had to leave*

as quickly as possible. I ran back to retrieve my tickets which I had just returned. And just in time; the office had filled up with people, I met all of St Petersburg there seeking tickets for boats. Luckily, I was able to recover mine.

The next day, Odessa did indeed fall to the Reds for the second time since the start of the Civil War. They would remain in control in the city until the pendulum swung back to the Whites again in August. Olga's husband got away to the White forces. It seems Nikolai went with him or he may already have been with the troops. Olga was able to sail to Constantinople, but she was worried about leaving her mother and her brother's family: my grandmother Nadezhda, her sister and young Alexander. Nikolai's propaganda work for the Whites made the situation very dangerous for them and Olga feared for their safety. She did not explain in her memoirs why they stayed behind.

Olga travelled with her two-year-old daughter and nanny on a Russian ship. She wrote that as soon as the crowded boat was ready to sail, the crew declared a strike and went ashore. She did not indicate reasons: perhaps they were upset at the overloading or sympathised with the Reds. The captain decided to proceed, along with four sailors who remained, but he needed the help of the passengers. So it was that "all our gentlemen were there working the shovels" to keep the boilers fed.

Olga had been able to obtain a cabin. Many travelled on deck, though for some it was not the money that was lacking but the space for the number on board. She was able to eat in the ship's restaurant, presumably stocked in Constantinople, as she noted that they served food items which had been unavailable in Odessa for the three months she had been there. Others could not afford the restaurant, but they did not go hungry, being fed simple sailors' fare. Among these was a cousin of hers; she gave him a silver spoon (which he would later return) to raise cash. In spite of fears over those left behind, "everyone was relieved to have been able to escape". The atmosphere was enlivened by the chance presence of two well-known singers on board, who gave impromptu recitals. Amid their sadness and uncertainty, the passengers briefly found relief in the beauty and familiarity of the music.

The travellers were excited when they could see Constantinople. But the authorities had misgivings about letting them land. Olga believed that hers was the first ship so crammed with Russian refugees to arrive and there were fears over who these Russians were: might they be Bolsheviks – or Communists as they were now calling themselves? Constantinople had been going through turmoil itself. Turkey had fought the war alongside the Central Powers and their defeat had led to its occupation by Allied troops. They no doubt had enough headaches without having to house all these new arrivals and to sort out their status. The revolving door of changing regimes across the water meant any passports the passengers carried might have been issued by administrations which no longer existed, or if they did, might disappear from one day to the next.

So the passengers were not allowed to get off. They remained on the ship at anchor for ten days. Olga remembered that this was not an unpleasant time. There was no shortage of food and small Greek and Turkish boats came out to the ship to sell chocolate and canned goods from the supplies the Allies were bringing into Constantinople. In the evenings, the ad hoc concerts continued.

Meanwhile, many other vessels "filled to the gunwales with

refugees" arrived and clustered around. Finally the authorities dispatched the ships to four islands in the Marmara Sea, just south of the Bosphorus Strait, an hour's journey away. The passengers disembarked and were provided with accommodation until decisions on what to do with them could be made. Their conditions were not very strict. Olga was soon able to move from the island to which she had initially been assigned to another; but then she still had money and past connections were likely a help.

When Nikolai and Nadezhda left Russia permanently, probably sometime in 1920, they too went via Turkey, on their way to Western Europe. However their movements during the first part of 1919 indicate they were still wavering in their plans, at least judging from the few mentions of my grandparents at this time in Olga's memoirs. She told how while she was still on the islands, they came and spent some time with her in the spring. How they were able to leave Communist-controlled Odessa is a mystery.

They arrived just before Orthodox Easter. Olga described how they celebrated the most significant holiday in the Russian church calendar. Their re-creation of age-old traditions on foreign soil was, unbeknownst to them, a rehearsal for what would become a lifetime of similar efforts in exile. During this uncertain time and later, the continuity and familiarity of such customs – which still reverberated two generations on in my Canadian family home – provided comfort:

...as we [Russians] were numerous on this island, we found a priest, a choir and a Greek Orthodox church where we could celebrate the [Easter] midnight mass, so highly cherished by all Russians. The church was located on a hill and we got there by donkey in the

CHAPTER SEVEN

middle of a spring night, warm and sweet-smelling, under a starry sky which was enchanting: it had a beauty and an impressively poetic feel... It was incredibly soothing, in spite of the anxiety, which never gave us peace, over the fate of Russia and of those whom we had left behind there.

It is possible my grandparents had come to Turkey expecting never to go back across the Black Sea. But they did, at some point, as Nadezhda's diary description of the retaking of Odessa several months later by the White forces demonstrates. According to Olga, Nikolai's reason for returning was to seek information on relatives still there and generally on the events. But then it seems he resumed service with the White forces. Why Nadezhda went back, especially to Odessa, still under the Reds, is less clear. Perhaps with the losses of loved ones she had already experienced, she feared that if she and Nikolai were too far apart, they might become permanently separated and she would lose him too. There were continuing hopes that the Whites would win the war and this likely played a role in her decision.

The next time my grandparents and their son Alexander travelled to Turkey, along with Nikolai's mother and Nadezhda's sister, there was no hope of a win in the Civil War and no going back: that trip took them away from Russia for good.

My maternal grandmother's sister Evgeniia also secured passage to Turkey, though I don't know when. It seems she was able to go ashore at Constantinople, so it was probably somewhat later than Olga, at a time when the authorities had established procedures for Russian arrivals. But it was likely before very large numbers of

Russians landed, as Evgeniia was able to get a job in the French Embassy as a secretary and translator. The French she had learned at the institute she and Natalia had attended in St Petersburg had become very useful.

Late in 1919, the White forces were at the closest point to Moscow they would reach, some three hundred kilometres south of the capital. Then things started to go badly for them. Defeats and retreat followed, and it became increasingly evident how the Civil War would end. Natalia's brother Vladimir found a vessel to take her and my mother to Constantinople. It seems he himself did not travel with them, but he too would eventually make his escape. My mother was too young to have any memories of her own of the experience but she relayed the great fears Natalia held over the trip in the small boat, which "was incredibly overcrowded – she really wondered whether it would make it across the water."

The quality of the boats used for the crossing varied, from large and secure vessels like the one Olga had taken, to small ones in a condition close to unseaworthy. From the impressions my mother gained from her mother's stories, the boat they took tended towards the latter. But Natalia is not likely to have had much experience of travel on the water so her fears may have reflected this, as much as the condition of the boat. Whatever state it was in, the overcrowding would have been a common situation and cause for concern.

Natalia and Irene made it to Constantinople safely. I wonder whether Natalia knew she had left Russia for good or whether she had any idea, however vague, where this first leg into exile would eventually take her. Perhaps she did not dwell too much on the future at this point, for she had more urgent matters to attend to: she had still to locate her husband, my grandfather Alexander.

CHAPTER SEVEN

October 1922 is sometimes given as the date for the end of the Civil War. That's when the last resistance by the Whites collapsed. This remaining group on the Pacific coast could not hold on after the withdrawal of Japanese forces which had supported them. But the Civil War effectively ended in November 1920 when the anti-Bolsheviks in the south lost their last bit of territory on the Crimean peninsula. This prompted the biggest surge in the exodus. About 150,000 White troops and civilians – though some historians say many more – sailed away on a flotilla of boats of every size, shape and purpose, their overflowing cargoes of people destined mainly for Constantinople.

There have been many analyses of why the Whites were defeated, listing a combination of factors. There were logistical problems: smaller numbers of combatants, and their sections widely scattered – greatly hampering coordination. The lack of access to resources made it very difficult to obtain sufficient food and equipment. There were political failings: they lacked an attractive or even coherent platform to offer the public, beyond anti-communism and a belief in reinforcing Russian dominance (this only served to antagonise many in areas where they fought, which were often populated by various non-Russian ethnicities). Numerous further reasons and nuances have been cited by historians.

For those getting away, the time to ponder how and why it all happened would come later. The first priority now was to seek countries that would accept them, and where they could make a home. The travellers to Constantinople, as well as to other areas adjacent to Russia, would eventually continue on to various parts of Europe, to China, to the New World, and to countries all around the globe. They were now refugees.

Olga had realised for the first time that she and her fellow passengers were seen as "just refugees" when they were still on their ship off Constantinople waiting for permission to land. The helplessness implied by this was amplified by outrage, which she expressed, when already on land she refused food brought to the Russians by the Allied troops: "They considered us to be destitute refugees... I did not like these donations as I did not want to consider myself a refugee, this offended me."

Olga was fortunate to still be in a position to be able to reject the assistance. This was a luxury not available to everyone, even if they shared Olga's feelings of distress and indignation at finding themselves labelled refugees. Many of those who fled came from the nobility or the wealthier layers of the merchant and professional classes; some would say their loss of wealth and position was deserved. Whatever one's opinion, these people's sudden powerlessness and their need to accept handouts were shocking and painful to them. The financial difficulties would only grow, even for those like Olga who had left with a reasonable supply of funds.

Between one and three million people are believed to have left Russia over the period of the Revolutions and the Civil War, and the next few years after it. They would face plenty of hardship. But those who stayed would suffer even more over the coming years.

The refugees fled a country first decimated by world war, revolutions and civil war, and then ravaged by disease and hunger. Epidemics of typhus, cholera and other illnesses swept through populations weakened by poor nutrition. A couple of bad harvests, combined with the draconian requisition policies of the government, meant increasing numbers of people went hungry. By late 1920, Russia and

Ukraine were on the verge of a devastating famine.

One of my relatives who remained was Nadezhda's cousin Anna. She had intended to head to Kiev soon after her husband travelled there in late 1918. He had managed to send her Ukrainian papers so she could cross the border. But her plans had been thrown into disarray. She had written a letter to a relative to tell of her imminent departure. It was to have been hand delivered, but one of those passing it on had been detained and searched and the letter read by his interrogator. For weeks she anticipated being arrested for plotting to escape. Finally she was able to breathe more easily, her name had somehow been bypassed. She was sure this was only because the regime was not yet very organised. She had torn up her Ukrainian documents; she was trapped.

Already in the winter of 1918-1919, living in the *dacha* her husband had rented on the outskirts of Moscow before his departure, Anna struggled with severe shortages. Those who lived in country areas could grow some food, but others had a hard time obtaining provisions.

Over the winter, she managed to feed her two sons, but often there was not enough for herself and their nanny Masha. (Anna had tried to convince Masha to return to her village where food was more available but the nanny was determined to stay to help care for the boys. The servant who had moved to the *dacha* with the family did return to her home village.) Anna looked for ways of distracting herself from her hunger:

> *There was one occasion when there were five days when we ate nothing – absolutely nothing, because there was nothing to eat. The small amount of provisions that remained – flour, grain –*

> were exclusively for the children. I remember cooking semolina porridge for the children and at the same time reading The Scarlet Pimpernel because I feared I would not be able to restrain myself and would suddenly gobble up their food – that's how hungry I was. I had to taste it two times a day – a little bit on a teaspoon and I thought "my goodness, how tasty this is..." I gave the children their food and I turned my back to them, because I so desperately wanted some – at least for the first three days, on the last two days I had already lost my appetite.

On another occasion, their landlord caught a hedgehog and they ate it with gusto, imagining it was all the delicious things they wished they had. Their landlady became sick with typhus and quickly died. Somehow, in spite of their weakened state, Anna, Masha and the children did not catch the illness.

In the spring, things were a bit better, with wild mushrooms to pick and carrot tops for sale; they were bitter and unappealing but they filled their stomachs. Money was almost valueless and she had pretty much run out of things to trade. When her last supplies of flour and porridge for the children were about to finish, in desperation Anna took a piece of fabric that had been given to her in times past and walked to a nearby village to try to exchange it for food:

> I went from house to house offering my material, but no-one needed it. At that time people could get better than pieces of material – women took milk to Moscow and came back with emeralds surrounded by diamonds – people gave away everything they

CHAPTER SEVEN

had for some milk. So a piece of lilac fabric was not of any interest to them. When I got to the very last hut and realised there was nothing more I could do, I said "For the love of God, please give me something for my children." The woman immediately replied, "Why didn't you say that right away. Mercy, of course, something for the children." They grabbed my basket and in one minute they had filled it with flour, eggs, a bottle of milk, even butter I think. I hardly managed to drag it home... [There] I sat down... and started to cry. It suddenly seemed so strange to me to find myself forced to beg. And at the same time I had the thought – well, that is entirely fitting... one must experience everything in life: both giving and receiving, in equal measure.

As a religious woman, Anna saw the hand of God in the charity she was shown. Her strong faith was to continue to be an important support for her as time went on, for things would get harder rather than easier.

Beyond increasing difficulties obtaining food, there were other causes for constant apprehension. Arrests became a regular feature of day-to-day life. Anna often learned of relatives or friends being taken into custody and sometimes held for long periods of time or exiled to remote regions. She realised she had to abandon, at least for the moment, any thought of joining her husband in the south. Anna began to search for a job and was soon hired as a clerk with the Red Cross in Moscow, where her stepfather worked.

On moving to the city, Anna was self-conscious about the

shabby condition of her clothes and the holes in her shoes. Thread had not been available for some time, so it was impossible to mend or remake well-worn clothes. But she quickly noticed that everyone walked around in rags; no-one gave her and her tattered family a second look.

They went to live in the apartment of an uncle. Their arrival brought the number of occupants to ten, including Anna's mother and stepfather. Anna's oldest son started kindergarten. He was fed there, and his teachers, taking pity on the family, regularly gave him food to take home for his little brother. Those in the household with jobs were given small rations of bread and potatoes. But those without official work were pretty much left out of the food distribution system. Masha was not allowed a ration either, as she was considered a "stooge of the bourgeoisie". The workers in the apartment shared their rations and were always on the lookout for any affordable items of food for sale.

Another thing they had to watch out for was theft, greatly on the increase. Anna said people were sometimes stopped in the street and stripped on the spot of all their precious clothing. It was particularly frightening in winter when accumulated snow provided screens behind which thieves could prey on pedestrians. The snow on the streets was not cleared away; it was pushed to either side of the footpaths and they became like trenches, hemmed in by ever-higher icy walls, effectively hiding any nefarious activity from view.

In sharp contrast to the poverty and struggles of daily survival, the cultural life of Moscow was rich, with performers willing to brave obstacles, such as lack of heating, to provide distraction. Anna said it helped to be young to be able to forget everything and appreciate the opportunities:

CHAPTER SEVEN

> *Youth has its effect. In spite of all the difficulties of this life, still somehow [there was much that] was interesting... for example, you could go to concerts, which were free. That is how we heard [bass singer Feodor] Chaliapin and [soprano Antonina] Nezhdanova, who sang in cold premises wearing warm fur coats, while the accompanist played the piano, hands blue with cold. After all, this was a diversion.*

Anna would spend about two years in Moscow. Then in 1921, she and her two sons and their faithful nanny Masha moved to the country where Anna became a village schoolteacher.

They managed to scrape through the famine years. Many did not survive: about five million people died between 1920 and 1922 from hunger and accompanying diseases (and many more would have perished, but for the foreign assistance the regime was grudgingly forced to request). Historian Richard Pipes states that "It was the greatest human disaster in European history, other than those caused by war, since the Black Death of the fourteenth century."

This toll came on top of those which resulted from all that happened before the famine, the events that had followed one after the other from the start of world war in 1914. The estimates of the numbers who died up to the end of the worst of the famine vary from source to source, from about ten million to well over twenty-million – figures impossible to grasp or comprehend. Few people would have got through those years without losing someone from among their family or friends.

For those who left, news from their homeland over the next period was devastating, but they could no longer be players in these events. For them, including my relatives who had reached Turkey, it was time to consider their next moves as migrants.

These were the relatives whose stories I heard in fragments when I was growing up, from whom letters would arrive from various corners of the world. I came to believe that everyone in my family either left Russia or perished there. It seemed inconceivable that anyone who was in the same social group as my parents' families could survive under a Communist regime: the rulers made it brutally clear that there was no place for such "former people" in the new order they were establishing.

It was only in later years that I started to hear about those who had stayed in Russia. There had been letters from some of them too. But these had stopped after a time; their writers either died or became too frightened to keep corresponding. In 1990, seven decades after the end of the Civil War, a relative of my father's from the Soviet Union found my family and came to visit us in Canada. This re-established link gave us a glimpse of the life we might have had if my grandparents had not left. And it helped us find out what had happened to some of those who had remained there. Various additional avenues of information opened up, allowing us to discover the fates of others. But for many more, their ultimate destinies remain unknown.

In my grandfather Nikolai's direct family, only his father Alexander remained in what would become the Soviet Union. After Sergei, the last of the family to see him, escaped from Petrograd, my great-grandfather also left. The wish he had expressed to his son – to

CHAPTER SEVEN

die in his favourite city – was not fulfilled.

According to Olga's memoir, Sergei's ever-faithful former batman Iakov found out the authorities wanted Alexander to take command of a Red Army unit in the Civil War. Knowing that he would refuse and that this would get him into trouble, Iakov helped him get to Tashkent, in what is now Uzbekistan, in the summer of 1918. In July, War Commissar Leon Trotsky did indeed launch his conscription of ex-tsarist officers. But my great-grandfather's service record, obtained from Russian archives since the fall of the Soviet Union, states that he was retired in March 1918 as he had reached the maximum age limit for an active role in the military. He was 56 years old.

Since Olga and other older relatives passed away, I obtained letters that my great-grandfather wrote from Tashkent to his wife in France. In these letters he gave no indication of why he left Petrograd, but he stated this happened in late 1919 and not in 1918 as the family thought. Alexander stayed in Uzbekistan until his death in 1928.

To urgings from his family in France to join them, he responded that he felt it was too late in his life for that. He was not old in years when he arrived in Tashkent, but perhaps because of his injuries from the 1905 war and the hunger and turmoil of the years after that, he had aged prematurely. Sergei thought of him as an old man when they parted company: "...he was no longer an elegant, hearty general, but an old person in civvies who had started to limp badly and with an ever more overgrown grey beard". Alexander also wrote in his letters that he did not want to be a burden to his children, already struggling to make ends meet in emigration. Then again, getting an exit permit from the authorities would not have been easy.

In the letters he often mentioned that he would like to go north to Moscow or Petrograd – feeling "a pull to the place where I lived and where I spent the happiest years of my youth." But he seemed to appreciate the warmer climate in Tashkent, especially as his health deteriorated, and often said he had accepted his solitude and was calm about his situation:

> ...*time goes by imperceptibly, there is no time to brood about the past and about the future of the family – the family I have lost seemingly forever. But what can one do, to each his fate and to grumble about it is useless.*

Alexander reassured his family that he was earning enough to live reasonably well. Indeed at one point he told of trying to send them money but of finding this impossible. He taught military subjects at university and was comforted in feeling these had some value:

> *My work is sustained by the awareness that I make just a small contribution to the reconstruction of my old homeland, to which I owe everything and which I will not betray till my last breath.*

He retired in late 1926, though he continued to give courses to supplement his pension.

In 1928 a friend of his wrote to the family to tell of his admission to a clinic because of severe respiratory problems and then of his death, at the age of 66. He described the funeral, the military band which accompanied the coffin, "drowning in flowers", and said there were plenty of mourners. The friend tried to obtain some of my great-grandfather's belongings to send to the family but the university where he worked seized everything that was in his apartment and the clinic took away what little he had while there. Among his papers, the friend believed there was a diary, but he was unable to get hold of it. He also wrote that Alexander had a reasonable sum of money in his bank account but that his relatives would not be able to access it – partly because under Soviet law the family "did not exist" as they had not been living with him.

In spite of his strong opposition to the Communist regime, it seems my great-grandfather had made his peace with the changed circumstances in his lonely last years, and had become accepted and even respected in his new situation. But it is hard to imagine the depth of pain and sadness – so often expressed in his letters – over being permanently separated from his family and over feeling he was no longer of any use to them or to anyone.

In the family of my paternal grandmother Nadezhda, her brother, another Sergei, remained in Moscow. My father's cousin who came to Canada was able to tell us something of his life, his times in prison, and his death in 1965. My father believed that this uncle of his was too tied to Russia to contemplate abandoning it, and perhaps felt less endangered as he had not fought with the Whites. However his prison terms demonstrate that he paid for staying, presumably because of his class origins. Two of Nadezhda's uncles who stayed spent much time in prison or internal exile too.

In the family of Natalia, my maternal grandmother, there were also those who never left, whether by choice or circumstance. Her sister Helen and her brother Alexander remained in Petrograd, where their mother Maria joined them after the estate in Mogilev was confiscated. My great-grandmother was able to keep in sporadic postal contact with her two daughters in France until the Second World War. There is a photograph from the mid-1930s of her sitting in front of a statue and fountain in Leningrad. Her pure white hair is pulled back behind her head, there is a determined expression on her squarish face and her eyes are deep-set and shadowed. With her is a woman, aged perhaps in her 30s, and a girl of about ten or twelve. My mother did not know who they were – they were as much strangers to her as they are to me.

After the Second World War, the family found out through the Red Cross that both my great-grandmother and her daughter Helen had died during the siege of Leningrad. They, like hundreds of thousands of others, had succumbed – to starvation, illness, or the cold. Did Maria regret her decision two decades earlier to stay, as she weakened and tried to calm the pangs of hunger, as she watched those around her fading to skeletons, failing to wake in the mornings, or stumbling and falling into the snow, too weak to ever move again? And yet, in spite of everything, she lived a couple of years longer than her daughter Natalia who had fled – my grandmother died just as the Germans were marching into France.

Recently I have learned something of the fate of an uncle of Natalia's – a brother of Maria's – who also stayed behind after the Revolution. Evgenii had risen in the ranks of the tsarist military and was awarded several high decorations. From 1918 he applied his engineering and military skills for the new Soviet regime, willingly or otherwise. He was stripped of his former rank but he attained senior positions in his specialty of naval weaponry. He won awards under this regime too – including two Orders of Lenin, the highest civilian decoration bestowed by the Soviet Union. But Evgenii was also imprisoned for five years, as was his then wife. He continued his work when he was an inmate and on release and was given the title of General Lieutenant in the area of engineering artillery.

As with my paternal great-grandfather Alexander, Evgenii's

past was not forgotten in his later life. But at the same time, he had been able to forge himself a trajectory under the new regime, gaining at least some acceptance by it.

As for her father's family, my mother had nearly no information. She believed her grandfather Ivan was killed by the Bolsheviks, possibly during the Civil War. She did not know anything about his wife Ekaterina's fate. My mother knew Alexander had several siblings, but she knew only that one of them went to Serbia – an older brother whose name she thought was also Ivan, and that a sister had perhaps ended up in Shanghai. As for the rest, she knew nothing about what happened to them, whether in Russia or abroad.

The bits of information that have come to light about relatives who remained in what became the Soviet Union, have filled out a small part of a past landscape that had been mostly blank. Yet these people remain ghost-like, with many details about them missing. And the fate of others is still a complete mystery. Much searching would be required to fill the absences in the family record.

The outcomes for those who left Russia and made it as far as Eastern Europe were mixed. My mother's Uncle Ivan, the brother of her father, was lost from sight during the Second World War and contact was never re-established. Serbia had joined in a union of territories, which in 1929 had been given the name Yugoslavia. Over the war years the country was subject to occupation and civil war. Thus it is not surprising that contact with many people was severed and that it never became known whether people like my mother's uncle survived. Even those who did get through the war may then have fallen foul of the Communist regime which took over after it ended.

It is a similar story for Natalia's brother Vladimir, who had helped her and my mother flee to Constantinople. He went to Czechoslovakia, where he worked as a government engineer. But during the war contact was lost and my mother never knew what became of him. Many in the Russian émigré community in Czechoslovakia disappeared, either during the German occupation, when they were sent to forced labour in Germany, or after, in 1945, when the Soviets shipped many of them off to their labour camps. Long after my mother passed away, I learned a bit of Vladimir's fate. He had survived the war, but died soon after, in 1946 in Prague. I do not know the cause of his death.

Irina, the sister of my paternal grandfather Nikolai, had moved to Montenegro to work as a nurse during the war between the Balkan states and Turkey in 1912-1913. She married an aide to the King of Montenegro and continued to live there with her husband and their daughter in the inter-war years. It too became part of the new Yugoslavia. In her case, in spite of all the upheaval during the war and subsequently, there was occasional contact after the end of the conflict. She had one daughter, who in turn had one son. Irina died in 1971.

Nikolai's brother Sergei was another of the family who lived in Yugoslavia between the wars, in Serbia. But unlike his sister Irina, Sergei fled before the Soviets moved in. He, his wife and young daughter managed to get to the American sector in Germany. They ended up in a Displaced Persons camp and in 1949 were accepted for settlement in the US. They went to live in Brooklyn, New

York. Sergei was able to get work in the Russian Department of the United Nations. When he retired he wrote his vivid memoirs. Their daughter continued to live on the east coast of the US until her death in 2011. Her surviving children remain in different parts of the US.

My grandparents on both sides – Nikolai and Nadezhda, Natalia and Alexander – ended up in France by the mid-1920s, after travelling through and occasionally settling for a time in a variety of countries along the way. Their siblings Olga and Vladimir (Nikolai's), Annochka (Nadezhda's), and Evgeniia (Natalia's), as well as my paternal great-grandmother Varvara, also all arrived in France around this time.

Nadezhda's cousin Anna would eventually come to the West too – but she did not manage to find a way to leave the Soviet Union until 1925. Her father died before her departure, but she left behind her mother, who died in Moscow in 1932.

Like many Russian émigrés, some of these relatives may have held on to hopes for some years that they would one day return to live in their homeland. None did, with one exception: Nadezhda's sister Annochka returned to the Soviet Union in the late 1930s, never to leave again. The surprising events surrounding her return – involving a spy scandal and an assassination – are a story for a later chapter.

Heading West

When I was born, my papers identified me as a refugee. By the time I was old enough to have any inkling of what that meant, I was no longer a refugee. I was a Canadian – and my parents often reminded me to be grateful for this. After more than thirty years of not officially "belonging" anywhere, they had been granted citizenship, and obtained it for my brother and me. Canada may have been very alien at first, there had been difficulties in adapting to a new society and language. But they never forgot that it had let them finally grasp that bit of paper taken for granted by so many, which signified they could stay as long as they wanted, that they had somewhere they could call "home".

To my parents, the word "refugee" had many meanings they were happy to leave behind: it was a label and a reality they had carried – my father from his birth, my mother from soon after hers – since their parents' fitful journeys from Russia to the West.

For my mother and her mother Natalia, that journey had begun when they had sailed away from Odessa, probably sometime in 1920, Irene still a toddler. In Constantinople my grandmother continued the search for her husband, whom she had not seen for the preceding year or two. They moved in with Natalia's sister Evgeniia, whose job at the French Embassy meant they had some financial security. Other refugees were having a hard time getting by; with so many Russians flooding in – often with few suitable skills to offer – the job opportunities were very limited.

CHAPTER EIGHT

The sisters almost lost their financial base over a cross-cultural misunderstanding. While my mother did not remember very much that her mother had told her about their stay in Constantinople, there was one story Irene knew well. She said that her aunt's husband almost caused a diplomatic incident when, having travelled ahead to France, he sent his wife a telegram at the embassy. He did not speak French and had cobbled together the message out of a dictionary – the result was nearly incomprehensible. It was intercepted and those reading it concluded it was in code; the protagonists being Russian added to the perception there was some sort of espionage involved. His words could have been taken to mean: "why are you not revealing anything, this is disturbing". Evgeniia's employers questioned her, but fortunately she was able to convince them that her husband had not been looking for secret information, that he had just meant he was worried at not having heard from her. My mother liked the story for its humour, but clearly it had a serious side, reflecting the suspicion refugees often elicit. With a Communist regime in place where they had come from, the climate of mistrust towards Russians would have been even more pronounced.

With huge numbers of Russians swamping Constantinople, organisations emerged to assist with their practical needs, run by western governments or international aid groups, or set up by the refugees themselves. Natalia approached these, hoping to find someone who knew where Alexander was. She also tapped the many informal links which quickly develop in any migrant community. It seems there was not yet a fear of revealing details about oneself, a fear that would later make people connected to the Soviet Union reluctant to share personal information. My mother well understood the value of this sort of unofficial network, which she later experienced in the Second World

War in France, when people also lost each other amid the upheaval:
> *During and after both this war and the next, people had a habit of telling each other where they came from, their names, who their families were, and so on – maybe the information would pass from one to the next to the third and eventually help someone find relatives. So, in this way, my mother eventually found out that my father was in Gallipoli.*

Gallipoli is a name of particular significance to Australians (and New Zealanders), because of its place in those countries' history. When I was growing up in Canada, it was also familiar to me, but for very different reasons. It was the place where Natalia and Alexander were finally reunited after their long separation, during which neither had known the fate of the other.

The Allies administering Turkey had provided a couple of locations for the defeated Whites fleeing from Russia to set up camp. One of these was at Gallipoli. The last commander of the southern forces, General Wrangel, wanted to keep them together, in the hope of going back to try to overthrow the Bolsheviks. For the Allied authorities, the large number of demoralised troops presented problems with practicalities of accommodation and control. Keeping them together, under the discipline of their military leaders, was a good solution for them too.

In Gallipoli, Natalia found Alexander in hospital; he was suffering from shrapnel wounds to his spine. One of his colleagues, a cavalry captain, who had become a close and devoted friend to him, found space for Natalia and Irene in the camp and helped them survive. Having left behind his own family – his parents and siblings – he was to become virtually part of my mother's family, later

CHAPTER EIGHT

living with them in France. To Irene he would always be "Diadia" Misha – "Uncle" Mikhail.

...he helped us get settled, finding us room in a tent, he helped with food, and so on... "Uncle" Misha and others used to go help harvest corn – I remember how good the corn tasted, cooked in coals in the evening. I believe [local] people's attitude to us was good... So the Russians harvested, and did other odd jobs, and were paid in food. My father was too ill to work, but "Uncle" Misha was very healthy... There was nothing in Gallipoli – there were just very poor people who had very little... Being so soon after the war, many men had been killed or wounded, so young men who could work... were welcome.

Not long after Alexander was released from hospital, my grandparents and mother left Gallipoli. This was likely sometime in 1921, judging by the date of a certificate accompanying a medal Alexander was later awarded for his loyalty to the White forces. A new government in Turkey from 1920 had been gradually retaking territory run by the Allies; a treaty in 1923 would confirm its renewed control. Anticipating the departure of the Allies from areas where the White forces were camped, General Wrangel received permission to move sections of his army (in units, but as civilians) to several countries, among them Bulgaria. This is where my mother's family went, but whether they moved with Alexander's unit or travelled independently, I do not know. Bulgaria was one of the countries taking in large numbers of Russians. Here too, the deaths of many men in the war had created a shortage of workers, so their arrival was welcomed. The government even provided help with resettlement.

My mother said they went to live in a small town, and she believed that they spent more than a year there. The main local occupation was sugar production, and this provided both her parents with jobs. Because of their shift work, my mother, then four or five years old, was left to her own devices much of the time:

> *My father worked at night, my mother during the day, at the sugar beet factory. The work was very heavy... My father slept all day... I had to disappear... We rented a small room – at a farm, I think – from some very nice people. They kept an eye on me, there were other girls my age, so we played all day. I was not supposed to go into our one room until dinner, as the room served all functions. When it rained, things were worse... I read a lot at this time, my mother taught me the alphabet and to read at a very young age. I read in Russian, or looked at pictures [in Bulgarian books]... My mother would come home around dinnertime, we all ate together, and then my father would go off to work for the night and arrive home again early in the morning... then she would go off to work for the day.*

There was instability in Bulgarian politics, and gains by the Communists. A Communist uprising in 1923 was followed by the party's suppression. No doubt these events made my grandparents nervous. They left before economic conditions worsened too much and Bulgaria became less welcoming.

Their next stop was Serbia, where they stayed in the home of Alexander's brother Ivan. He was managing a large estate and farm for a woman who had been widowed during the war. This was in

CHAPTER EIGHT

Palic, near the town of Subotica, in the north of Serbia near the Hungarian border. Perhaps part of the reason they sought him out was that Alexander's wounds were again causing him problems. During the time they lived with his brother, neither Alexander nor Natalia worked. My mother said her parents were uncomfortable that her uncle refused to take any money from them, though it is hard to imagine they had very much to give him.

Alexander's health must have improved over the year or so that the family lived in Serbia. France, another country trying to overcome a shortage of workers after its war losses, was recruiting labourers from among the Russian refugees in several countries. Alexander decided to go work in France.

In 1921 the Soviet government had revoked the citizenship of those who had fled (though while cutting adrift its opponents who had managed to get out, it stopped allowing opponents still in the country to leave). For my grandparents and others like them, this final severing of their official ties to their homeland must have been painful.

The travel document used by Natalia, Alexander and Irene instead was a Certificate of Identity issued by the High Commissioner for Russian Refugees of the League of Nations; it still remains among my family's papers. It contains the stern warning that it would cease to be valid if the bearer should at any time enter Russia, as well as forbidding return to the issuing country, in this case Serbia. The smudged visas and stamps on the tattered certificate depict the route they took, through Austria and Switzerland, to France.

The document has a photograph of the family, one of only a couple which survive where they are all together. All three stare fixedly, Natalia and Alexander not quite at the camera. My mother looks right at the photographer, her fingers appear to be fidgety; she seems apprehensive. It is hard to define the expressions in her parents' eyes – fatigue, maybe resignation or vulnerability – but then perhaps I am reading into the photograph feelings that I imagine they must have had as they prepared to move to yet another new country.

Nikolai and Nadezhda, like Natalia, were lucky to have family in Constantinople when they arrived there, probably in the first half of 1920, after leaving Russia for the last time. Nikolai's sister Olga was living in a building that belonged to the Russian Embassy, with her husband and daughter, and my grandparents stayed there. Many countries would not recognise the new Communist government for a few more years, so ambassadors appointed by the Provisional Government, or even by the Tsar, continued to occupy Russian diplomatic premises. These provided assistance to the increasing number of refugees. They also housed representatives of the White forces and it was in this capacity that Olga's husband had been given an apartment in the Constantinople complex. He had arrived as part of an official mission which aimed to seek more support from the Allies for the White troops in the Civil War. Olga left the island in the Marmara Sea where she had been living, for a time able to discard the hated label of "refugee" as she joined her husband in the official apartment. She again found herself providing beds or meals for a parade of friends and relatives passing through or still seeking their own accommodation.

Nikolai and Nadezhda arrived with his mother, her sister Annochka and Alexander – now about two years old. Annochka's daughter Anika many years later told me her mother often recalled the situation in the Constantinople Russian community: it was unhappy and tense, they were in an "...unfamiliar country, with an unknown language – it was not clear how things would turn out – everyone's morale was terrible."

Staying with Olga meant that, materially at least, they were in a better position than many others. But their outlook on the Civil War must have already been gloomy, for Olga recalled that my grandparents stayed in Constantinople only a short time – not waiting for the defeat of the Whites a few months later – and moved on to Bulgaria. Olga wrote that there they settled in a small house with a garden, in the capital Sofia. In his turn, Nikolai would take in her family for a time when they later followed.

This happened after Olga and her husband had to leave the Embassy compound in Constantinople when her husband resigned his position. He had found it impossible to work with a new head of the White forces mission there, who he felt was undermining efforts to gain foreign assistance for the increasingly beleaguered troops in Russia. He was unable to find other work, among the numerous refugees also seeking employment. In the meantime, the Civil War approached, in Olga's words "a complete debacle, with a general stampede of all those brave men who had wanted to save Russia from chaos". There seemed little prospect of a renewed role for her husband with the opposition, so they left for Bulgaria.

Olga's and Nikolai's brothers Vladimir and Sergei also soon arrived in Sofia, being among those White forces who, she wrote, by some "miracle" succeeded in escaping Russia after their final defeat.

My grandparents spent about a year-and-a-half in Sofia. During that time Nadezhda had a second child, a girl, in the summer of 1921. Like her, her mother and her grandmother, the baby was given the name Nadezhda, or Nadia. My grandmother took up her diary for the first time since Odessa to describe the depths of her love for the tiny, helpless new addition:

> *The birth of a child is always happiness and mystery...*
> *I looked with pleasure and delight at these little hands,*
> *little feet, little hairs, little eyes... And my miserable,*
> *weakened body thrilled in an indescribable bliss*
> *of peace.*

During their time in Bulgaria, it is unclear whether Nikolai worked, or how they survived, though my grandmother did mention in her diary selling a sapphire just before her daughter's birth. So clearly they still had some valuables to trade.

Olga's family had run out of funds in Turkey. In Sofia her husband was able to get a job in a bank, while Olga started a business as a seamstress. Her creations proved popular among the foreign delegations that were in the city sorting out war reparations. Soon Olga was hiring others. At first she took on Russians. She wrote that these women, refugees too, had not yet become accustomed to their changed circumstances for "they concealed their activity which they judged to be unworthy of the wives of officers..." Unused to working for a living, they proved "unsatisfactory" and before long Olga replaced them with Bulgarians. She too would not have been in the habit of working to survive or running a business, but she took to it readily. Her involvement in fashion design would continue to sustain her throughout her life. Later, in France, when she and her husband split up, she would support herself, first employed by others in the clothing trade, then setting up her own business, this time as a milliner.

There is no record of my grandparents' thoughts on Bulgaria, no way of telling whether they agreed with the negative assessment Olga gave it. She found it a very poor place, suffering various shortages, and with theft prevalent. She did not like the Bulgarian language, and the question of her daughter's education was pressing as she approached school age. Olga also bemoaned the locals' taste in clothing – they did not buy her designs. But she conceded they did not need the type of clothing she made, mostly dresses for the glittering social activities of the foreigners, ostentatious displays considering their mission in the poor, war-damaged country. When the foreign delegations completed their task and went home, Olga's business dropped off and her family also decided to leave. Olga did not mention political events in her list of reasons for moving on, but perhaps they were a factor. A 1923 coup and the assassination of the prime minister were followed by more political violence – by the time of the failed Communist uprising a couple of months later, the family had left Bulgaria. They were now four: a second child, a son, had been born in 1921. They travelled by train and ship to Paris, which became their final destination.

Nikolai and Nadezhda had left Bulgaria some time before Olga and her family moved west. But their destination was Germany. Once more, the only clues as to how they got there come from an old travel document remaining in family files. It is creased and torn, with corners missing. The passport seems to have been issued to Nikolai by a Russian diplomatic mission in Sofia in 1920 in the name of the Armed Forces of Southern Russia. Later stamps identify the Organisation for the Protection of the Interests of Russian Refugees – perhaps endorsements or further extensions of the passport. Judging by bits that are decipherable, the family seems to have first travelled to Belgrade, in Serbia, where they may have seen Nikolai's brother Sergei who had settled not far away. Then they continued on through Hungary and Czechoslovakia, finally arriving in Bad Bruckenau, in Bavaria, in late 1921 or early 1922.

Germany, like Bulgaria, was experiencing a period of much

instability, including a series of uprisings – both right-wing and communist – as well as numerous economic woes resulting from the war and its aftermath. My Aunt Nadia believed my grandparents chose to go to Germany primarily because Nadezhda had an aunt there of whom she was very fond. This woman was married to a wealthy local man; they took in many Russian refugees on his large estate. My father was born there in February 1923. My grandmother once more took up her diary to record the birth of the child – her third. She wrote that the newborn was "...very sweet and promises to be very handsome..."

One month later my father was christened. Like Nadezhda, the name Dimitri was a tradition in my grandmother's family. Her father and her older brother, who had died in battle in 1914, were both named Dimitri. The great-aunt in whose home my father was born became his godmother. According to the christening certificate, the godfather was Nadezhda's brother Sergei. But my father believed his uncle never left Russia. Was he there after all or did someone else stand in for him during the service? This remains a mystery (*).

Again, I do not know how the family supported itself in Germany, though while living with my grandmother's aunt, there would have been substantial material help. There are numerous Bruckenau stamps on my grandfather's passport for dates in 1923 and 1924; these presumably reflect a requirement to regularly report to the authorities. Other stamps point to visits or stays in Munich and Berlin. My Aunt Nadia believed her parents contemplated settling in Berlin, but Nadezhda took a dislike to the city, even though it was the first – and still – major post-revolution centre of Russian emigration.

Nadezhda grew fond of Bruckenau. She wrote in her diary about leaving it for the last time in August 1924. Her relationship

CHAPTER EIGHT

to nature and its ability to echo her much-missed home would only have increased the wrench of leaving, and added another layer to sadness over past departures and loss:

I did not realise how deep that attachment has been... I have become aware of it now that... I must say goodbye forever, as I said goodbye to my kinfolk and loved ones in Russia...

An August day, bright and radiant and quiet. Around are fields of rye, low wooded hills, to the right green elm trees... The fragrances of the rye, of the forest, of the last flowers and of much else, are so strong in the warmth of the sun, it seems that I myself am dissolving in this scented sultriness, in the perfect blueness of the bright August sky. I walk and dawdle and I melt into these fields, hills, the road, all so dear and close and monotonous and somewhat tiresome – it reminds me of how I used to feel in Russia, when in the country...

Hardly anywhere in all our wanderings, past and to come, was there and will there be more left behind of ourselves, of our souls, than here in this dear, old house... it seems to me that in the rooms, in the halls, out of all the corners, emerge various memories, that everything is imbued with them. I look out the window at the familiar views... They are such bright canvasses from that chain of pictures which replace each other on the path of life...

The pain of farewelling the place where the family had spent the most time since leaving Russia – more than two years – was sharpened by the death of Nadezhda's beloved aunt.

Circumstances in Germany at this time were encouraging many others to leave too. It had at first harboured the largest number of Russian refugees. But by 1924 the cost of living had risen dramatically, and through the 1920s their numbers fell to about a third of those who had originally sought refuge there. Numbers would continue to drop as the political and economic situation became more difficult in the years leading up to the Second World War.

The next destination of my father's family was France, where some of their relatives were already living. They were among the many Russians who settled there since the end of the Civil War: some moved to properties they had owned before the Revolution, or pursued other long-term connections. Many from the upper classes already spoke the language, among them my grandmother, though my grandfather's French was poor. The numbers arriving in France were boosted further by the departures from Germany and other intermediate countries. The result was a burgeoning of Russian expatriate activity, providing practical support, as well as social and cultural opportunities. France now became the centre of Russian migration – the venue of "Russia Abroad".

It is not clear how my grandfather was able to get permission to bring his family to France. While my other grandfather had to sign a work contract to be allowed to settle his family there, for Nikolai this was not an option; with only one arm he could not take on manual labour. It may be that the last wife of Nadezhda's grandfather Prince Galitzine smoothed the way. The Prince had passed away before the Revolution, and his widow had inherited his properties both in Russia (which were later confiscated) and in Western Europe. She offered Nikolai work, helping to manage her holdings. Perhaps she signed French papers vouching for him and his family.

CHAPTER EIGHT

Compared to their descriptions of life and events connected to Russia, there is little recorded from my grandparents' generation about how they experienced their later years as migrants. Thus from the time of my parents' arrival in France with their parents, the narrators in this chronicle shift. In the case of my mother's family, she remained the main source but her story now came increasingly from her own memories, rather than from what she was told. In my father's case, it was mainly he and his sister who now took up the story on that side of the family.

This generational change of narrators comes with the increasing use of a different type of source: interviews which I conducted with members of my parents' generation. This brings with it a different way of remembering. Rather than a process consciously aimed at recording for descendants a time lost to the past, their recollections of experiences and events witnessed came in response to my questioning. There was no planned choosing of what to include or systematic editing of memories. Sometimes the result was less polished. (For instance my father preferred to be interviewed in English, even though it was his third language – leading to sometimes unusual but unique ways of conveying experiences and thoughts.) But the more spontaneous expression was a significant compensation. And interviews provided the opportunity for further questions.

The shift in the sources coincides with the move by both families into a major new phase – as migrants now settling into a long-term stay.

(*) All indications are that Sergei remained in Russia till his death in the 1960s. However a French legal document from 1924 places him at a Berlin address. Perhaps he did briefly leave Russia and may have been at the christening in 1923 after all. There is no-one left of whom to ask that question.

Alexander Popov, the grandfather of my paternal grandmother. He raised Nadezhda and her siblings after their parents' early deaths. Early 1900s.

Nadezhda (Galitzine) Popov, the mother of my paternal grandmother Nadezhda, 1890s.

My paternal grandmother's other grandfather, Prince Sergei Mikhailovich Galitzine, about 1910.

Prince Galitzine was instrumental in the funding and building of the Russian Orthodox cathedral in Nice, still an important landmark in the French city today.

Nadezhda and Dimitri Popov, the parents of my grandmother Nadezhda, early 1900s.

Varvara (Arapov) Apouchtine, the mother of my paternal grandfather, late 1920s, France.

My paternal grandmother Nadezhda and her siblings, from left: Annochka, Nadezhda, Sergei, Dimitri. Early 1900s.

Idyllic summer days at Piatnitskoe, the estate of the Popov family.

Piatnitskoe estate.

*My paternal grandmother's brother Dimitri.
Just a few months after this photo was taken,
he was killed in the war in November 1914. He was 22.*

Ekaterina (Goussarevitch) Kouprianoff, the mother of my maternal grandfather, probably just before the First World War.

My maternal grandmother Natalia and her mother Maria (Berkaloff) Tcheboutcheff, about 1910.

My maternal grandfather Alexander, December 1914.

My grandmother Natalia as a wartime nurse, 1915.

My maternal grandfather Alexander, second from the right – with military colleagues, 1916.

My paternal grandfather Nikolai with all his siblings except Sergei.

Front row: Vladimir and two unknown friends; back row: Olga, Nikolai and Irina, 1916.

My paternal grandmother Nadezhda, a widow at 20 years of age, 1915.

Family members leaving Piatnitskoe at the end of the summer in 1916, very likely unaware they would never again return to the estate.

The ashtray from the imperial porcelain factory that the Tsarina gave my great-uncle Sergei during the Revolution. It is now with his descendants in the US.

My grandfather Nikolai, in France in the mid-1920s.

My mother Irene with her parents Natalia and Alexander, from refugee travel document issued in Belgrade, 1925.

Alexander at the time when he was working in the steel works in Imphy, France, 1926.

Irene and Natalia, 1920s.

My father Dimitri with his siblings.

From left: Dimitri, Sasha, Seriozha and Nadia, Nice, 1926.

*Sunny days in Nice with the governess, Tiotushka, at left.
In front: a friend and my father Dimitri, Nadia and Sasha are behind,
about 1927.*

*My paternal grandparents
Nikolai and Nadezhda,
Paris, about the 1930s.*

*Russian summer camp in southern France,
where my mother met my father's sister long before she met him.
Irene is fourth from the left, Nadia is at the far right.
Early 1930s.*

*My grandmother Nadezhda's
sister Annochka in 1938.
She returned to the Soviet Union
in 1937 after her husband
was involved in a spy scandal.
She was never able to leave again.*

Irene dressed for a costume party, late 1930s.

Irene and Dimitri's wartime wedding in Paris, 1943.

My father Dimitri in 1939.

Dimitri with my brother and me in 1950 at the property on the edge of Paris where my parents planned to build a house – until they decided to emigrate to Canada.

New Canadians: Irene and Dimitri with my brother Alexander, me, and my baby sister Helen, 1954. On this land north of Montreal, they would build their summer cottage.

Faltering New Beginnings

The Russian Orthodox Cathedral in Nice, in southern France, might never have been built were it not for my great-great-grandfather Prince Galitzine. He played an important role in the construction of St. Nicholas: he donated large sums of money and was the chairman of the committee which oversaw its completion. It was consecrated in 1912. Unpredictably, it became a monument to a society in a distant land that was about to disappear.

The cathedral is a major tourist attraction. It is a colourful, ornate confection: columns, onion domes, gilded spires and crosses, high arched windows enclosed within scalloped and carved trim, and walls decorated with mosaics and golden painted icons.

When my sister and I visited in 2001, we were dazzled by its beauty and at the same time, felt squeamish when we thought of its improbable link to our family. We were certainly not the only visitors. Some were moving in a group, following an earnest young woman who explained the origins and significance of the major icons. Others carried large laminated cards in the language of their choice, which led them through the highlights of the church.

The extravagant decoration of the exterior is more than matched by the overwhelming interior: elaborately painted frescoes on the walls, icons encrusted with precious stones, silver liturgical accessories and a high iconostasis blinding for the amount of gold leaf and paint on it.

The tourists wore shorts and sandals, with cameras and beach

CHAPTER NINE

bags on their shoulders, and in spite of efforts to speak quietly, created a constant voluble hum. My adherence to Russian Orthodoxy had lapsed long before. Yet there seemed something improper about all this gawking. My religious upbringing was too deeply ingrained for me to be comfortable with such informality.

The cathedral was the result of long ties between Russia and Nice. When the area was still part of the Sardinia-Piedmont Kingdom, Russia was given permission to build a naval base on the waterfront close to the city. The Russian presence gradually spread, as wealthy families bought land and built homes, among them the Tsars and their relatives. Many of these people spent only part of the year in Nice. Yet the number of Russian residents by 1900 – permanent and part-time – was such that even though there was already a church, it was felt a cathedral was needed.

St Nicholas continues to hold regular services. But it has not escaped the politics which have surrounded it almost since it was built. A six-year legal battle over its ownership ended in 2011, when the Russian Orthodox administration in Moscow took it over from an organisation that represented Russian churches in the West. The Kremlin has since provided funding for restoration. This has not mollified critics of the Russian government who believe it is trying to fuel patriotism at home by reclaiming examples of its former greatness abroad. The Nice cathedral is among several churches that the Moscow government has recovered.

My family's link to the building was difficult to fathom; the wealth and prominence of Prince Galitzine reflected a reality from my family's past that I could not comprehend. My father too had often expressed difficulty in making the connection to this previous affluence, not only because of his family's subsequent dire poverty, but also because of his strong views critical of wealth disparities.

In his early years in Nice, the cathedral was a place Dimitri would have often frequented. His parents were religious and the family would have attended many services there. Living on the boundary between being somehow still associated to all this past wealth, and the new more difficult circumstances taking hold, must have been confusing. Yet the cathedral's extravagant architecture, and the luxury of the Russian villas nearby, were not what left the strongest impression on young Dimitri. It was the natural setting of these buildings which was prominent in his reminiscences in later years.

My father's first memories were of his family's time in the city. On arrival in France, probably in late 1924, he and his parents, his brother Alexander – or Sasha, and sister Nadia, had briefly lived in Paris. There Nikolai started work for Prince Galitzine's widow. They then moved to Nice, where she had a number of properties. Dimitri was about two years old; they remained there until he was six.

To him, "Nice was like a dream – the kind of beauty of that place, you can only read in fairy tales... it's amazing." The family initially moved into the basement of the Villa Montebello, one of the properties of Prince Galitzine, in the possession of his widow.

Their stay in the villa was short. The descendants of the Prince were to inherit the house after his widow died. Much younger than him, she did not anticipate this would happen quickly (indeed she lived until 1950). She was aware that many of those named in the will were struggling financially, while she had other sources of wealth. So she sold Montebello and shared the proceeds.

Nikolai, Nadezhda and the children moved to a neighbouring

CHAPTER NINE

property, also owned by Russian émigrés – the Villa Theodore. They did not live in the main house, but rented part of a smaller one on the property. This may have been a gatehouse or a residence for staff in former times. Although there was no electricity or heating, they lived in what were probably the most comfortable circumstances the family would experience in their whole time together in France.

The Villas Montebello and Theodore, and their gardens and woods, were located on Cimiez hill behind Nice. The city and its bay were spread out below. The area is now occupied by the University of Nice Sophia Antipolis, with affluent suburbs around it. The beauty of the neighbourhood had retained its enchantment for Dimitri many years after his family left. He returned a couple of times to seek out the places he remembered from his early childhood. His last visit had been in 1997, three years before his death.

In 2001, my sister and I went in search of the locale of our father's fond recollections. He had brought back photos, which we clutched as we tried to match his stories and memories with what lay before us.

We wandered around the campus of the university and its spacious lawns and gardens, with their pond and scattering of statues amid buildings old and new. We could not find the Villa Montebello, though several of the older buildings seemed possible candidates. Apparently Dimitri had also not located it during his last visit as there were no photos of it.

After climbing up and down the hilly terrain amid a maze of winding streets and paths, patches of trees and high stone walls, we found the smaller house that had been part of the Villa Theodore property. There could be no mistake, it matched Dimitri's photos.

He had told us how amazed he had been to find the exterior hardly changed when he revisited it for the first time more than forty years after leaving Nice:

> *When I came back in 1972 to see the place, everything was the same – that little old house in which we were living was exactly the same. There was a big glass canopy there with broken glass, and it... [still had] broken glass. I had permission to walk in the place... in the gardens and so on, and I saw that alley where we were playing with kids, an alley bordered with palm trees and it was the same, except that the palm trees were huge, because so many years had passed. So it was something to [make you want to] cry.*

The beauty of what he saw was what sparked his emotion, but the fact that some of it had remained seemingly frozen in time must also have brought back visions of his past.

When he returned in 1997, again he was astonished at how little the house had changed since his family left in 1929. It was still a private home in 2001, with a high fence around it. My sister and I could only peer through the metal railings and speculate about the garden and the wondrous views from the upper balcony that Dimitri and his sister Nadia had described.

There was an indication of how big the property of the Villa Theodore had been, because a variety of buildings now stood between the main house and this smaller one. The large house, just outside the university grounds, was clearly visible from the campus, dominating the scene from higher up the hill. Three many-windowed storeys, a square tower with a pointed spire, a rust-red shingled roof with multiple chimneys, carved stone balconies – all hinted at interior lavishness. We skirted a couple of ugly round university residences to get a closer look. But a man and a woman suddenly appeared and admonished us for invading private property. Our protestations about our family's historic link to the building fell on deaf ears. After heated Gallic gesticulations were exchanged, we gave up. We could only hark back to my father's description of the way he, as a young child, had viewed its imposing presence:

> *After our house, the road was still making a couple of hairpins and it was arriving at... a kind of entrance where you could park ten cars at least, that was the back of the house. The house was huge... Those people owned it before the Revolution, but by the time we were there, they themselves were occupying only a few rooms in the basement because they certainly didn't have the means of occupying such a house – not the means nor the reason... [A] huge living room was leading to a balcony... with huge stone stairs leading to the front lawn... After that, there was a cliff, and I remember there was a stone colonnade, and from that cliff you could see the whole of Nice and the sea behind. It was something so grandiose, you just cannot describe.*

The unfettered views both the main house and the gatehouse would have enjoyed in the 1920s were now broken by newer buildings in spreading suburbs. There were many more roads, and buses linked Cimiez hill to the rest of Nice. Yet one could still appreciate the feeling of being perched high above crowded streets and traffic, detached from the bustle, with impressive views of the city and the sea stretching to the horizon.

My Aunt Nadia remembered the family's time on Cimiez hill like living in the country. There were scattered villas but no suburbs, and the road leading there was narrow and unpaved. She and her siblings "...always went barefoot, there was that huge garden and we played Indians... in general, [it was] a marvellous life." For Dimitri, a small boy by the time they were living on the Villa Theodore property, there was lots to explore. He recalled

>...*some little vegetable gardens and vineyards...*
>*I remember the grapes were very good to eat, table*
>*grapes – but [mainly] it was just a rich property,*
>*a park which was made up of meadows, forests,*
>*and rocks.*

Among the games the children played in this large domain, there were plenty of opportunities for mischief. Nadia remembered her younger brother playing chicken, when occasionally they were sent down the hill to a small grocery store – the *épicierka* (*). Cars might not have been frequent and they no doubt travelled slowly on the winding road, but Dimitri would still succeed in frightening his siblings by running across, at the last moment, in front of vehicles. He also was in the habit of upsetting his parents and the gardener on the Montebello estate by turning on all the taps in the gardens and leaving them running, in the process getting soaked. Nadia said his energy and exuberance were boundless: he was "...round-faced, with a nose like a button... and very cheerful, bubbling with life... a very lively, joyful child..."

Dimitri's good health was in marked contrast to that of his younger brother. Sergei – or Seriozha – was born to Nadezhda in 1925, her fourth and last child. He had club feet and his early years were filled with doctors, hospitals and operations. Her son's suffering deeply affected her and she would always remain extremely protective of her youngest child.

At this time the family could still afford a governess, a widow who had been a teacher in Russia and had emigrated after losing her daughter in the turmoil of events. With Nadezhda preoccupied with Seriozha's medical requirements, the children spent a lot of time with Tiotushka – Aunty – as they called their governess. An image of her supervising the children remains among a scattering of Nice photographs. She sits among trunks of palm trees, their implications of sunshine and heat an incongruous contrast to the unsmiling woman dressed in severe dark clothing. Dimitri, Nadia, Sasha and a playmate are surrounded by toys, but are not smiling, perhaps impatient to return to their play. My father is only about four years old, but his toy, a long stick with a small wheel attached at the end, seems to presage his lifelong interest in things mechanical. I can picture Dimitri running off the moment the photo was taken, pushing the homemade contraption along paths and hills.

The governess was strict, a strictness even her employer sometimes questioned; Nadezhda was of the view that one had to explain things to children, not just order them to obey. Yet the children were very fond of Tiotushka; indeed my Aunt Nadia subsequently kept in contact with her for several decades. Perhaps for them the governess was a reassuring presence, against a background of growing worries and uncertainty in the family.

Nadia started to learn to read and write from her. By the time Dimitri was ready to become a pupil, Tiotushka had left, due to the family's financial constraints. She had become attached to the children and offered to continue without pay, but my grandparents could not accept this. They knew her value and the demand for her services elsewhere. So my father had his first experience of education in a kindergarten at a school run by the Russian community.

The governess's departure came as other links to the old way of life were quickly disappearing.

Dimitri and Nadia would piece together the practicalities of the family's time in Nice in later years, often from others' memories. Nikolai made a good living while he was manager for the widow of Prince Galitzine. But this job ended abruptly, in shameful circumstances, which Nadia only started to learn about some years after her father died. My father probably never knew the story as she did.

Nikolai's weakness for gambling – which had caused him strife when he was studying to be an officer in Russia – came back to again wreak havoc in Nice. Perhaps he found the family's circumstances hard to accept, forced to live less well than he would have liked. Maybe Nikolai believed that he could win enough money to provide more comfortably for them. Whatever the motives, Nadia told me that her father lost a large sum of money. Worse than that, it was not his money, but his employer's. He promised to repay her every penny; Nadia did not know whether he ever achieved this. This incident left him unemployed and when he did find other work, the debt must have greatly added to the financial strain.

Still, it is hard to judge whether in the long run the lost money was of such an amount to have truly made a big difference to the family's situation. Certainly my Aunt Nadia always believed it did. She also felt my grandfather paid for his mistake many times over through remorse and guilt:

...I started to feel very sorry for father, because of what he must have endured, that he had placed

CHAPTER NINE

the family in such an awful, desperate plight.
Mother never reproached him – never!
Nikolai started working with another Russian who had a shop that sold jewellery and antiques. My father remembered him "bringing home pieces of jewellery, and he was examining [them], weighing the gold, and weighing the stones..." Whatever he may have lacked in business skills, Nikolai worked hard, his partner complemented his abilities, and they did well for some time. But in 1927 France went through a recession, after the government revaluated the franc. Tourism dwindled and hotels in Nice started to close. As many of the shop's customers were visitors, the business went downhill. Then Nikolai's partner died of a heart attack, and my grandfather decided it was not worth continuing on his own.

The economic situation would have made employment openings scarce. Dimitri believed Nikolai's war disabilities made the job search even more difficult:

He was not capable of doing much physical work, because he had one arm cut to the shoulder during the war, so his physical abilities were very limited... He also had wounds all over his body, one very bad [one] in the back – I remember him showing the scar, a huge scar across the back. So... of course he was a great invalid, and he couldn't do much.

A doctor's report in Nikolai's military record from March 1917 backs this up. It states that besides the loss of his left arm, his war service left him with wounds to the shoulder blade above the amputation, his stomach and his right arm. And a later certificate – issued in Paris in August 1935 by the Union of Disabled and Invalid Russian War Veterans Resident in France – said Nikolai, having been wounded four times in the war, was eighty percent incapacitated for work.

But according to Nadia, he had learned to do everything with one hand, and there were many jobs he could have performed well. In the difficult climate there were other handicaps working against him: his knowledge of French was poor, and suspicious attitudes towards Russian migrants did not help.

My grandparents decided to move to Paris, hoping to find more opportunities there. Yet this move would herald the beginning of great poverty for the family, with Nikolai only able to pick up the most menial of jobs. Also the move marked the beginning of the family's enforced splitting up, in a physical sense; the cramped accommodation they could just afford meant it would be difficult for the family to live all together in future. As Nadia put it, their "untroubled life ended... [and] the family fell apart, never again to unite the way it was in Nice." It is not surprising that she and my father retained such fond memories of Nice: beyond its physical beauty and space, the time there represented an era of carefree togetherness. And as young children the siblings were probably only vaguely aware of the anxieties and hardships behind the scenes of their sunny days.

Dimitri and his older brother Sasha stayed behind, while their parents, with Nadia and Seriozha, went ahead to Paris to seek work and a home. Sasha stayed with friends. Dimitri travelled west a short way to the home of Nikolai's brother Vladimir, who had settled in the little town of Théoule, across the bay from Cannes (he would remain on the French Mediterranean coast all his life). Nikolai and Vladimir's mother Varvara was also staying there. Dimitri is said to have been one of her favourites among the grandchildren,

CHAPTER NINE

so her presence must have cheered the six-year-old. Vladimir made a comfortable living as a chauffeur and mechanic for a wealthy Englishman. The job provided accommodation, a cottage on the sea, "...a regal place for a chauffeur...", Dimitri said.

My father had had little contact with non-Russians and spoke virtually no French. So when he resumed school in Théoule – this time a French public school – he had some catching up to do:

I went to the local... one-room school, where all the classes were together... it was not always fun for me, because I spoke only Russian, so it was hard, but still I have a good memory of those few months I spent in that school, because it was real fun. All the time the kids were just playing, and yelling, and throwing things at each other, while the teacher was busy with a small group at a time. So when she finished with one group, OK, that one could join the fun, and she was taking care of the next group. It was nice, very nice.

My father usually saw the positive side of things, so he focused on his memories of the children's enjoyment at the teacher's expense, while playing down what must have been a difficult adjustment. In the same way, he emphasised the beauty of the area, yet in his description there is an undercurrent of loneliness:

I was in Théoule just one winter – so I never saw Théoule in the summer. Even [of] that winter I have a very good souvenir... I was spending most of the time alone – they had a dog, so I was roaming around the countryside with that dog. The countryside is mainly all mountains, I remember climbing those mountains with that dog for days on end.

*And you know – Côte d'Azur in winter, it can be
very beautiful, particularly with those mountains,
the blue sea...*

In the coming years Dimitri would live apart from his parents and siblings more often than with them. His stay in Théoule was a taste of times ahead. But in his telling about his life many years later he never complained or expressed any resentment over these long separations from his family.

My mother Irene and her parents arrived in France in September 1925, when Dimitri's family was still living in relative comfort in Nice. Natalia and Alexander did not have a choice of where to settle: the contract he had signed in Belgrade at the French mission assigned him his job and location.

After time spent in Turkey, Bulgaria and Serbia, the family – like my father's – would have found France appealing. Natalia had learned French in Russia and it is possible Alexander also spoke it. Many Russian refugees – probably including Natalia's sister Evgeniia – had already made their way to France, with all the possibilities of mutual support this implied.

But having to accept living wherever they were sent meant they could not head to an area where Russians were well established, like Paris or Nice. In addition my mother told me that her mother had been very much against Alexander taking on what would be heavy physical work. Natalia worried his war wounds would worsen with such labour.

Rapid industrialisation and a dropping birth rate in France had resulted in a shortage of workers for its factories, mines and farms even before the First World War. This was exacerbated by the loss of nearly one-and-a-half million people in that conflict. Thus businesses and the government were keen to recruit migrants, including refugees.

But refugees are not usually in a position to negotiate and the French government had very clear ideas of where and how it wanted to use foreign labour. The aim was to fill jobs unwanted by the French, not to import competition for better-paid work the locals preferred. As a consequence, migrants were directed to the most unpopular jobs, regardless of any skills they may have had to offer.

My grandfather's contract was for unskilled labour in the steel industry. It stated that he was to receive the same salary and work in the same conditions as any Frenchman prepared to do the same work. There would be deductions for accommodation that the company arranged. My mother told me that the French government paid their way from Serbia and that these travel costs were also deducted from Alexander's salary. It does not seem unreasonable that the family should have had to pay its own transport. Yet it angered my mother. This probably had more to do with what she saw as the demeaning treatment of her father: an educated, intelligent man forced to work in hard, dirty circumstances for tiny wages because he was a refugee whose previous experience was not recognised.

Another point which illustrates the negative memories my mother held of this first stage in France was her unwavering belief that her father's contract was for three years, that when he became increasingly unwell he could not afford to buy it out and slogged on for the full term. In the family documents that still exist, I can only find evidence of him working in the steel industry for one year. What seemed such an eternity for my mother can be explained by her young age. But there is also no doubt that her memories were shaped by the fact that Alexander would be a very ill man, never able to work again or do very much else, by the time he finished his steel job.

Like so many refugees before them and since, the Kouprianoffs had very limited options. There is no record of what they later felt about their decision to sign on, whether they thought it had been the right one. But my mother's very mixed feelings about their adopted homeland – ambivalence familiar to many migrants in many places – were perhaps a hint of how they might have looked back: bitterness blended with affection for a country that allowed them to settle, resentment over the official view of people like them merged with the need to accept the reality that there had not been much choice.

Alexander was assigned to Imphy, a small town about ten kilometres from Nevers, a historic city in the middle of France. Metalworking had been important in Imphy since at least the seventeenth century. Not long before the family arrived, the town had had a moment of glory: Charles Edouard Guillaume won the 1920 Nobel Prize in physics for creating several new steel alloys, in collaboration with researchers in Imphy.

I wondered what my grandparents felt when they saw the grey industrial town that was to be their first home in France, when I myself saw it for the first time more than seventy years later. While the physical layout and structures would have been similar, the atmosphere must have been very different. For in contrast to the constant production then, steel activities had been much reduced. It being a Saturday afternoon when I visited with my sister, there was a strong sense of abandonment. Apart from a small supermarket near the centre, the whole place seemed shut down and the streets were empty. Old mills and factories loomed at every turn, but were silent, either no longer in operation or stopped for the weekend.

At the train station there was a young man behind the ticket window. His laconic manner gave way to friendliness in response to our questions. Stations in small localities in France often hand out tourist pamphlets, but he was bemused by our request for printed information. There wasn't any – tourists did not come to Imphy. But he dug out a tattered old map for us to consult.

We explored the main street, lined with somewhat rundown mostly two-storey houses, some with shops on the ground floor. According to what appears to be a certificate of residence signed by their landlord at the time, this is the street where my mother and her parents lived, though there is no house number on the document. Irene's memories of Imphy were patchy. She said they rented a room in a family home. She remembered that conditions were cramped but that the family treated them well. They used the same kitchen as the woman of the house. Irene and Natalia often helped her make conserves and jams, which she would then share with them.

As is common in France, the buildings on this street fronted the sidewalk and it was hard to tell whether there were yards or courtyards hidden behind. As we tried to guess which one had housed our grandparents and Irene, we hoped it had had such an internal courtyard, perhaps with some plant life in it, to bring a touch of green.

Adjacent to one part of the main street was a warren of tiny lanes with lopsided old buildings, rotting wooden shutters and miniature yards. Rusty bits of unidentified equipment lay scattered amid unruly weeds. In one courtyard there was an ancient ironwork well, similar to ones we had seen preserved outside historic buildings, but this one was crooked and encrusted with layers of blistering rust. Many of these houses appeared to be still inhabited. A more current version of low-priced housing was visible a few blocks back: the group of identical non-descript concrete apartment buildings seemed hardly more appealing than the decaying old workers' homes.

At the edge of town, there was a newer suburban neighbourhood. And before the main street moved into farmland, we came across a large modern supermarket. Here things were more lively, a contrast to the ghost town feel elsewhere, though the gaudy signs and lights seemed an incongruous juxtaposition to the rest of town.

My mother started her formal education in Imphy. She was seven, but she had never been inside a classroom – though her mother had taught her much at home. Through her family's travels since leaving Russia, she had also picked up a smattering of several languages. As is often the case with children, she found it easier to learn new languages than did the adults around her; thus she had often acted as a go-between or interpreter for her parents. But she knew no French, so as she went off to a government primary school, she was starting from scratch yet again. Irene was lucky – she found her first teacher sympathetic and helpful:

> *I knew Russian, Turkish, Bulgarian, and a bit of Serbian, and trying to pick up a fifth language totally confused me. But my teacher was very, very nice – I used to walk around with a big [Russian-French] dictionary, and she would show me things and name them in French, and I would immediately look them up... because at that time I already read and wrote very well in Russian. So in a month I could already speak a little bit with the other girls, and in a few months I could already do the lessons.*

Several schools of the appropriate vintage remained in the town, close to the main street, but my sister and I had no clues to help us guess which one Irene had attended. We also did not know in which of the steel mills Alexander had worked. We found them in rather decrepit condition – except for their shiny signs, gates, and security booths. These locked entry points prevented us having a closer look, but it seemed large parts of these plants were abandoned.

The dreariness of the crumbling factories, mills and smoke stacks which dominated the town was accentuated by gloomy weather when we visited, though their silence muted the harsh industrial landscape. But what would the town have been like with all the plants working at full pelt and disgorging smoke and other nasty by-products? In the twenties there would have been few anti-pollution laws to fetter production, or regulations to limit noise.

Nowadays, Imphy has a population of about 3500. In years past, there were at times many thousands of workers, keeping the mills running day and night. In the 1920s many of these were migrants, including numerous Russians. Alexander's former military colleague "Uncle" Mikhail, who had been so helpful in Gallipoli, was among them. The influx of large numbers of non-French apparently shook up Imphy's established residents at first. But in my mother's memory, their misgivings over the new arrivals gave way to a measure of acceptance:

> *[There] were many, many Russian people... Few had families like my father, many were on their own, like "Uncle" Misha... single men. They would get their pay every two weeks and get terribly drunk – through the night they would walk around singing Russian songs. At first, the people of Imphy were not too keen*

on them. But they were good workers and also helped out with everything, and when... they all started to leave, our landlady said: "Imphy will never be the same again."

Social contact between the foreigners and other townsfolk was probably limited. Yet a few of the refugee workers married local women and stayed. Many others, like Alexander, left when they had completed their contracts. They preferred to try their luck elsewhere – Paris in particular.

I have found only two photographs of my grandfather from this time. In both, his face is expressionless, his mouth a straight thin line, denoting patience or disinterest in the camera's work. He looks drawn and tired, but perhaps my impression is coloured by my knowledge of his deteriorating health. Whether Natalia's prediction had been right that the work in the steel mill was too heavy for him, whether his wounds would have brought him grief regardless of his work there, is impossible to know. By the time the family moved on to Paris, Alexander could never again hold a job. He would live out the nine years until his death in poor health and constant pain, much of the time in hospital. My mother would always lay part of the blame for Alexander's terrible last years on the town of Imphy.

(*) The word *épicierka* provides an example of the way the émigrés often mixed their languages – *épicerie* is French for grocery store, the *ka* ending gives it the sound of a Russian word.

10

The Paris Years

Looking back in later years on Paris in the inter-war period, former émigrés – and other Parisians too – have sometimes made the comment that all the taxi-drivers in the city at the time were Russian. This is of course an exaggeration, but it indicates the way the Russian presence had made itself evident.

For if France was a magnet for the Russian refugees, Paris – as the capital of "Russia Abroad" from the mid-1920s – was even more so. After the First World War France took in more refugee immigrants than any other country, among them Russians, numbering somewhere between 100,000 and 200,000. While exact figures are elusive, what is not in any doubt is that the Paris district received the largest proportion of these.

With the émigrés at times conspicuous, the ways in which they were perceived by others were often somewhat skewed, as historian Robert Johnston writes:

...the stereotype common in the 1920s... envisaged the Russian community... as made up of impoverished aristocrats. All were deemed wildly impractical, exotic, and frenetic. To this mixture might be added a brace of Cossacks, a mournful choir, two or three onion-domed churches, ex-grand dukes driving taxi-cabs, and more than a touch of the suffering Slav soul... That the image did not invariably correspond to the reality of exile life was just one more liability the refugees were obliged to endure.

Many of the émigrés did indeed come from the noble classes. But there were also professional and business people, former military men, writers and artists, and clergy, "along with those of every class who had simply been caught up in the whirlwind of defeat and evacuation," writes Johnston. What was common to most was opposition to the Bolshevik regime, but even here, there was a wide range of political gradations: from monarchists, to democrats and socialists.

Yet one aspect of the stereotype was accurate: most of the post-revolution émigrés found themselves in difficult material circumstances.

So it was that the majority of Russians arriving in the capital had one overriding preoccupation: to find a way to make a living. Between a lack of appropriate skills for the French job market, and impediments to the recognition of ones that might have been useful, many émigrés had to settle for unskilled, poorly paid work. Amid a limited array of opportunities, being a cabbie was among the better jobs. But while myths grew up around those able to get this work, taxi-driving only accounted for a small proportion of the arrivals. For many, factory work or other heavy manual labour were more likely.

Both my parents arrived in the city in the late 1920s. In the two families, driving and factory assembly lines were not open to the adult males. My paternal grandfather Nikolai could do neither with only one arm and had to settle for even more undesirable jobs and spells of unemployment. My other grandfather Alexander suffered increasingly poor health after his stint in the Imphy steel mill, which prevented him from working altogether. He entered hospital about a year after the family's arrival in Paris, and it seems he never left it again.

CHAPTER TEN

Natalia became the breadwinner in my mother's family. She applied the sewing skills she had learned in Russia. First she worked at home, making clothing for individual customers. Irene remembered how she and her father had to squeeze into the tiny kitchen during fittings; these were done in the only other room in their apartment, which served as bedroom, lounge and sewing room all at once.

Natalia also did piece work. My mother said everyone pitched in:

...we used to stuff [toy] puppies. Mother would sew the little fabric dogs on her machine, father would sew on the eyes and tongues, and I had small hands, so I would stuff the paws.

When Alexander was hospitalised, Natalia got a job in a sewing workshop. Like many before her and since, she learned that having a co-national as a boss is no guarantee of protection from exploitation. For her employer was another Russian émigré. Her business, my mother told me, was:

...mostly "lingerie de luxe"... it was a small sweat shop, mother earned peanuts there... They passed the sewing on... to have embroidery done on top by hand. It was all Russians working there... The clients were mostly Americans, who came to France in winter or just before winter and then went south to the Côte d'Azur, very chic then. They ordered all the stuff and then picked it up on their way home. Things like nightgowns... in real silk. Mother, because of the sweatshop conditions of her work, categorically refused to teach me to sew. She said God forbid that you should ever sew [for a living].

Natalia probably had few other employment alternatives, for she stayed in this job for ten years, till she became too unwell to work, at the start of the Second World War.

During all the years of her husband's hospitalisation and after his death, Natalia was helped by her sister and others close to her. She also took advantage of various avenues of assistance to send my mother to schools, summer camps, and other programs. These were run by the Russian community, but sometimes there was also backing from the French government.

This made it all the more painful for my mother to recollect the treatment her mother received at the hands of her long-term employer. Even as it became clear that her mother's health was failing, and then as she was dying, Natalia's boss never offered any assistance, after a decade of what Irene felt had been underpaid labour. The woman being a member of the supposedly mutually supportive émigré community made this particularly hard to accept.

In my father's family, his mother Nadezhda was occasionally employed taking care of children or doing housework. Her sister Annochka, who often lived with the family, contributed to the household budget through her work, also looking after children. But Nikolai remained the main breadwinner, though his handicap very much narrowed his options. Dimitri remembered that his father's first job in Paris was selling newspapers at a subway entrance:

> *He was outside the metro outlet with a kind of crate that he was using for a counter... He was getting up about 4:30 or 5 o'clock in the morning and he was walking several kilometres to get his bundle of newspapers and he was carrying that bundle on his back with a strap to that metro station to be there*

CHAPTER TEN

> *around 6, 6:30 – he had to be there to get the people who go to work... Then in the afternoon he had a break – only from about 2 to 4, something like that and he was going home and having a sleep [and then returning to work]... So that was not a funny life, and in winter it could be hard. He was completely outside, no shelter, so he had huge raincoats, and umbrella, it was a strange arrangement. But that's the only job he could find, and he did that for several years. But he developed a clientele, he was very good with people, and [among] his clientele, there was a fidelity... he was joking with his customers, and so on, so it was not too bad.*

When I went to the Botzaris subway station in 2001 with my Aunt Nadia, she said it was still very much like it was when her father worked there. Like many entrances into the Paris metro system, it consisted of just a staircase descending into the ground, surrounded by a wrought ironwork fence and sign, and adjoining a park. She said that across the street there had been a bakery, where Nikolai would exchange the coins he had collected for bills to lighten his load, and shelter from rain or cold – though briefly, as he could not afford to miss customers.

Nikolai's job ended when he caught pneumonia. He was in hospital for a time, followed by a recovery period at home. Then he set out looking for work once again. This time a member of the Russian community had a positive role to play, using her influence within a department store company to help, as my Aunt Nadia told it:

> *Father got work selling tickets for the... national lottery, which was divided into ten sections.*

228

> *And I think it was the tenth section... that was reserved for the wounded from the Great War, those wounded in the face. Father was not wounded in the face. But a Russian woman, who was the lover of the director of all the Printemps department stores, she asked that he allow that Russian – only Russian invalids – sell those tickets at all the... [stores of one group owned by the company]. And so father got the best spot, because it was on the Champs Elysées, and there it went well, very well, for him.*

Besides the affluence of the area and thus good sales, there was another plus: Nikolai's position in a doorway provided shelter from the rain. My father said his father's gregarious nature again helped:

> *...every time I was going to see him there, he always had a chat with a customer, a friendly chat, and there – they were quite wealthy people – so finally they were casually buying tickets more for the pleasure of having a chat with him than for the fact of the ticket...*

Another job my father remembered Nikolai having for a time was as doorman at a "very fancy cake shop and tearoom". He would escort customers to their cars with an umbrella and open doors for them, for which he would receive tips. A bonus was that he would bring home pastries, left over at the end of the day.

The jobs Nikolai was able to get provided very little income, but in his children's memories, he always made the best of them, deploying what was by all accounts his charming personality. My father described one incident to demonstrate the customer loyalty Nikolai inspired. It occurred when his father was selling newspapers at the metro:

Once I was playing around his little counter, and one of his regular customers came and he took me by the hand... to a toy store just nearby... It looked like he was a wealthy person, and he said to me: "you choose any toy you want, anything you want – big, small, medium – anything is yours." So being a child of seven or eight... it was such a dream, that I was just looking around [overwhelmed]. Finally I chose a big locomotive about thirty centimetres long... After that he took me to his place... he gave me some cookies and fruit juice...

The poor pay my grandparents took home from their employment was reflected in the living conditions of both families.

My father, after spending a winter in his Uncle Vladimir's home in Théoule, joined his parents and three siblings in Paris. For Dimitri the contrast between the sun and greenery on the Riviera, and the miserable hotel rooms in Paris which were the family's first homes, was a shock:

...we were living in a hotel, a tiny dirty hotel, we were the whole family in two tiny, tiny rooms. There was no proper bathroom, one of the rooms had a sink and a stove, and I think there was a toilet for the whole floor, something like that. It was small, it was not too clean... [and] remember my father had one arm, so... things men do in a house – paint a wall or repair a piece of furniture, stuff like that – my father could never do, so we were stuck... So we were living in that hotel, we moved about ten times from place to place, gradually trying to improve our lot.

The family lived in hotels for a total of four or five years. They did move often, but not quite ten times. The number of these places may have been inflated in Dimitri's memory because when he and his older brother were at boarding schools and came home for holidays, rooms in separate hotels were sometimes rented as there was no space for them to sleep with the family. So in fact he may well have experienced that many different hotel rooms.

The hotels often did not have showers or baths, even to share, so the family regularly trouped to a Paris institution – municipal baths. Eventually the family was able to rent an apartment, though my father said the space was still cramped and had to be allocated efficiently:

> *It was an amazing apartment – we had one room in the basement, and another on the ground floor... and I remember I used to go to bed... on the ground floor, and during that time, the older people were eating dinner, and washing dishes and all that downstairs. And later, when they'd finished everything, they'd move me... I went to sleep in someone else's bed, and in the morning woke up on the divan in the basement.*

After Nikolai's first bout of pneumonia, the family returned to a hotel. With time and help from relatives, they finally were able to leave hotels behind for good and live in apartments, some better, some worse, depending on finances. When Nikolai died in 1938, the family moved for the last time, again having to squeeze into smaller accommodation; this apartment would be rented by various members of the family for the next fifty years.

My mother's family also started off in hotels. They too could not raise

CHAPTER TEN

the large payment of rent in advance required to lease an apartment. Most of the time they lived in the 15th *arrondissement* (district) of Paris, which after the Revolution quickly became a major Russian émigré area, according to Hélène Menegaldo, a Russian scholar in France:

> *...there are soon more than 4000 in the XVth "arrondissement", that is about ten percent of the population. The regrouping happens by streets and buildings, some of these being almost entirely populated by these new arrivals.... One can still [in 1998] find representatives of the second generation there, sometimes married to "Soviet" Russians.*

On a visit in 2001, after disembarking from the subway in this southwestern part of Paris, my sister and I immediately came upon a Russian restaurant. Otherwise there was not much obvious evidence of a Russian presence.

We had a few addresses for hotels around Paris where our parents' families had lived – most no longer served that function. But here, at one address there was still a hotel, though it had a different name from the one on a document from our mother's files. It was a plain but clean looking six-storey building, with a two-star rating advertised on dark green awnings. A half-hearted attempt had been made to beautify the cream-coloured facade, with small bunches of flowers in some window planters.

After puzzling over its newish appearance, in spite of feeling somewhat self-conscious, we finally succumbed to our curiosity and went inside. By a strange coincidence, the man at reception spoke Russian. But he had come by his Russian rather differently to us: he was a Bolivian who had lived in Cuba, where he had studied the language. In spite of a political background radically different from ours, he was keen to tell us all he knew about the hotel's history. It had indeed changed identity – twice in fact, since it was the Modern-Hotel – to become the rather pretentiously named Hotel Prince Albert Tour Eiffel. He believed the only original features remaining were the staircase and lift.

The man told us that the 15th *arrondissement* had been quite a poor area, but had recently been undergoing gentrification. He said there were still stories around about the days when the area was full of émigré Russians who lived in hotels.

Our Bolivian-Cuban-French informant invited us to have a look around so we climbed the spiral staircase, with its decorative ironwork railings. We managed to peek into a room being cleaned; it was tiny, with no bathroom, the double bed filling nearly all the space. But with all the renovations that had occurred over the years, there was no way of knowing whether it in any way resembled rooms here more than seven decades before. Even with the cleanliness now in evidence, the notion of living in such a place for months, sometimes years, was daunting. In dirtier circumstances, with children, and cooking often having to be done in the room, the idea was even less appealing.

Natalia probably moved into the Modern-Hotel alone, for judging by the dates in the document we had, this was when Alexander went into hospital. As for my mother, she was sent to live with relatives in the south of France. As in the case of Dimitri's parents when they dispatched him to live with his uncle, the decision was no doubt made to spare my mother cramped conditions and a stressful time.

She travelled to the outskirts of the naval port city of Toulon, on the Mediterranean coast, about 150 kilometres west of Nice. Irene

CHAPTER TEN

was about nine or ten years old when she moved into the home of her mother's uncle and his wife and two adult sons. He had been a military officer before the Revolution and both his and his wife's families had been wealthy.

As with others lucky enough to have had holdings outside Russia, their property in France provided for them after the Revolution. By moving from their original French home into a smaller house, they made some money to live on. Later they repeated the process, again making some profit. They supplemented this by gradually selling remaining valuables. Irene's uncle also raised rabbits, pigeons and chickens to take to market.

The company of extended family muted somewhat the pain of this first long separation from her parents. Irene became particularly close to one of the sons, in spite of their age difference. But her homesickness is poignantly clear from a bundle of postcards and letters between Irene and Natalia; from my mother's side, in childish, clumsy handwriting, there are constant queries about when Natalia would be coming south to see her.

But Irene would have to resign herself to living away from home, even when she left Toulon after about two years. For she was then sent to a Russian boarding school, though at least this was close to Paris, allowing for visits in both directions.

During the time Irene was in Toulon, her mother got together with her sister Evgeniia and Alexander's close friend "Uncle" Mikhail to share, first a small, then a larger apartment. Evgeniia, who had divorced her first husband, remarried. Privacy, even for newly-weds, was a luxury, and it was accepted by her new husband that when he went to live with his bride, the others would remain. My mother would eventually also move in. What was lost in space and privacy was made up for in closeness: this group would become my mother's surrogate family when her parents died. Her Aunt Evgeniia and her husband Peter would remain in the same apartment until their own deaths in the late 1960s.

The flat was relatively roomy and comfortable. The four adults were able to afford it by pooling their incomes from their various jobs. Over the inter-war years Evgeniia worked selling chocolates, testing light bulbs, in a hairdressing salon, as a masseuse, and possibly in other jobs my mother did not remember. Her husband drove a taxi. "Uncle" Mikhail had reasonably well-paying employment stencilling patterns onto fabric.

It was strange to see the building in 2001; after hearing my mother so often mention events connected to *rue* Boucicaut over the years, the very name had taken on a mythical aura in my mind. The street itself – one dead-end block – was incongruously tiny compared to the prominence it held in my imagination. But the building was quite grand: typically Parisian, seven storeys high, with intricate ironwork railings in front of tall windows. The large wide entrance door was framed in carved stonework, and above, the architect's name was cut into the wall along with the date of construction: 1912. Some of the matching neighbouring buildings were having their facades sandblasted: rich pale golden stonework was emerging from under layers of grime. Number three would doubtless have its turn. Whatever stages the building may have gone through over the years, it was certainly a respectable address now. This was somehow reassuring.

While my mother's family was centred in the 15th *arrondissement*, my father's family lived there only once. Mostly their hotels and apartments were in the 19th *arrondissement*, across town in the northeast of Paris – a poorer area.

While it may not have been as Russian as the 15th, there was one very important community institution there: the St Serge Theological Institute and Seminary, which became a major centre of religious thought and education among the émigrés. It had been established in 1924, as the climate in the Soviet Union became increasingly hostile to religious scholarship and the training of priests. The closure or destruction of churches in Russia by the government had discouraged not only those who might have liked to study theology, but also many in the population, fearful of the repercussions of showing their faith.

My father spent much time at the St Serge seminary and church, but this had little to do with religion. He went to play in the seminary's yard with other Russian children. The young students would sometimes join in between classes, and even the dean of the institute would have time for the youngsters when they burst into his office as he worked on theological texts.

While my father was too young to realise that he and his playmates were interrupting the work of one of the leading authors in Orthodoxy at the time, or to understand religious issues and debates, he did admire another aspect of those connected to the seminary:

Those people, they seemed to live with a total disregard to anything material. Sometimes at evenings, in our dirty hotel rooms, we had some professors from the Institute coming, and discussing with my father with loud voice and huge words and so on, probably about making a better world, I don't know what. But they were totally disregarding the sordid decor

> *surrounding us... and then we were sharing some poor food between us, like if it was a big feast. Those souvenirs are very precious to me, because those people in that Institute, they were really on the margin of the material world, things material were absolutely... meaningless for them... those big discussions with my father... were on another plane...*

Escape from the realities and poverty of daily life, through focusing the mind on ideas with congenial company, would have been enjoyable respite. Whenever Nikolai found himself unemployed, in-between seeking work he pursued such activity further, obtaining permission to sit in on courses at the seminary.

On Thursdays, when French schools had a day off, it was the children who went there for classes. The aim was to teach them Russian reading and writing, history and religion. Dimitri attended for just a short time before being sent away to boarding school, so perhaps that is why he mostly remembered these classes as an opportunity to be with his friends, and for the tea and biscuits the children were given.

St Serge still teaches young men courses in Russian Orthodoxy. The church is charming and beautiful. Carved wooden balconies and staircases lead to doors framed in religious painting, while inside almost every bit of wall is covered in frescoes. I attended part of a service there with my Aunt Nadia in 2001 and in spite of it being a weekday, there was a fairly solid attendance. Afterwards we spoke to the aging choirmaster and he remembered playing with my father in the grounds when they were both "mischievous boys".

The garden which surrounds the church was smaller than I had imagined from my father's descriptions of his hours of joyful play there. But the enclosed grounds, among Russian-speaking children and young seminary students, would have represented a safe and friendly haven. And the yard would have been expansive compared to the family's various hotel rooms.

Yet even there, both Dimitri and Nadia remembered that – like those who took part in the impassioned debates in their rooms – they did not mind the poverty of their living conditions, the closeness of their family life overcoming material shortcomings. My father said the contrast between then and his later life – not luxurious by any means – was huge, and yet his memories were good ones:

The way we live now in all our wealth and grease, we would not tolerate such conditions of living, and yet we were... really happy there. My souvenirs are only happy souvenirs of those times.

My Aunt Nadia said the children were aware of difficulties, for instance understanding they could not have as much to eat as they wanted. Yet no-one ever complained about things being hard, because she believed their home could not have been happier. Their parents' success in providing this sense of security amid difficult material circumstances was an achievement. Years later my aunt learned of her father's despair at not being able to better provide for his family – a despair with which he did not burden his children, instead taking his sorrows to his sister's place.

St Serge was among dozens of places around Paris where Russian émigrés could seek help and support, or meet with their fellow refugees. Organisations and venues proliferated to cater for a wide range of their needs – material, cultural, social and spiritual. It was support that was crucial to many, including both my parents' families.

11

Russia Abroad

As the émigrés struggled to build new lives in France, many never gave up on one day returning to Russia. Thus the death in January 1924 of Lenin brought a glimmer of cautious optimism – in some quarters, even celebrations. But others realised that it was unrealistic to think that Lenin's passing would bring a change of regime and they were proven right. Any hopes of a transformation of the one-party state quickly evaporated.

More bad news was to come. Émigré leaders lobbied western governments on the Soviet Union's untrustworthiness, warning of the dangers of it exporting revolution to the West. They also reminded them of their stated commitment to human rights, convinced those were being trampled in Russia.

But all their efforts failed to counter political pragmatism. One by one the Western European nations gave the Soviet Union diplomatic recognition. In France this occurred in October 1924. To add insult to injury, the French government handed the former Russian Embassy over to the Soviets. The pre-revolutionary tricolour slid down the flagpole, replaced by the red hammer and sickle. In Russian-French author Henri Troyat's words, the refugees feared that "They would no longer have any official existence. They would be the citizens of nowhere."

There were rumours that stateless Russians would be repatriated or forced to choose between French or Soviet citizenship. But those fears did not eventuate. In fact, the French government allowed diplomats who had been appointed by the Provisional Government to continue to act on behalf of émigrés through a Central Office on Russian Refugee Affairs.

Though politics had a way of intruding into many aspects of life in the Russian community – sometimes in a divisive way – the importance of education with a Russian focus was a unifying factor. It was seen as critical whatever the future brought. The community pulled together to set up facilities, from pre-schools to secondary schools, along with a variety of less structured courses catering to all ages.

Funding was always difficult, and the French government was persuaded to provide a share, as well as certification. That, along with donations, kept the schools going and allowed them to offer financial assistance to the many who needed it. Their dual tasks, parallel to other exile communities, were to educate the children, while passing on the heritage and language. As Russian-French scholar Hélène Menegaldo put it, the latter was the "carrier of the essence of 'Russianness', guarantor of the transmission of culture and memory". There was also a wider goal, especially in the early years, when a return to Russia still seemed possible, as historian Robert Johnston writes:

> *All sectors of émigré opinion acknowledged the importance of the struggle against the loss of Russian national feeling in the young. Both for their own and Russia's sake, younger men and women of the emigration must not surrender to the alien culture around them... Once freed of her yoke, their country would require "well-prepared human material"*

for the gigantic job of restoration in all areas of the state and the national economy.

Among the educational institutions set up by the émigrés was the boarding school where my mother was sent when she returned from her stay in southern France. It is unlikely that her parents had any thoughts of a possible future role for her in rebuilding Russia. But the Boarding School for Russian Young Girls, set up by a relative of the Tsar in the town of Quincy, provided many advantages: familiar language and customs creating a comfortable living environment, teaching on Russian heritage, and importantly, the availability of financial assistance. It overcame other practical difficulties too: everyone in Natalia's shared apartment worked, and she did not want Irene there alone outside school hours.

The stated aims of the school point to an effort to be broader in outlook than some other émigré institutions, which had a tendency to teach through the prism of the past. Most of the instruction was in Russian when Irene attended, and a book about Quincy written in 1991 by Olga Efimovsky, a former pupil, says the majority of the girls were Russian Orthodox. However the school's policy was to welcome children of all classes and religions, in an effort to instill tolerance and respect for others. It also encouraged the pupils to discuss contemporary political and social issues, to teach them to examine all sides of arguments and form opinions. These policies and the overall goal of producing "young girls endowed with strong personalities" apparently sat uncomfortably with some of the more conservative members of the community.

But the school did not neglect instruction in Russian-related subjects, such as, in the words of its director Princess Irène Paley

CHAPTER ELEVEN

Théodore of Russia, the "cataclysm which is wreaking havoc in their country, about which we try to explain the causes and the events with as much objectivity as possible."

The small town of Quincy, thirty kilometres southeast of Paris, is half-an-hour's travel on a suburban train. The school was housed in a château, thanks to the generosity of the French count who then owned it. When my sister and I travelled there in 2001, we had photos of the distinctive 1890s building. Yet strangely enough, most of the staff in the Quincy train station did not recognise it. Eventually someone, half-jokingly, declared that the château was haunted. We thought of the scores of girls who had passed through its doors six or seven decades before, to then travel to many corners of the world to unknown fates. We could visualise a haunting, but of a different sort.

It was surprising that the rail men were unaware of it, for the château housed a police detachment and was only a short walk away. We gazed at the large brick and stone structure and its busy architecture through a metal fence: round turrets, steep slate roofs with porthole-like windows, large windows lower down with stone lintels depicting faces and flounces, and a grand staircase to the main entrance. In front of the château stretched a vast lawn, scattered with spreading trees.

In spite of our pleas, we were prevented from entering the grounds beyond a few metres by a policeman on duty. But after we had taken some photos, a commander appeared from inside the building and, to our surprise, invited us in. As he led us up the stone staircase he said letters regularly arrived here, and occasionally visitors, from around the world, interested in the château's current state. Becoming curious, he had researched the building's history:

the school had closed in 1939, and for a short time it served as a Jewish children's home. German troops requisitioned it in 1940, and in 1951 the police took it over.

Inside the entrance, two large lions guarded another massive staircase of heavy dark wood. The commander showed us a few ground floor rooms, once classrooms and dining halls, used by the police for meals or recreation. These retained the original ornamentation, each with a different theme and colour pattern on elaborate painted ceilings and papered walls, some with plasterwork and large fireplaces. The tall windows made the rooms bright, in spite of the rain outside.

Our mother spent four years here, from the age of eleven. We tried to imagine her sharing a desk, or sitting at a table at mealtime, chatting with companions, in these rooms, surrounded by the same wallpaper and ceiling patterns. There are a couple of photos of her at the school. She wears her uniform, a loose long-sleeved smock-like garment, tied at the waist with a sash and topped by a white collar. Her blonde hair is tied in pigtails or braids, framing her smiling face.

The commander did not take us upstairs, where the dorms used to be, so we could not place this smiling girl in her living quarters; these we had to visualise from the photos and information we had. Up to eighty girls lived here in dorms of seven or eight. These seem to have been quite plain compared with the ground floor: for each girl, a narrow bed, a chair and a small curtained night table for her treasured possessions.

The book about the school tells of sports in the large garden, of dancing lessons, music and theatre. A program reproduced in its pages contains Irene's name in a list of actors in a 1932 dramatic production. The play depicted an old tradition whereby the Tsar "chose his fiancée from among the most noble, the most beautiful and the best-connected young girls in the country." My mother played one of the potential fiancées presented to the Tsar's envoy.

Irene remembered her schooling here as being primarily in Russian, but by the time she left Quincy in 1933, it was sending the girls to nearby French schools most days of the week. This was perhaps seen as more practical for their future, but there were financial considerations too. The increasing economic difficulties through the 1930s reduced the school's funding and its ability to pay its own teachers. Such economic constraints affected many of the community's educational establishments, resulting in closures or limiting of services.

Irene's last report card shows she did well in her studies. Attending a Russian school had drawbacks. Girls who wanted to proceed further had to write government exams, but there were logistical problems arranging these for schools outside the mainstream. Irene was delayed a year in continuing because of this, though she later made up the time. There were higher Russian institutions which did not require exams but they were not accredited for university entrance, and my mother was keen to go to university.

There have been endless debates that continue today about the pros and cons of a bilingual education, in Canada and elsewhere. My mother does not seem to have suffered any disadvantages besides the delayed exams. On the contrary, her already demonstrated ability for languages may have been enhanced by her years at Quincy.

In spite of his stint at school in Théoule, my father's French was still not fluent when he resumed his education on arrival in Paris.

In 2001 I saw the French neighbourhood school he attended: a four-storey brick building with elaborately carved stone lintels and tricolors above the large wooden doors. The children who poured out at lunchtime chattered in a variety of languages. The school was not as multicultural back in the 1920s; yet when my father attended, he found the teachers and children alike tolerant of his difference and initially, his language problems. Still it would have been a relief for him to join his Russian friends at the St Serge Seminary after classes and to lapse into a language that was easier and more comfortable.

After my father had spent about a year in the neighbourhood school, his parents also decided to send him to boarding school. But they enrolled him in a French institution, believing this would better prepare him for the future. By coincidence the school they chose was in the same direction as Irene's, though almost twice as far from Paris, in the town of Melun.

There were practical issues in his family too: the need to ease their overcrowded hotel room homes. Nadia was kept at home to help her mother, Seriozha because of his health problems. So it was decided that the two older boys – Sasha and Dimitri – should go away to study, presumably with financial assistance from the community. My father said he could see the logic of this because of what his little brother was going through with his club feet, undergoing many painful operations, and the toll this took on his mother.

It was not unusual to send children away to study at a young age, but leaving his close family would not have been easy for the eight-year-old; being wrenched from an environment where the familiar Russian language and customs dominated would have made it tougher yet. There was consolation for Dimitri in that a sizeable group of Russian boys attended the school and an émigré woman worked as their monitor:

> ...*she always knew when a kid had some problems – problems because the parents are far away and so on, she could feel that. I remember one winter evening after classes when I was in a sad mood, she came to me and we went together... [to] an old old house, where there was a Russian family living... and there I had supper with that family... [other times] she would take one or two boys in her room after classes and she would give us some candies or some jam or something – just little touches like that.*

Not surprisingly though, Dimitri was always thrilled to go home:

> *We were living in that single room in a hotel, we were three in a bed, some on the floor... and yet... the pleasure and the joy of being in my family again was fantastic.*

For Dimitri's older brother Sasha, infrequent visits home were not enough to temper his homesickness. He was continually running away from schools. These were usually on the outskirts of Paris, and he had many hours of walking to get home. One time it was the school that expelled him because he took an interest in the Communist Party. Nikolai would not have been impressed with his political dabbling, but beyond that, he himself had attended boarding school and felt it was good for his sons, even if the separation from the family was hard. So another school would be found and he would be sent away again.

When it came to secondary education, his parents sent Dimitri to the only boarding school from which his brother finally had not fled: the Practical School of Commerce and Industry at the Cyprien-Desgroux Professional School. Sasha's persistence had to be a good sign and indeed my father did enjoy his technical training there. But Dimitri would have preferred to have gone to *lycée*, to work towards school leaving exams which would have allowed him to continue to university. Dimitri said his father was obsessed with making sure that his children acquired practical skills, applicable anywhere. His own education in Russia had proved useless in France and he wanted to avoid this for his children:

> *He couldn't accede to any civil service or anything like that, or military job, things for which he had training in Russia, because we were foreigners... His knowledge of French was not academic, so he couldn't very well go into places where a thorough knowledge of the language is necessary. So that's why he had that idea we have to learn a trade – the kids – in order to be able to make a living.*

Perhaps Nikolai intended for my father to take up further education after he had mastered practical technical abilities, because my Aunt Nadia said he always spoke of making an engineer out of Dimitri. My grandfather's early death and the war would disrupt any such plans.

The school was located further this time – in Beauvais, some eighty kilometres north of Paris. With the technical training, it also provided the regular high school subjects. The combination of courses meant nearly sixty hours of class time and supervised homework a week.

Two report cards survive from my father's first year at Beauvais. He did best in workshop subjects and industrial design, though his gregarious nature sometimes got in the way, one teacher noting that he was too talkative. Russian was listed as a subject, which is surprising. My father told me the last time he took any Russian at school was with the monitor at Melun. Perhaps the lessons here were perfunctory. Considering the school's main goal was teaching technical skills, it is also surprising that it was here that my father acquired a lasting deep appreciation of literature. The library master set out to acquaint the boys with the classics – not only the French ones, but others in translation. My father said he would promote books with "such an enthusiasm, gesture, and high voice" that his zeal was infectious and irresistible.

Eventually the boys had to choose a specialty. My father was interested in ceramics, perhaps a hint of his later enjoyment and artistic skill in working with his hands in a number of materials. But in the end he took electricity, again probably influenced by his father.

After three years at Beauvais, Dimitri graduated in 1938 with a couple of diplomas in the electrical trades. He then attended another technical school in Paris until mid-1939. Dimitri's education was interrupted by the outbreak of war, though he did take night courses during two years of the conflict.

My father was a great believer in lifelong learning. Beyond the formal courses he took after emigrating to Canada, he always pursued self-education – at work and away from it – in spite of always putting in long hours in his jobs. Dimitri frequently found himself doing work which normally required higher official qualifications than he had. His constant thirst for knowledge, along with his prodigious memory, often led people to believe he had studied at university, something he always wished he'd been able to do, had circumstances not intervened.

While my father was in Beauvais dreaming of studying in a *lycée*, my mother was fortunate enough to have begun attending one. It was in Paris, so she finally got to live with her mother in her shared apartment. The secondary school, French this time, was almost next door to the building which housed the sewing workshop where Natalia was employed. She could see the school from its windows and Irene would often go to have her lunch with her mother.

In the early 1930s, fees for secondary schools in France were dropped. Thus it was that my mother was able to attend the Lycée Molière from 1934. This was considered among the better such schools in Paris and the 1880s institution is still well respected. Exploring it in 2001, my sister and I found the exterior of the huge building fairly ordinary. But inside we discovered an enclosed world centred on a large courtyard, filled with trees. On three levels, long corridors with multiple archways and classrooms along them lined the courtyard, as in a cloister. When we arrived, the sound levels were anything but cloister-like: it was recess and the voices of exuberant teenagers echoed all around. The activity helped us feel more inconspicuous as we explored, uninvited, wondering whether we might be thrown out. While much of the original structure remained unchanged, a third storey had been added since our mother's time, accommodating more students, and boys had been admitted to the once girls' only school.

Among the subjects my mother studied were English and Russian. The school still offers English, along with a variety of other European languages, but it seems Russian is no longer taught.

Irene attended the Lycée Molière for three years preparing for her baccalaureate, or school leaving certificate. For my mother, surprisingly, one of the hardest exams was the oral part of her

CHAPTER ELEVEN

first level Russian. Irene said that her being a native speaker was a handicap, because she knew what was right by instinct, not by rules:

...the way I know Russian... when you are asked why you write it that way, or say it that way, you answer – it has always been that way – why? I don't know. So I was very worried.

In the end, Irene successfully passed both levels of the baccalaureate. The higher level, which she completed with distinction in 1937, allowed her university entry. She applied to the Sorbonne University with the aim of becoming a teacher and was accepted, but then discovered barriers. As a non-citizen, Irene faced quotas getting into some courses; there would also be quotas at the end of the degree, limiting access to certain jobs.

As it turned out, her time at university would last only a few months. While Irene was still at *lycée*, her father Alexander died. Not long after she finished, her mother's health began to fail. While attending the Sorbonne, my mother also did secretarial courses. With Natalia's illness worsening, Irene's priority became to find work. The practical need to bring in money would have been mixed with terrible anxiety over the future. With her father gone, she must, at such a young age, have lived in dread at the prospect of losing the person to whom she was closest – her mother. In addition, there was the approaching war – whatever hopes she may have held of resuming university were buried for once and for all.

The community's efforts at passing on the Russian language and culture continued in the summer breaks. During holidays while she was at school, Irene was sent to various camps run by émigré organisations. Their intention was to spare children the heat and dust of the city, taking them to places where they could enjoy the country and the company of other children. They also aimed to further promote Russian heritage and customs, for instance teaching them songs and poetry and other forms of cultural expression, and arranging Orthodox church services for them.

It was at one of these summer camps that my mother met her future sister-in-law, my father's sister Nadia. There is a photograph from about 1934 of the two of them, in their mid-teens, with other girls. Both have long braids, my mother's blonde, Nadia's dark. The girls wear uniforms, yet their casual poses and carefree expressions indicate this did not cramp their summer enjoyment.

It was a Russian organisation also which arranged trips for refugee children further afield. Here the goal was more outward looking, providing them with exposure to other countries and cultures. During two summers, my father travelled to Switzerland through this organisation, staying with a farming family.

The trips were planned by members of the Zernov family, prominent among émigrés who helped their fellow refugees in a variety of ways, somehow always able to raise money for their efforts. In a joint family history written by several members of the family, Nikolai Zernov noted how numbers of poor children sent abroad under this program grew over time, from 50 in 1935, to 600 four years later. It aimed not only to provide the children with a rare opportunity for travel, but to also make people in participating countries "aware of the tragic events, suffered by our homeland".

My father had fond memories of his two trips away, of the beauty of the farm among the mountains where he stayed, and the enjoyment he got from going out with the livestock into the hills. And as the Zernovs hoped, he found his host family warm and welcoming. His siblings Seriozha and Nadia also had summer visits to Switzerland under this scheme.

My mother too went overseas, to England, with a program run by the Zernovs, when she was in her teens. These trips were a combination of holiday and work for families, to help the young people pick up English and other skills. Zernov wrote they also "opened up different perspectives for these young men and women and tore them away from daily émigré life."

Irene crossed the Channel two or three times, her experiences varying depending on the family which took her in. Certainly improving her English would be a huge help to her, not just in her work, but in her future life in Canada, a place in which I am sure she could not imagine she would one day live.

As they got older, there were many other avenues for my parents to take part in community activities. The cultural life of the emigration was dynamic and vibrant. What was dubbed a Silver Age in the arts had begun in Russia late in the nineteenth century, and Russian literature, music, ballet, art, and so on, had also found recognition across Europe. Many of those active in cultural endeavours became refugees and they pursued their creativity in the West. This resulted in émigré organisations where people could study and participate in cultural production or take advantage as spectators of the pool of talent on offer. These activities spread beyond the community: they made their mark on the artistic life of France in the inter-war years, leaving a lasting legacy in terms not only of their output, but also their influences and the institutions they created. The émigrés felt particularly vindicated in the eyes of the world, in their goal of retaining a culture under threat of disappearance in the Soviet Union, in 1933. That's when the first

Nobel Prize awarded to a Russian went to an émigré, author Ivan Bunin receiving the literature prize.

Such cultural pursuits, along with a variety of recreational clubs and less formal social networks, provided many opportunities for meetings among Russian youth. My mother had an active social life before the war. She was an attractive young woman, petite, with long wavy hair. Among several photos from this era is one of her dressed for a costume party, sitting on a high stool, showing off slim, stockinged legs. In another photo, she wears a fedora hat, perched fashionably at an angle, from under which her large, dark eyes look out dreamily.

Irene's path had not crossed my father's at this point; their age difference meant he was just reaching the time when he might have joined such social activities when the war began. But she did meet Dimitri's older brother Sasha. It surprised both my parents, that when my father introduced his bride-to-be to his family a few years later, it turned out she already knew two of his siblings. Yet perhaps it is not that surprising; the webs of friendships, relations, and connections within the Russian community seemed to link everyone in some way, in spite of the large numbers of émigrés and their dispersal, both geographic and social.

This closeness among the émigrés, and their efforts to perpetuate their Russianness through their children have been blamed for some of the difficulties they had in being fully accepted in the wider society. But as with immigrants everywhere, it was a two-way street: sticking with their community did help keep them separate; at the same time, lack of acceptance also pushed them towards others like themselves. Among parts of the émigré community there was certainly the will to keep apart. For others though, this was not the aim. And being educated in France and fluent in the language did not necessarily help bridge the difference.

My Aunt Nadia said she and her family "stuck to Russian friends and everything Russian; we... felt ourselves to be different." This feeling was sustained by the French with whom they interacted. In my aunt's experience, this was rarely done in a hostile way; only occasionally did she face negative attitudes, such as the accusation by a fellow pupil at school that foreigners took away jobs from locals. On the whole, she "saw much that was good from the French."

My mother felt her separateness from those around her keenly. During her nearly three decades in France, she said she had few close relationships with French people, though when occasionally the ice was broken, the resulting friendships were warm:

>...in France, we lived for so many years, and yet I was hardly ever... invited inside a French home, that hardly occurred. And yet, among all sorts of foreigners, it was very common... But if you made friends with [the French], for instance there was [a woman]... with whom I worked – she was very nice to me... for her there was no difference what nationality I was or anything else, in fact she found it very amusing that I was not Catholic. But, in general, we had little [social] contact with them.

Irene too had her occasions when her difference was pointed out to her in not very subtle ways, such as when she encountered the expression *sale étranger* – dirty foreigner. These hurtful words appear in the memories of other refugees, including in the writing of Henri Troyat, a Russian and prominent author in the French language. His novel *Aliocha* (a nickname for Alexis) is the story of the difficulty an émigré boy has in understanding his situation, caught between two worlds:

> *He remembered the former caretaker of the building who, two years ago now, had called him "dirty little foreigner" because he was playing with some friends, in front of his quarters. The insult had remained wedged in him, like an arrow. What hostility there had been on the contorted face of the janitor! Would he have been so insolent if the parents of Alexis had been French?*

Although the book is fictional, it draws on Troyat's own childhood as the son of Russian émigrés in 1920s France. As an adult, the author wholeheartedly took on his identity as a member of French society, and it took to him: he was elected to the French Academy. Yet he often returned to Russian themes in his writing, both historical and centred on the émigré period. Troyat wrote *Aliocha* many decades after he experienced the feelings which inform the book, but his depiction of the misery his protagonist suffered in trying to reconcile the two parts of his life is still poignantly expressed.

The relatives of my parents' (and Troyat's) generation who remained in France did, it seems, come to accept and be accepted. The French are said to have become more open to different cultures after the Second World War, at least those originating in other parts of Europe. And with the shift of generations, the migrants themselves increasingly left Russian ways behind. But during the inter-war years, for émigré children, the divergence between their two worlds – one of which they only knew through their parents – must have brought confusion and dismay.

As historian Marc Raeff writes, this was further underlined by questions surrounding the official position of the émigrés, as their "...legal status gave palpable form to the differences that separated the exile from all others."

Regulations for migrants changed often over the two inter-war decades, influenced by the numbers of refugees arriving at various times, as well as by the evolving economic situation and popular or political reactions to it. But one thing which was constant was the distinction maintained between residents who were citizens and those who were not.

The position of the Russians was shared by refugees and migrants from a range of countries – and the French restrictions on such people were no worse than those imposed by other governments across the continent, indeed they were often less stringent than elsewhere. Each group faced complicating factors in any efforts to improve their legal standing, depending on the politics of their country of origin and the evolving situation in a Europe moving towards war. For those of Russian descent, their circumstances were often influenced by the changing attitude among the French towards the Soviet regime: they fell in and out of favour depending on whether the left or the right had the ascendancy in local politics. At the same time, some always saw them as reactionaries against what they believed was a progressive experiment in the Soviet Union; others consistently thought of them as potentially dangerous suspects because they originated in that same country.

In the inter-war years there were various espionage scandals, a couple of kidnappings involving the émigré community and Soviet connections, and the 1932 assassination of French President Paul Doumer by an apparently deranged Russian migrant. None of this helped efforts to shake politically linked opinions of the community among the French.

The community itself and harmony within it was tested when it came to politics, which mirrored many of the past divisions in their homeland. Politics also led to splits in the Orthodox Church, with different groups arguing over whether they should remain under Soviet church leadership or create their own. But the multiplicity of organisations and groups catered for all shades of opinion and taste, and certain factors – such as language – often overrode other differences.

The émigrés did gain one major form of support, which was not accessible to other refugee groups – at least at first: the Nansen passport. When Moscow declared émigrés non-citizens and, further, when the West recognised the Soviet Union, the émigrés became stateless. In response, the League of Nations created the passport in 1922, an initiative of the High Commissioner for Refugees, Fridjof Nansen. But even among countries recognising this document, such as France, rights under it were not always equally granted, either in matters relating to movement between countries or indeed in local laws and rules.

Regulations for non-citizen residents of France required renewing residential and work permits often, the difficulty of these processes varying, again depending on prevailing economic and political circumstances. They also required many visits to police stations to have certificates issued or stamped: when one moved house, for instance, or when one left town, as my mother remembered:

...every time you went away for more than 24 hours, you had to go to the police, and say – "I live here... I am going there and there" – but that was only for

CHAPTER ELEVEN

foreigners. Just going from one town to another in France. When I went to camp, after I turned sixteen, I would go to the police, and say... "I am leaving for so much time and here is the address", they would stamp it... you would arrive in the other place, you'd show this [to the police there], they would stamp it [too].

This constant paper chase brought anger and frustration that such rules still applied after so many years of living in the country. But it also engendered insecurity, and sometimes fear, among people always vulnerable before these regulations and those who applied them. Émigré author Vladimir Nabokov wrote in his autobiography *Speak Memory* that these procedures would repeatedly...

> *...show us who was the discarnate captive and who the true lord. Our utter physical dependence on this or that nation, which had coldly granted us political refuge, became painfully evident when some trashy "visa", some diabolical "identity card" had to be obtained or prolonged, for then an avid bureaucratic hell would attempt to close upon the petitioner and he might wilt while his dossier waxed fatter and fatter in the desks of rat-whiskered consuls and policemen. "Dokumenti", it has been said, is a Russian's placenta.*

These encounters with the bureaucracy could have serious results; for instance, the threat of expulsion was always present. For the émigrés, who had no homeland to which to be sent, this usually meant being taken to the border, where they would be turned back by neighbouring countries and would often end up in a French prison.

One could also be jailed for just forgetting to carry one's identity papers, something that happened to a friend of Irene's:

> ... *he was a student... a Hungarian, and once he did not turn up for a rendezvous, and he always, always turned up, and I was a bit worried. We had no telephones then, so I went to where he lived... to find out what had happened and they said they didn't know. They were also all foreigners, afraid of the police, there were constant raids in the "Quartier Latin" where they would catch all sorts of illegals. So I went to the commissariat of police... They said "Oh, he didn't have his papers – we arrested him because he didn't have a certificate of residence with him". He was receiving a stipend from the French government, and from the Hungarian government to study at the Sorbonne, and he did not have on him a certificate for where he lived, so he sat there [in prison] for 24 hours.*

My mother managed to get her friend released by pretending to be his fiancée and vouching for him. But the regulations were more difficult to overcome in other areas, such as entering certain professions, as my mother learned. During the war, the émigrés would also find that the regulations discriminated in areas like rationing and war widows' compensation. And the constant threat of new restrictions being added, or of penalties in cases of perceived or real breaches, brought reluctance to speak up for one's rights or openly espouse controversial political views.

Becoming a French citizen generally provided an escape from these restrictions and official discrimination (though even naturalised

CHAPTER ELEVEN

foreigners faced official quotas during part of the 1930s). But obtaining citizenship was not always easy. According to historian Gary Cross, naturalisation was not particularly encouraged in France before the Second World War. Although the procedure varied over the interwar years, much of the time there were major financial and bureaucratic obstacles: the process could be very expensive, it could take years, and it was often applied arbitrarily.

For many émigrés in my grandparents' generation there was also an emotional obstacle. Some of Nikolai's friends urged that he apply for citizenship, as that would have given him the right to more government benefits. But my Aunt Nadia said he felt it would be wrong to swear allegiance to France for such motives:

...he did not want to take it – he could not, because he could not be dishonest before his conscience – he knew he was not French, that he was Russian, that it would be a deception... many said our life would be a lot easier, but he could not do it.

But my grandfather did not discourage his children from becoming citizens. The family was able to obtain citizenship for the youngest child Seriozha, assisted by the fact that he was born in Nice. And when the oldest son Sasha decided to join the French Army, he too was able to get through the procedure, his application likely facilitated by his military intentions. Nikolai approved his son's decision to join the forces; as Nadia said "...father understood, that for us, Russia was apparently finished."

Nadia herself tried to get citizenship just before the war, partly to improve her employment possibilities – even to be a salesperson in a shop was difficult for non-citizens. My grandmother Nadezhda put aside her misgivings and applied with her. But the arrival of the

German occupation army interrupted that attempt and Nadezhda never tried again. Shortly after the war, when my aunt had her first son, she and her husband tried to get him naturalised; she said French newborns in the post-war period were entitled to an extra government allowance, and they were also thinking of securing his status for the future. But they encountered a maze of requirements that defeated them. In the end, my aunt and her family remained refugees until after they emigrated, as did my parents and the children they had before leaving France: my brother and me.

Becoming a citizen might have eased official restrictions, but it did not guarantee complete acceptance. So whether one became naturalised or not, community and family continued to be crucially important.

With so many families fragmented and scattered in numerous locations, whether in Russia, Western Europe, or beyond, those relatives who were together in one place cooperated as extended families, sharing accommodation, pooling incomes, or helping each other with the care of children.

In my father's family, Nikolai often put in long hours of work. My Aunt Nadia saw so little of him that she sometimes felt she hardly knew him: for days on end, he would leave for work and return again when she was sleeping. Thus the relatives in the children's lives were integral to their feelings of family support and solidarity. Nikolai's mother Varvara moved among her three children who were in France, particularly giving much time to his busy home.

She helped care for the children. Also, she proved very capable at picking up skills useful to the household, in spite of her lack of experience in such chores previously in Russia. Others from the aristocracy, who had also had servants in the past, found the adaptation difficult. But Varvara enthusiastically took to new tasks, everything from picking up a hammer or saw to do minor repairs, to bringing holiday cheer to dismal homes, as my Aunt Nadia recalled:

I remember [one] Christmas, on the landing on the stairs, [she] put up a Christmas tree, and it was very beautiful, because she knew very well how to make everything beautiful... [she] had golden hands, she knew how to sew, cook, anything at all, she could do... Generally, I think she took an interest – when in Russia they had a cook and a servant and all the rest – but she probably used to go to the kitchen to watch, she was probably generally interested in all that.

Another person who often lived with the family and helped out was my grandmother's sister Annochka. Even when she got a live-in job with another family, she contributed financially and spent time with her niece and nephews.

The family web spread wider, with a more distantly related uncle taking the children on regular outings. When he was home from school, my father remembered walks with this uncle on the Champs Élysées, where he would buy them pastries. When the square in front of the Town Hall of the 19th *arrondissement* hosted a fair, he would treat them to the rides. One time he won a bird at the fair and gave it to the children. They adored the red songster, but my father – perhaps feeling sorry for it – let it out of its cage one day to fly around, and it took the opportunity to disappear through an open window. The uncle also took some of the children to the Colonial Exhibition; Dimitri was dazzled by the exoticism of this showcase of France's African and West Indian colonies.

The warmth and closeness in Dimitri and Nadia's home was echoed in my mother's extended family in Paris. This was a smaller group than the relatives who surrounded my father, consisting mainly of those who shared the apartment in which Natalia lived, and also Irene when she was not away at school.

But in their teenage years, while still studying, both Dimitri and Irene had to face terrible loss: the deaths of their fathers.

In Irene's household, Alexander had been an absent presence most of the time the family lived in Paris. He was in hospital for nearly eight years, in pain and increasingly immobile. My mother did not know whether the shrapnel that had lodged in his spine during the fighting in Russia had ever been removed. But it had left her father with a damaged back, which deteriorated over time. She said that when he was offered a new treatment, he felt it was worth risking:

>*He got worse and worse – he developed all sorts*
>*of sores, because he had to lie on his back. He could*
>*hardly move because of the pain and the fact his spine*
>*could not hold him. The shrapnel had smashed one*
>*of his vertebra and there was nothing left of it so he*
>*could not stand or turn. He was really suffering. So*
>*when they offered him an operation, one of the first*
>*transplants, which would involve taking bone from*
>*his leg and putting it in his spine – he agreed. He died*
>*from the after-effects of that operation. The operation*
>*itself was a success, but he developed an infection*
>*and there were no antibiotics at the time.*

Alexander died in July 1935. He was 45 years old.

Nikolai too died for lack of what would later become common: antibiotics. He contracted pneumonia once again, and this time, was unable to overcome it. He had managed to survive being left for dead on the battlefield during the First World War, his sister Olga bitterly lamented, but he succumbed to an illness she believed was brought on by his poor working conditions:

> *Saved [previously] almost miraculously in dramatic circumstances, [Nikolai] was taken away... by a banal pulmonary congestion contracted when, as a poor émigré responsible for a family and with no external assistance, he sold outdoors, in all weather... penicillin was not yet available for sale and the cupping glasses I went to apply to him every day did not succeed in saving him. We were all in despair.*

My grandmother recorded the painful two weeks of Nikolai's illness in her diaries: the high fevers, the breathing difficulties and coughing, the wasting away. She wrote that he seemed most agonised to be leaving his family to fend for themselves, by fears over how they would get by. Nadezhda turned to her faith to carry her through the loss of the man she had once hesitated to take as her husband, but had come to love deeply over two decades of marriage.

Nikolai died in January 1938, at the age of 48.

While my parents' families mourned the private tragedies of the deaths of Alexander and Nikolai, a broader tragedy, which would engulf a large part of the world, was brewing: the Second World War.

12
Troubled Ties

When I was very young, I thought Communists were three metres tall. Everything that was said around me about them implied they were monsters, to be feared and hated. Maybe I was also influenced by the monumental statues seeming to dominate every scene in every photo I saw of the Soviet Union.

In the tense and unsettled inter-war years, many in Europe did not know what to make of the new Soviet leaders. As for those Russians who had fled Communist rule, to them they would have seemed like giants: a huge obstacle to their dreams of political changes in their homeland that might allow them to go back. Every development there was of great interest to the émigrés. But as time went on, it became increasingly difficult to get a clear picture of what was going on in Russia. Those who had current information to offer inevitably added their own biases, depending on which end of the political spectrum they inhabited. At the same time, there was growing censorship and manipulation of information by the Soviet government.

One source of news came from Russians continuing to leave the Soviet Union through the 1920s, and in lesser numbers in the 1930s, either expelled or getting out because of their opposition to the regime. Clearly the versions of events told by these people were not unbiased either, but they provided alternatives to official or censored reports from Moscow and variations on the contradictory information available otherwise. And they carried the weight and

CHAPTER TWELVE

persuasiveness of personal experience, especially to the émigré audience hungry for news.

Anna, the cousin of my paternal grandmother Nadezhda, left the Soviet Union for the West in July 1925, bringing plenty of stories about kin who stayed behind and the life there in the five years or so since many of her relatives had left. The situation of the refugees might have been tough, but her descriptions of the famine, material hardships, arrests and fear in their homeland would have given them pause if they had any doubts over having fled.

Anna's departure had been thwarted in late 1918 when a letter outlining her plans had been intercepted by the authorities. Fear of the consequences if she persisted in trying to leave had led her to forget such notions for a time, in spite of her husband already being out of the country.

She had managed to get her two small sons, their nanny Masha, and herself through the first part of the famine, working and living with relatives in Moscow. In the autumn of 1921, she took a job in the country as a teacher. The village she moved to was a few hundred kilometres north of Moscow, in her words on "an endless snowy plain". She found the remoteness daunting; she had resigned herself to the reality that it was almost impossible to get any news from her husband abroad, but here even contact with her relatives in Moscow was difficult. She gave classes in English, French and natural sciences. Never having taught before, she would work late into the night preparing zoology and botany lessons. There was little kerosene for lamps; she worked with the light of burning twigs, gathered by Masha. In her latter years she blamed her growing blindness on these long work sessions with only dim, flickering light.

The education system was in some confusion, with the new regime having discarded much from the past, but not yet having set up a coherent alternative more suitable to its ideology. This uncertainty made teaching difficult in practical terms; in political terms, it brought apprehension. Anna said that not long before she arrived, a government official had paid a visit to the village school:

> *[He] said to the children... that they were free, that they could throw out their teachers, that there were no marks and so on. The teachers feared the students, as they were teachers of schools from before; they were completely at a loss over what to do...*

Yet Anna found she was able to establish a good relationship with her pupils. She won their respect in class, which was enhanced by her willingness to give them extra tutoring outside school hours. Anna gained satisfaction in feeling she was fulfilling an important role, regardless of the difficult context:

> *I consider that over my whole life this was my most productive position because I truly worked for the benefit of my Russian people whom I so loved and love and will love always in spite of everything, because the government is one thing, the Russian people is another...*

Anna's words reflect her personality, one of firm and unwavering conviction in both her religious faith and her loyalty to Russia, regardless of what happened. But they also represent the strength of the connection to their homeland that many émigrés of that generation retained all their lives – not an uncommon emotional link also felt among exiles from other countries. There was perhaps some reassurance in the certainty of such strong attachment. But it also

CHAPTER TWELVE

intensified the suffering from the inability to be in the place with which one so closely identified. And it would make it difficult to feel at home elsewhere.

Along with fulfillment in her work, Anna often felt loneliness and deep sadness over everything that had transpired, as well as frequent despair over the future: her own and that of the country. One consolation was that her father was living not far away with a relative, in a mill. This had belonged to the family and had been nationalised, but they were permitted to remain as long as they operated it for the benefit of surrounding villages.

At one point a friend with connections found an excuse for her to visit Moscow by organising a school excursion. For the children, most of whom had not ventured much beyond their village, this was a wondrous prospect. For Anna, it was a welcome opportunity to see relatives and friends. She found the mood in the city had improved, there was more food, the hunger had subsided. One early morning on a walk past the Kremlin, she spied Vladimir Lenin taking a stroll within its walls. This former lady-in-waiting at the Tsar's court recorded just one observation about a man she despised: when the clock in the Kremlin tower struck the hour, the Soviet leader checked his watch.

While the situation in Moscow seemed more hopeful, it was not just her glimpse of Lenin which reminded Anna that things were now very different. On the way home she was arrested because of a mix-up with her train ticket. The threat by her guard of three weeks' incarceration would have been horrifying enough, but Anna was also carrying a letter for her father which she feared might be incriminating. She managed to get permission to go to the toilet and disposed of it. In the end she was neither searched, nor imprisoned;

the episode just gave her a fright. She felt this type of arbitrary arrest was a threat that hung over everyone, every day.

Indeed soon after, the arrest of a friend of Anna's had more serious consequences. The man was sent to Siberia for supposedly being part of a covert monarchist group. What was particularly shocking to Anna was that it was a former student of hers who had denounced him.

She was appalled at the young man's betrayal, especially as he had been one of those to whom she had given a great deal of extra help. From what she was able to discover, the youth had been in a group of rail workers threatened with execution over the theft of a carload of flour during their shift. Their only salvation was to offer the authorities some useful information, so the ex-student invented the story. And since the denunciation apparently included her and others as participants in secret meetings, she lived with the daily expectation of being detained or seeing other friends taken into custody. Yet somehow, they all escaped arrest.

Anna taught in the village for three years and she might have stayed longer were it not for another development reflecting the times. Being forced to ignore God in her teaching was hard enough for such a believer; being pressured to reflect the official anti-religion line was too much for her. When all the teachers in her village received a probing questionnaire, she knew she would soon be leaving the school:

> Each of us had to answer all sorts of questions, among them: what is your attitude to... faith and to anti-religious propaganda in school. This was very frightening. We all understood that just to say we believed meant we could lose our jobs. Where to go, what to do, how to act, we did not know.

CHAPTER TWELVE

Anna debated with herself for days on how to respond, but finally decided she could not lie, as some of the other teachers did:

> *[I] wrote that I was a believer and regarded this to be a personal matter, that I considered that for me anti-religious propaganda in school was impossible. I did the sign of the cross on the questionnaire and handed it in, and thought: come what may... At any rate, I understood my days here were numbered.*

Anna's youngest son had nearly died of pneumonia during her last winter in the village. She herself had had a severe bout of flu which had left her with a damaged lung. Fuel shortages made heating hard to maintain. The school was particularly draughty because village children had broken most of the windows while playing ball. Glass was hard to get so pictures of the Tsar and his family, which had previously hung in the classrooms, were put to use to block the holes. But they were ineffective against the bitter winter cold. All this reinforced her decision to leave.

In spite of her initial misgivings over the difficult conditions in the village and its remoteness, Anna had managed to cope. She was sad to leave it – and her father nearby. She was touched by the large numbers who came out to farewell her. As her cart set off to the train station, crowds of children ran after it waving. It is hard to know whether Anna had any inkling that this journey was the first stage of a longer one out of the country. On the one hand, her adaptation to the village showed she was capable of getting used to a life radically different from her past experience. On the other, the political aspect of her decision to leave must also have been a warning over just how far that adaptation could go. How much one had to compromise, especially when the safety and material survival of one's dependents was at stake, would have been a difficult question facing many as the new regime consolidated its power.

Anna's description of her move to Moscow provided insights into another range of issues for the Paris émigrés hearing her stories. For if their own living conditions were tied mostly to economic factors, they learned that in Soviet Russia, there were political elements as well as financial constraints in the ability to find a home.

Anna recounted that when she arrived in Moscow, she knocked on dozens of doors, seeking a place to live. She was close to despair when her cousin Sergei (my grandmother Nadezhda's brother) proposed a solution. He had just split up with his wife and had a room to himself in an apartment, so he offered it to Anna, while he would share with a friend. But then he discovered that if he left, it was possible strangers would be moved in with Anna. It was part of a policy to force the formerly wealthy to share their living space, as much to punish them for the past as because of housing shortages – a policy sometimes applied with vengeful vigour by members of building committees.

To forestall more occupants, Sergei stayed in his room when Anna, Masha and the two boys moved in. Their having few possessions – and the difficulty of obtaining furniture – became something of a silver lining as they all squeezed in. Their lack of chairs meant the children always ate standing up and had cheeky responses for their mother whenever she tried to tell them to "sit still". In spite of the cramped conditions, with several people living in each room (including the former bathroom) of what had been a one-family home, relations were cordial among the inhabitants of this example of a growing Soviet phenomenon: the *kommunalka*, or communal apartment.

CHAPTER TWELVE

Anna found the New Economic Policy (NEP), introduced in 1921, in full swing. A temporary relaxation of moves to outlaw the free market, this was initiated by the government as a distasteful necessity to get the country back on its feet after the Civil War and famine. There was now plenty of food for sale. And even continuing arrests, Anna said, seemed less terrifying:

When I arrived in Moscow I found it greatly changed... Of course it was a long way from the way it had been before the Revolution. Mainly there were lots of stores with provisions... These stores were even open in the evenings so that people coming home from the theatre could buy themselves wine, snacks, anything they wanted.

Searches and all sorts of repressions... of course continued, but they did not slow down our lives as before. True, in the evenings when we sometimes sat, gathered together... suddenly we would hear the rumble of a vehicle outside. This would be after eleven – until eleven everything was completely peaceful, but from eleven people began to worry a bit. This loud sound of a motor heralded a black "raven", a huge truck into which those arrested were gathered. When it went past... we froze – music and conversations – until it continued on. Thank God, people would think. They would cross themselves, and then continue on as if nothing had happened.

This equanimity in the face of the constant threat of arrest seems hard to believe, yet presumably it was necessary for survival and retaining sanity. It was helped by people – adaptable as ever –

finding ways of learning where searches were most likely to occur. Anna said information was somehow obtained and passed along the grapevine on which professions or other groupings were being targeted on any given night. Another warning sign involved the supply of electricity: it became known that when the power was turned off in the evenings, areas of the city where it was kept on were very likely to be searched that night.

Fear of arrest and imprisonment or exile was not a new phenomenon in Russia: punishment of those thought to oppose the government had occurred all too regularly during the tsarist era also. But those doing the arresting and those targeted had changed, and Anna and her friends were now in a particularly vulnerable group.

It was a fragile equanimity, easily destroyed. Anna remembered an occasion when she had friends over and someone ran in to say that the building was surrounded by armed soldiers. Everyone threw together whatever papers, addresses and so on they had with them and flushed them down the toilet. It turned out her room was not of interest this time, but the group only found this out after being ordered to stay put and sitting in trepidation for several hours while another room in the apartment was searched. The inhabitant was taken away. Anna learned the only incriminating evidence found was a line in a notebook next to the date of the October Revolution, identifying it as the anniversary of the beginning of suffering. The man was sent north and, as far as she knew, was never heard from again.

While the NEP brought quick profits to some, Anna found it heartbreaking to see the large numbers of beggars in Moscow. Many of these people had fled famine and chaos in the countryside, but had been unable to find jobs in the city and often lived on the street.

CHAPTER TWELVE

By contrast, Anna, with her knowledge of languages, found herself in demand on the job market, as many of those with similar skills had fled. She first got work as a governess for a family of the new elite, and later taught languages at a tertiary institution and gave private lessons.

Anna had an active social life, regularly meeting with friends to enjoy conversation and music. Theatres and concert halls again had busy schedules and she took advantage of this cultural renewal. Because of her work she was even able to move up in the hierarchy of living space allocations, with the authorities finding another room for Sergei in their building so she, as a tertiary instructor, could have more room for herself and her family.

Amid all the difficulties and anxieties of a city and country struggling with new circumstances and trying to regain some normalcy, she was able to establish for her family a settled and reasonably secure existence, at least for a time.

In January 1924, Lenin died. While Anna did not mourn the passing of the man who had turned her world upside down, the death cast a terrible pall over everyone:

> *[It was] as if some evil spirit had been released from a bottle. In the whole city there was gloom, dread. I, who never feared ghosts, felt queasy in the dark. I even tried to pray for him – because I thought here was a soul standing before God, someone with nothing but sins – but my prayer seemed to rebound, like a ball... I understood it was not my affair. He himself had to answer for his terrible deeds.*

Anna said she was fortunate to be able to avoid participating in the public mourning. But many of her friends were among those obligated or expected to visit Lenin's coffin, amid temperatures of thirty degrees below zero and colder:

> *During three days all of Moscow had to go pay their respects to him. His open coffin stood in the Hall of Columns [in the House of Unions]. At a time when there was hardly any fabric to be had, all the walls of the huge, high-walled hall were stretched with black crepe de Chine – where this fabric came from... is a mystery. An orchestra, of course the best orchestra in the city, played funeral marches of all the famous composers... Luckily I was not in a government job and did not have to go, but... many others, in terrible freezing conditions, had to stand in the queue for hours to get into the hall to walk around the coffin. On every intersection stood ambulances, bonfires burned so people could warm up a little but often people fainted and they were taken into the ambulances and given some sort of alcohol to drink and then returned to their spot...*

Many people were genuinely grief-stricken by the leader's death. Yet Anna remembered this did not prevent a whole series of jokes and mocking poems about Lenin's corpse and its fate being passed around. Of course these were only whispered between trusted friends and it did not pay to have any written down, as being caught with such evidence was severely punished.

The regime set about reinforcing the "cult" of Lenin, in an attempt to fill gaps left by the toppling of pre-revolutionary heroes and by the discouragement of religious observance. The elaborate

CHAPTER TWELVE

ceremony around the Soviet leader's death had included many echoes of traditional customs of mourning, which led observers to liken it to religious ritual. The comparison became even stronger when the decision was taken to embalm Lenin's body and keep it on display permanently. The regime which had so strenuously attacked saints' relics, in effect turned Lenin's remains into something similar, as historian Catherine Merridale writes:

> *The rebels who had forced open the coffins of the Orthodox saints now jealously preserved a relic of their own. They strenuously denied the continuity with religion, with the past, but the irony was inescapable. The empire was built upon the bones of a saint...*

Another death which occurred while Anna was in Moscow, while played down by the authorities, sparked much grief in some quarters. The Patriarch of the Russian Orthodox Church, Tikhon, died in April 1925. In the position since 1917, he had tried to find ways of co-existing with the regime. But he had also attacked measures introduced against the church and the widespread use of terror generally. He had been held under house arrest on a couple of occasions.

Some saw Patriarch Tikhon as a martyr to the regime. For others the source of grief was wider – for the church generally and its victims in the government's "war against religion". If it was not always for the official hierarchy and dogma as such, then at least for the comfort religious practices had for so long provided.

Anna joined the queue to pay her respects to the religious leader. She said that for three days, there were constant church services all over the city, which became imbued with a spiritual atmosphere. During the actual funeral, every church bell pealed and people stopped what they were doing to cross themselves. Whether this religious feeling was indeed as broadly felt as Anna perceived, public demonstrations of it on such a scale would not be repeated in future. After Tikhon, many church leaders not killed or banished complied with the government, cowed into silence. Or they made accommodations to allow at least something of the church to survive. The population meanwhile, increasingly hid any religious feeling it retained.

Anna and her family remained in Moscow for about a year-and-a-half. Amid their apparently routine existence, there were always reminders of how precarious it actually was. Arrests continued, among them those of friends and relatives of Anna's; for instance both her cousin Sergei and his former wife were held for a time (and in later years would again be arrested, with more serious consequences).

Anna's sons were ten and five when they moved to the city. At their school, a whole new host of problems cropped up. Perhaps picking up on conversations he heard in Anna's group, her older son had begun to make disparaging comments about Communists from a young age. As he got older, he refused to get involved in the Pioneers, an almost obligatory association for youngsters and the first part of the path into the Communist Party. He did not buy a medallion of Lenin when the leader died, something his fellow pupils did not fail to notice. He became interested in the church and volunteered to do odd jobs at a local parish and then became an altar boy. And he persisted with his habit of making dangerous comments in front of the wrong people. Anna was at a loss: she did not want to discourage his questioning mind and his religious inclinations but she understood that he could one day get the family into trouble.

Anna's father, still in the country, died suddenly. Anna's mother was living on the outskirts of Moscow with her second husband and Anna realised if she left Russia she would probably never see her again. But increasingly she felt her children's future was her first priority and she started looking for a way to go abroad.

It was difficult to get out legally, though the NEP period provided a few more possibilities than before. In what Anna saw as a "miracle", the government introduced a scheme for teachers in higher education to go abroad briefly if they needed specialised medical treatment. Unofficial networks, even among those seen as enemies of the regime, could still provide crucial assistance. A friend of Anna's put her in touch with a friend of his, a senior nose and throat doctor in a hospital. He came up with...

> ...*an illness such as no-one else would be able to identify [easily]... He also called in some head of the hospital, having told me in advance what to say about the illness, and both decided that of course I had to go to Vienna, because only there could the [necessary] operation be done... The doctor said that no-one would be able to analyse this at any station if they stopped me on the way, as to find particular symptoms would be too difficult. They gave me this frightening certificate, and with that I was able to make all my applications.*

Another friend helped with contacts at the Austrian Embassy and soon Anna had a visa. She had to queue up at many other offices to obtain a slew of approvals, the most terrifying being an interview with the GPU (the renamed secret police). Many awkward questions were asked about her background, the whereabouts of her husband, and the role of Masha, who signed with a cross and whose illiteracy had to mean she was a servant, a class which officially no longer existed. But Anna clearly told her story convincingly, for soon after she learned that her exit visa was being prepared. In the meantime, Masha sold anything that could bring in a few *kopecks*, to pay for the trip.

When she left in the summer of 1925, Anna could not tell anyone she was not coming back, though she felt many realised this. The pretence of joy over an opportunity to travel abroad made the final parting even more painful. As if to underline the instability and fear that characterised the country she was leaving, shots rang out in the train as it started to move out of the station; instead of getting a last look at those waving to her on the platform, her final moments in Moscow were spent sprawled on the floor over her sons till the shooting – whose origin remained a mystery – stopped.

In spite of the pain of separation from her mother and other relatives, Anna later did not regret having left when she did. When the NEP period ended, the borders tightened again. Another famine and intensified repression were on the way.

At the same time, Anna's life abroad would not be easy. She found her husband, but their marriage did not survive seven years of separation and she never remarried. She settled in Belgium and brought up her sons with the help of Masha, who never left the family; she cared for Anna's children, then their children, and died in Brussels at nearly one hundred years of age. Anna's knowledge of languages, especially English, once again came in handy, helping her find a variety of jobs over the years.

On a number of occasions in her latter years, I spent time with Anna, a perennially active, enthusiastic and optimistic person. I had never met three of my grandparents; the fourth – my father's mother Nadezhda – I did not have a chance to get to know before her death. Thus her cousin Anna provided a vital family link for me to that generation and their times. For her, there was sadness but also joy in telling me about my grandmother, their past in Russia and their lifelong friendship. Anna credited her own strong faith for always having supported her to get by. It also helped that she had an invincibly positive personality with which to tackle whatever was thrown her way. Anna died in 1982, at the age of ninety.

Back in 1925 Anna's accounts provided a connection to their past for her relatives in the West with whom she was reunited. They were still trying to come to terms with what increasingly looked like a permanent separation from their homeland; the perspective she provided on developments both known and new to them would not have been reassuring.

The émigrés at first tried to maintain contact with those who had remained in Russia through the only link still available to them: the post. Later that too became difficult, as historian Marc Raeff writes:

In the 1930s the contacts between émigrés and Soviet citizens decreased and they ceased for all intents and purposes after 1934. Soviet citizens were afraid to have links with the outside world, especially with émigrés.

Generally what mail there was focused on personal news, as both sides feared the censors. But whatever efforts the Soviets made to cover up material shortages and other difficulties, information still filtered out one way or another. My maternal grandmother Natalia and her sister Evgeniia heard enough about the problems there to be concerned about their mother, living with another daughter in the city renamed Leningrad. Although they themselves were struggling financially, they managed to put aside enough money to send assistance to her, though as my mother remembered, there were always doubts as to what actually reached her:

> *At the time, the Bolsheviks wanted hard currency and they opened a special bank so people could send money from abroad. So when my mother and her sister… located their mother, every month they would go there and consult a catalogue and buy this and that – every month both of them gave a large portion of their salary… Later they learned from many people – though they had suspected this all along… that very little actually got to their mother, maybe only half, but at least she got something. My mother used to order basics – for example sugar, butter – then over there, the recipients were given coupons with which they could buy the food.*

A letter and a few yellowed postcards sent by my great-grandmother to her daughters in the 1920s and 30s have survived among my mother's papers. They tell of children's progress at school, illnesses and other small dramas; anything broader is not mentioned, though sometimes the great distance between the two parts of the family is lamented. The many questions about the French side of the family denote a thirst for contact, whether expressed in a few simple words or implied in other ways. The pain of separation and the sense that the writer is well aware that it is permanent, speak out from each of these cards a hundred years later.

My mother said if there was any doubt that the censors were

checking the mail going back and forth, this was dispelled when a letter arrived with a photo enclosed. The text spoke of the children pictured, but in fact, what was in the envelope was a photograph of unknown elderly men, presumably swapped from another letter in error during the censorship process.

My father's family too managed to keep in postal contact for a time: with my great-grandfather in Tashkent until his death in the late 1920s, with my grandmother Nadezhda's brother Sergei in Moscow, and others. The knowledge that these close relatives were getting through the upheavals of the early Soviet era would have been a relief; the details of how they were doing this would remain a mystery for years to come – or in some cases, would never be known.

On the western side of this divide, the pain of split families was augmented by homesickness. As the years wore on and the Communist regime not only persisted, but became increasingly entrenched, any thought of going back would require acceptance of the new order. This, and the passing of time, led some émigrés to begin to question their assumptions. Where earlier there had been a range of political opinion from right-wing to left, there had been one common factor: rejection of the Soviet government. There were now some who were prepared to seek positives in the regime. Soviet-linked organisations, like the Union of Return to the Motherland, helped woo them, painting a picture of the rosy life they claimed awaited returnees. A trickle of people chose to go back.

One relative of mine was among them, but it was not her own politics that brought about her decision, nor was she enticed by any Soviet public relations effort.

Anna, the sister of my grandmother Nadezhda, was the youngest in their family – she was always known by the diminutive Annochka, even in her latter years (she is not to be confused with Nadezhda's cousin Anna who appears earlier in this chapter and left Russia in 1925, never to go back). Annochka's siblings had been protective of her from the time they were orphaned in Russia as small children. When the grandfather who took over their upbringing also died, she was fourteen. Nadezhda and her brother Sergei, in spite of their own recent marriages, took her into their homes by turns.

After the Bolshevik Revolution, when my grandparents fled south, they were joined by Annochka. She subsequently travelled with them to Turkey and then Bulgaria. There she met and married a fellow Russian refugee, but their union was short-lived. Soon she was back with my grandparents again, this time in France.

My grandmother had been in many ways a replacement mother to her sister. Now as Nadezhda and Nikolai struggled in their new life in Paris, Annochka lived with the family and helped out, in turn becoming something of a second mother to her sister's children. My father remembered her with great fondness: helping in every type of task at home and going out with his father to sell newspapers on the street.

Eventually she got a job caring for and educating the young child of another Russian family. More than sixty years later in Moscow, Annochka's daughter Anika told me what she could remember of her mother's stories about her life at this time. Anika said Annochka moved into her employers' home, but did not abandon her sister's family, handing over most of her salary to them and helping in other ways. The household where she worked was a wealthy one, though it was a puzzle at the time as to where this family's money came from. By the 1930s, even many of those émigré families who

CHAPTER TWELVE

had had property outside Russia or had managed to bring some of their valuable belongings with them when they left their homeland, found their funds running out. Unable to get work, or having to settle for poorly-paid jobs, whatever they had salvaged gradually dwindled away. But this was not a problem in the household where Annochka worked.

Through her employers, she met another Russian émigré, Vadim, who worked as a taxi driver. Soon they were in a serious relationship.

Vadim had been in the White Army, had fought against the Bolshevik forces in the Civil War, and had fled when the Whites were defeated. But according to Anika, even after more than fifteen years in the West, the man who would become her father was homesick. His circle, Annochka's employers and other friends, were among the handful of émigrés who increasingly saw the Communist regime as an idealistic – and attractive – experiment: so much so that they became involved in Soviet espionage, which Anika believes explained the wealth of some in this group. Vadim too became an agent:

> *Because in principle they were all good people, but they of course very much loved Russia and Russians and were very homesick for it. Secondly how it all happened – they approached the Russian Embassy to ask for permission to return. At the Embassy they said: "you are guilty, you took part in... the White Army, and you need to atone for your guilt. Work for us, earn the right to return to the homeland and then we will allow you to."... They did it only in the hope they could return... also they were full of enthusiasm, that this [Soviet regime] was such a good new system,*

and fair. That is, they could not imagine how terrible everything really was over there.

Their spymasters eventually handed out a deadly assignment: the assassination of Ignace Poretsky, also known as Ignace Reiss, a man who himself had been a Soviet agent. The group given this task included Vadim, but Anika believes he did not know the ultimate objective of the assignment. Her inquiries and reading on this incident over the many decades since have also reassured her that her father was not directly involved in the actual killing, which took place in September 1937.

Reiss, who was then in Switzerland, was a Pole who had worked for Moscow in a variety of western countries, and had lived for a time in the Soviet Union. But he had become disenchanted with Stalin, expressing his sentiments in an uncommonly frank letter, criticising the leader and what Reiss saw as his betrayal of socialism and the working class. This was a time of purges by Stalin and even without the letter, Reiss had already joined the numbers of formerly trusted servants of the regime marked for liquidation.

The assassination went off as planned, but one of the group was picked up by the police and the rest were identified through their questioning of her. A few of those involved were apparently arrested but then released, including Vadim; only a couple of them served short prison sentences. The others fled and made their way to the Soviet Union, among them Vadim and Sergei Efron, the husband of the poet Marina Tsvetaeva.

In the autumn of 1937, my father was fourteen years old and home from boarding school, when his Aunt Annochka and Vadim came

CHAPTER TWELVE

to visit his family's apartment in Paris. What followed was a series of baffling events. It was only much later that my father and his sister Nadia were able to piece together the story.

Dimitri and Nadia were puzzled, but so were their parents. Even their aunt, at the centre of this mystery, did not know all the details and import of these events: through her love of a man, she had become entangled in a web of intrigue that was to radically and irreversibly alter her life.

The couple arrived unexpectedly in the morning as my grandfather was about to go to work. Vadim asked if they could stay that night and Nikolai said of course. But Annochka jumped in and said they would only stay if they could find nowhere else. My grandfather was surprised at her reaction. He told them how happy he was to see them, invited them to make themselves at home, and went off to work. My Aunt Nadia continues:

[I later learned that] all day long they destroyed papers by flushing them down the toilet. They were gone before my father returned from work. Annochka left her icon of the Mother of God in a silver mounting on the table. That was the last time they were seen in Paris. The explanation came the next morning when my father read in the newspaper that Reiss... had been killed. Among the names of people involved in the plot was Vadim's... My poor father was astonished. Who could have suspected that Vadim was a Soviet agent? He wondered whether Aunt Annochka was aware of it...

My father's memories of that day were patchy, but he acutely remembered that his favourite aunt left his life at this point: she disappeared and he never saw her again.

Nikolai went to the police to report that Vadim and Annochka had spent their last day in Paris in his apartment. He believed the police would find out and presumed his sister-in-law was already safely out of the country. To protect his own family, he decided it was best to pre-empt the inevitable enquiries.

Some months later, after Nikolai had passed away, Nadezhda was summoned to police headquarters for questioning about her sister and Vadim, a terrifying experience. But soon after, it seems the incident got lost in the wider issues of the looming Second World War.

The whole affair could have been difficult for my father's family, not just because of the sadness of separation. The awareness among the Russian émigré community of the family's connection to Soviet espionage and to the killing could have turned people against them – or at the very least, made people suspicious of them. But neither my aunt nor my father remembered any specific episodes which might have demonstrated any ostracism or criticism by others.

This was a time of much disagreement in the community over politics. As the war approached, divisions became ever more acute. There were those who were prepared to support fascism, in spite of its anti-Slavic elements, if this was the ideology which could bring down the hated communists. Many more were not prepared to go that far; they accepted, if grudgingly, that if it came to a contest between fascism and communism, they would support the Soviet Union as the lesser evil, and – after all – the site of the Russian nation. The debates aroused fierce passions and the Reiss assassination may have become submerged among them.

For Vadim and Annochka, the fall-out from the incident was much more drastic. Anika believes her father tried to convince her mother not to go back with him to Russia: she was, after all, not directly involved in the events. And he had tuberculosis and believed he was unlikely to live long. But she chose to stick with him.

Some time after their return, Vadim himself realised he had made a terrible mistake. He tried to arrange an escape for them by boat from Georgia, where the authorities had placed him in a sanatorium, but the plan was precarious and they did not go ahead with it. Vadim died of tuberculosis less than four years after returning. During that time, Anika was born, and Annochka was left to face the future with a baby, and with no legal status in the eyes of the regime. But although the regime did not seem to want her, it also would not allow her to leave the country. She lived until 1968, but she was never to see her sister and her family in France again.

As for the other members of Vadim's group connected to the Reiss assassination, Anika believes most were executed or otherwise met their deaths at the hands of the Soviet government, not long after Vadim succumbed to his illness. She said that the authorities tried to pin a coup plot on them, but that only one member of the group was coerced into stating that they were seeking to overturn the government. It was a time when many became victims of Stalin's suspicions:

> *First of all anyone who knew too much, they all perished... And secondly, at that time under Stalin... there was constantly a witch hunt, and they kept trying to make it look like they had uncovered some sort of conspiracy... [They] wanted to organise some sort of a show trial, that this was part of an organised*

conspiracy... [But] there was no trial... I think it was speeded up too, when they shot them, because... the Germans were already approaching in the war. If it had not been for the war, maybe... but as it was, they had to hasten things.

The Soviet and German governments had signed a non-aggression pact in August 1939, confounding both Russians in the Soviet Union and the émigrés, as well as many others. But six weeks before Vadim's death, Germany abandoned the pact and on June 22nd, 1941, invaded the Soviet Union. Suddenly, Stalin became an ally of the western nations fighting the Nazis. Annochka was far from the French branch of her family, but now both places faced a common enemy.

13

War and Occupation

There are many images that evoke France in the Second World War: from Adolf Hitler posing in front of the Eiffel Tower, to a triumphant Charles de Gaulle on the Champs Elysées; from the chaotic exodus of Parisians as the Germans approached, to Jewish families with yellow stars on their clothes trucked away. There are the familiar photos of the white moustachioed Marshal Pétain in his omni-present round cap. And of the women with shaved heads, paraded along streets, greeted by hissing and insults for their alleged affairs with German military men.

Yet iconic as these images have become, with their apparently clear distinctions among heroes, villains and victims, they come with many contradictions and shameful echoes of the time they reflect, that have continued to haunt the French. As historian Henry Rousso found when he set out to research the war and occupation some four decades later: "What surprised me most was... the *immediacy* of the period, its astonishing presentness, which at times rose to the level of obsession."

My parents witnessed some of these most representative scenes, which were interwoven with incidents from their own experiences, resulting in a more personalised set of images and memories of the war.

Their departure from France in 1952 meant they were somewhat removed from much of the later soul-searching, controversies and re-interpretations of this period of French history. But while they were not as immersed in these debates, the many reflections and revelations about the war since that time could not fail to have had an effect on their recollections and their significance to them.

The Russian émigrés who had settled in France experienced all the upheavals, deprivations and fears alongside the French. Being foreigners, they often faced additional anxieties and dangers. But everyone had one thing in common: whenever I asked my parents how they endured this terrifying time, they responded as people always seem to do to such questions – it was necessary to get through it, you just did. Nearly incomprehensible for those who have not had such experiences, it was a feeling shared by millions across Europe and beyond.

France was reluctantly drawn into the war against Germany with its ally Britain in September 1939. The declaration of war brought apprehension that Paris would immediately be bombed. My mother and her mother and aunt joined a flood of departures from the city, the panic foreshadowing the more numerous and notorious exodus that would take place the following year when the Germans marched towards the city. The husband of my mother's aunt Evgeniia hustled them into the taxi that he drove for a living. He took them about a hundred kilometres south to the town of Montargis sur Marne, and settled them into a rented room. They were away just a month. The expected bombing of Paris did not take place, and Natalia's increasingly poor health convinced them of the need to be near the city's medical facilities.

After finishing *lycée*, my mother had taken secretarial courses, bought a typewriter and found typing and translating work to do at home. A few months before the war she had landed a good job with

CHAPTER THIRTEEN

the Agriculture Ministry, as a secretary and undercover inspector of food shops, checking they did not cheat on the weight of goods they sold. But her office was among sections of the French government that moved away from the city to avoid attack. The deputy minister wanted Irene to come along, but as she was not French, he could not offer her the position on a long-term basis. He found her a willing bridegroom, promising to expedite a citizenship application if she married him; then she could join those moving away. Irene was not interested in marrying an unknown man, or in leaving her mother, so she declined. She returned to freelance work until early 1940, when she got a job with a company that produced seeds and agricultural chemicals.

But Irene's main preoccupation at this time was Natalia's health, which was deteriorating quickly. At first the doctors put it down to exhaustion from her years of long hours of work, or anaemia, and prescribed vitamins and other supplements. Finally they diagnosed pancreatic cancer, but an attempt to operate came too late.

Natalia died a painful death late one night in May 1940, at the age of forty-three. The loss of someone so close is hard to endure at any time; with the Germans advancing on Paris, Irene's personal emotions were framed in the broader feelings of fear all around her. She was abruptly reminded of this when instead of being able to go straight home from the hospital to share her grief with her aunt, an alert was sounded. She was hustled into a shelter, where she had to stay for several hours.

Natalia was buried next to Alexander, in a cemetery on the outskirts of Paris. It was a long trip by metro and bus to the various services called for under Russian Orthodox custom. By the fortieth day, when, according to the church's rituals, another memorial service is held, the Germans had arrived. Buses were not running; everyone had to hike six kilometres to get to the graveside.

Irene continued to live with her Aunt Evgeniia – her only remaining close relative in Paris, her aunt's husband Peter and her father's friend "Uncle" Mikhail. They provided her with support and affection, but it is clear that the loss of her mother was traumatic for this twenty-two year old. Over the years, right until her own death, my mother often talked about the night Natalia passed away, and the days and weeks that followed. It seems theirs was a particularly close mother-daughter relationship; no doubt the difficult years of emigration and the long illness and death of Alexander had tightened an already close bond. Coping with her loss amid the alarming developments in the war, my mother must have felt very alone.

When the war began, my father's family was still trying to adapt to the loss of Nikolai and the departure of Nadezhda's sister Annochka to the Soviet Union. Dimitri had come home from boarding school after his father's death. The family had shrunk to four: the oldest son Sasha had joined the French Army in Tunisia; Nikolai's mother Varvara had died in 1936. My Aunt Nadia, not yet twenty but the oldest child at home, had become the main breadwinner for her mother and two younger brothers. Like Irene, she found some employment options closed to her because she was not French. She got work as a sales clerk in the same department store outside which her father had once sold lottery tickets. She, as Nikolai had been, was hired because the director was sympathetic to Russian immigrants and found ways of bending the rules to hire non-citizens. But he urged her to become a citizen. Her attempt to do so would be interrupted by the war.

CHAPTER THIRTEEN

My father attended a technical college in Paris for several months, then in mid-1939 started to seek work to help support the family. At sixteen years of age, he had never had employment. This was a bad time for any immigrant to be looking for a job, never mind someone with no experience. In the lead-up to the war and as it began, perceptions as to who was the enemy were confused. There was also an influx of new refugees from places like Spain and Germany, which further heightened nervousness amid the instability; xenophobic feelings ran high. More established refugees, like the Russians, were generally less vulnerable than newer arrivals, but some émigrés who thought they were safe in their jobs found themselves suddenly sacked. And the August 1939 non-aggression pact between the Soviet Union and France's enemy, Germany, did nothing to enhance feelings towards Russians. Popular sentiment, and economic woes, were reflected in government moves: restrictions on foreigners were tightened. In this atmosphere, my father found the job hunt very difficult, though it is likely that as a refugee almost anywhere in Europe at this time he would have faced similar problems. Amid his search far and wide, Dimitri had a bicycle accident which left him in hospital with a broken leg for two months. Finally, not long after the start of the war, he got a job in a radio factory.

My parents both remembered the weeks before the arrival of the Germans in Paris in June 1940 as being full of apprehension. The months between France's declaration of war and Hitler's westward offensive had been a period of relative calm and unreality – the so-called "*drôle de guerre*", the "phoney war". The French government, recalling the scale of deaths in the previous war, at first adopted a primarily defensive policy in preference to any offensive action. The delay by Germany in pushing west reinforced a false sense of security over the ability of the Maginot Line and other defences to protect France. Internally, there were severe political divisions, and there were also disagreements between Britain and France on how best to act against Hitler. So when his forces swiftly moved through the Netherlands and Belgium in May, there was a lack of preparedness. The French suffered a quick succession of losses and the Germans moved rapidly towards Paris. Panic swept the capital.

Natalia's funeral took place as the French Army was being pushed back by Hitler's forces. On visits to her mother's grave during the first half of June, Irene witnessed scores of people fleeing Paris:

It was terrible, as the road went south, the big road... many people started to leave. And all these people in cars, on foot... the whole big road was jammed – cars that did not work anymore, mattresses and things that people had taken and thrown away. It was horrible, horrible.

This time Irene had no thoughts of leaving Paris. My father's family too decided there was no point in joining the exodus:

We were thinking – what does that mean, leaving Paris, where do you want to go... what the hell, what do you want to do on the roads... And apparently there were even bombings on those hordes of people... [they were] going somewhere south, just going south without knowing where they go... And I remember... the weather was beautiful – and we saw a huge black cloud, like a storm cloud, but it was not a storm cloud – it was smoke from refineries and factories that were burnt, either by the Germans or the French retreating. And the next day that cloud arrived on

Paris, and it rained on top of it, and the rain was black water... and through that black rain we saw those hordes of people passing through Paris...

It is thought that as much as three-quarters of the population of Paris fled. Perhaps memories of the chaotic departures from Russia in 1920 and a reluctance to relive such scenes influenced my parents' families. It seems they made the right decision. My mother said it was distressing to later watch people returning, some wounded, some having lost members of their families in bombings, most having left behind what they had taken with them somewhere on the road.

In his memoir about his time in France during this period, Hungarian-British author Arthur Koestler wrote about ads that appeared in newspapers for weeks afterwards as "fragments of families all over the country" tried to find each other.

While my father's family did not join the exodus, they moved briefly into the apartment of his Aunt Olga, in the centre of the city, for mutual moral support. She lived on a street parallel to the Champs Elysées, so my father saw the triumphant Germans marching into Paris on June 14th. It was clear that the city was considered a great prize, from the way they staged their entry:

When they arrived, they camped outside Paris, and they washed themselves, they cleaned, they shaved, and they entered Paris impeccable, "musique en tête" [music leading the way]... They arrived in a practically empty city.

In just over a week the French government signed an armistice with Hitler, which took it out of the war and divided the country. About forty percent of France would be governed for the next couple of years by the Vichy regime, though any independence this administration claimed it had under the Germans was illusory. Its leader Marshal Philippe Pétain was in effect a puppet of the Nazis. The rest of the country – the west and north, including Paris – came under direct German control.

Many businesses had barely paused during these events, but others closed for a time. Whether his radio factory did not reopen, or because of lack of work there for him, my father found himself unemployed once more. Again, the search was not easy. At one point, he joined casual workers trucked out of town to harvest abandoned crops. After gathering peas for two days, it cost him most of his pay to get the train back to Paris, so the next time he took his bicycle. A bonus was that he was allowed to bring back as many peas as he could carry.

Community contacts continued to be helpful. My father was eventually hired by a Russian immigrant who ran a car repair shop, to work as an auto electrician. It was the first of a series of jobs where he learned to improvise in the face of a chronic lack of parts. It was a skill he and many others would increasingly apply to a variety of facets of life as the war brought shortages of many things.

About half the employees were Russian immigrants. Dimitri said they practised another important skill to get through hard times: finding ways to briefly forget what was happening. They were helped in this by a professional actor employed there in the absence of Russian theatre work:

> *I can tell you, during our lunches in the canteen, he was talking – I don't know when he was eating – because he was telling us jokes. Any joke that you or me will tell will be flat, but when he was telling it, it was such fun, because he was a real comic artist...*

CHAPTER THIRTEEN

> *even the French people who were there, who couldn't understand anything, only his mimic[ry] was enough for them to have the laugh of the day. So that was during the German occupation, when food became scarce, when we began to have rationing and stuff, we had that kind of distraction.*

In my mother's case, her company resumed operations after a two-month closure. Because it produced supplies for agriculture, the Germans began paying regular visits. Irene found herself in a go-between role with representatives of the occupying army. The company had to provide weekly reports on its output and to show that its seeds and other supplies were being sent only to approved farms whose harvests were intended for Germany.

Irene's boss sent her to intensive German classes. Her unsettled legacy as a refugee child who had lived in several countries had helped develop her skills for picking up languages: my mother quickly mastered the basics. It would be a mixed blessing. Over the war years she would often intercede – sometimes with success – when acquaintances or fellow employees were threatened with being taken away for forced labour in Germany. But her knowledge of the language would mean she was also often compelled to act as an interpreter for the occupiers, a task she found harrowing, especially when it usually involved communicating distressing information or unpopular measures to the locals.

But in the early days of the occupation, my parents' encounters with German troops were not as threatening as they had expected. My father told of going to a local bakery once just as a regiment marched in. He decided to return later, but by then the whole day's baking was gone. It was the same in the neighbouring shops: the shelves were empty. The shopkeepers had watched the soldiers approach with trepidation, but they found the Germans courteous and to their surprise, willing to pay for everything. My mother's first experiences at her work were also more civil than she had anticipated: the low ranking officers delegated to keep an eye on her company did their task coolly but politely.

While initial contacts with the occupiers were often less frightening than anticipated, Parisians increasingly had interactions that were more alarming. My mother said the Germans were everywhere, and it did not pay to disobey the rules, such as curfews:

> *In Paris, it was very strict. The metro stopped at midnight, and everyone who was in the street after that, they were taken to the police station. And in every police station there was a German – and these Germans were nasty, very nasty. So you could not miss the last metro. I remember once I missed it, and was running home at night – I took off my shoes so I would not be heard – ooh! it was frightening!*

For others, encounters with the occupiers were much more threatening right from the start. Even before the arrival of the Germans, communists and some categories of foreigners – "undesirable aliens" – had been rounded up and jailed or interned. Among these were people who had escaped the Nazis to what they thought was safety in France. Arthur Koestler was one of these:

> *...the majority, like... myself, had been through prisons and concentration camps in Germany, Italy, Eastern Europe, or Spain... A few years ago we had been called the martyrs of Fascist barbarism, pioneers*

CHAPTER THIRTEEN

in the fight for civilization, defenders of liberty, and what not... Now we had become the scum of the earth.

Some of these internees were still being held at the start of the occupation, and the new authorities soon added to their numbers. The net of those targeted would gradually spread wider, and the measures used become more brutal, especially after Mid-1941, when terrorist acts against the Germans brought ever more severe responses.

Russian migrants of various political persuasions were among those rounded up, especially in June 1941 when Hitler abandoned his non-aggression pact with Stalin. On the very day that the Germans invaded the Soviet Union, the ex-husband of my great-aunt Olga was taken away to internment. He was held until February 1942 and then released as abruptly as he had been arrested.

Arrests and internment were accompanied by other measures against foreigners. In July 1940, a Commission for the Revision of Naturalisations was set up by the Vichy administration to review citizenships granted since 1927; some fifteen-thousand of these were revoked. In August, foreign organisations in the occupied zone were dissolved, among them some eight-hundred Russian cultural, educational and charitable associations. Various measures targeted other groups, but among these discriminatory moves, it was the Jewish population which faced the most severe and numerous decrees.

From the time the Germans arrived, they and the Vichy regime introduced measures removing the right of Jews to do a range of jobs and taking away their businesses and property. In the occupied zone, the first mass arrests of Jews occurred in May 1941 and systematic deportations began in early 1942. From the middle of that year those in occupied territory were ordered to wear yellow stars.

My Aunt Nadia said that however untouched she personally may have been by the occupiers, her growing awareness of their treatment of the Jews revealed to her the horror of the Nazis. Forcing people to be labelled with yellow stars, she felt, demonstrated the depths of the regime, singling out people for their origins in such a "humiliating" and "dreadful" way. Her memories may have been coloured by later revelations of everything that happened. But she said Parisians could not have failed to observe the convoys of Jews trucked to the Velodrome, before being sent to concentration camps, and to sense they were headed for a terrible fate. She would later learn about the underground work of some in the Russian community in hiding Jews, among them Russian Jews.

In March 1942, the atmosphere of dread was further heightened when air raid alerts, frightening in themselves, began to herald actual bombings. The first of these Allied attacks were on factories on the outskirts of Paris, causing extensive civilian casualties. The railways soon became targets too; my mother travelled to work by train and the possibility of a raid was a constant anxiety. Once a bombing did come very close, when my mother was already at work, with an explosion in a street adjacent to her office.

From late 1942, another danger faced those who till then had managed to avoid attracting the attention of the occupation authorities: people began to be taken to Germany to work. By the end of 1943, more labour had been taken from France for the Nazis' factories than from any other occupied country. This mass recruitment – the *Service du travail obligatoire* or STO – is seen as one of the reasons support for the Resistance grew from late 1942.

Some would never return, either dying in the poor working and living conditions, or killed in fighting or bombings. Many of those of Eastern European origin who were in areas that were taken over by the Soviet Army at the end of the war would be shipped to the Soviet Union, to disappear in camps there.

My parents said that being unemployed or caught in the street without the right documents often brought swift dispatch to Germany. But even a job was no protection. My father witnessed co-workers being told they had two hours to get ready to leave, amid warnings of severe punishment if they tried to slip away. One of Dimitri's cousins was among people he knew who were taken (he returned safely at the end of the war, though it was a close thing: he found himself in the Soviet zone but managed to escape).

In spite of the constant worry, people tried to maintain some semblance of a normal life. My father had long hours at his job, but managed to pursue his electricity studies at evening courses right into 1942. He faced many obstacles, including lengthy disruptions to transport because of bomb alerts, and working on assignments with frozen fingers in his family's poorly heated apartment. When he got a new job, as a draughtsman in the garage where city buses and metro trains were repaired, there was a bonus: the work was less physical so he did not get quite as hungry.

All principal foodstuffs had come under rationing in late 1940, but at first the amounts allocated had been reasonable. As well, the black market was initially not prohibitive, so even those who were not wealthy could now and again buy from the broad range of available items. But rations grew ever smaller with time, and the black market became too expensive for many. My father said hunger became a constant companion of ordinary people in Paris:

The meat ration was seventy grams without bones per week per person... or ninety grams of meat with bones, and that doesn't make a big steak! And sometimes you had to queue even for that. The butter ration was also something very small... everything was miniscule – every ration... There were strange things also – like sometimes, without tickets, you could buy some pâté. Pâté is very easy to accommodate because you can put in anything you want. So there was probably – for volume – some turnips and some other stuff that was easy to get, or some rutabaga, and some sawdust...
All that was very well pulverised, and it was good. Everything we ate was delicious, because we always had empty stomachs.

Beyond a shortage of farm workers, food scarcities were aggravated by the Allied blockade of France and by the shipment of much of the harvest to Germany. The situation, according to historian Robert Paxton, went from one of "austerity in 1940 to severe want in 1944", France becoming the "worst nourished of the western occupied nations". Other necessities, like coal and oil, were also in short supply, because imports were impossible and local production was mostly requisitioned. Dimitri said people improvised as they could, in the search for fuel for cooking and heating:

We got wood wherever we could find it – gradually all the wooden fences disappeared... there was a fence across the street [from us]... And one night I heard the noise of the broken fence, so the next night I was there too to get my share. And I can tell you, there was a little crowd getting their share, so in two days there

CHAPTER THIRTEEN

was no more fence... In the garage where I worked, there was a wood department – many cars had wooden structures in those days, so they were fixing [them] – so there was lots of wood being cut and there were piles of cut-outs of wood. And usually we were sharing and everyone was bringing home in his lunch bag two or three bits of boards, cut-outs...

Besides all this, the French were forced to pay the costs of the occupation: well over fifty percent of income gathered by the administration was handed over.

In late 1942, all of France came under direct German occupation.

My father decided to leave Paris for a job in Nantes. As it happened, my mother had just moved to the city too.

My mother went to Nantes after an unpredictable chain of events. She had quit her job with the agricultural supply company in mid-1942 because she developed severe allergies to the chemicals produced and used there. While seeking other work she received an urgent message that the occupation authorities had noticed her absence from the company; her ex-employers were worried that she was being considered for work in Germany. Irene's "Uncle" Mikhail was at that point in a senior position with a Nantes shipping company; he authorised a certificate stating that she worked in its Paris branch, though she never actually appeared there.

But fate stepped in. A secretary in the Nantes office broke her leg and needed a long recovery time. As a replacement was being sought, "Uncle" Mikhail became nervous about Irene's position as an employee who never reported for work. Though such devious arrangements were not uncommon, she was thought to be his niece

304

and this could have made the source of her "fictitious document" more suspicious. She had nothing to keep her in the capital and continued to worry about being drafted for Germany. So she agreed to go to Nantes, nearly four-hundred kilometres to the west of Paris, to fill the position of the injured secretary.

In my father's case, the motivation for the move was twofold: as food rations continued to shrink, he thought that perhaps away from Paris, closer to farmland, it might be easier to find supplies for his mother and siblings. And Dimitri also sensed that the danger of being recruited to Germany was growing; the round-ups of fit young people were increasing and he hoped that a less populated area would not be as frequent a source for such labour. Witnessing people around him being shipped away, he felt "that something had to be done to avoid being taken to Germany."

So when he heard through other Russians about a draughtsman's job at the company in Nantes that had hired my mother, he applied and was accepted.

Community links had played a part – yet again – in my parents' lives. The company that hired them was run by a Russian who had an unusual historical connection to the Revolution: he had been involved in the breaking up of part of the tsarist fleet. A section of the Black Sea fleet – more than thirty vessels – had escaped to Bizerte in Tunisia after the Civil War. They had languished there amid hopes of a White Russian offensive against the Soviet regime, with the officers and sailors living on board, prepared to join such an action. But then France – whose protectorate Tunisia was – recognised the Soviet Union. In the mid-1920s the ships were gradually scuttled.

One of the men involved in the salvage work had later pursued his shipping business in France; it was his company that my parents joined in Nantes. An actor at pivotal moments in history, he would eventually be overtaken by it: my mother said he was brought to book after the war for his work for the Germans. But at the time, the Russian migrants hired by this man were grateful for the opportunities he provided.

The Russian émigré network could sometimes weave a strange web. The war and her "uncle" combined to get my mother to Nantes; very soon afterwards the occupation took my father there too.

Another thread in the web led to his older brother Sasha. Before the war he had joined the French Army in Tunisia. There he met and married a woman who had spent several years of her childhood living on one of those Russian ships berthed at Bizerte, with her navy commander father and her family, before they were forced to abandon it.

My mother arrived in Nantes in January 1943, my father a month later. They met there for the first time.

14

Bombs and Punishment

Nantes and the surrounding area were the setting for many stories my parents told over the years. Perhaps not surprising, as fate brought them together there and it was the site of events that left indelible marks.

The intensive bombing of Nantes, my mother's fear and unease when compelled to act as an interpreter for the occupation forces, my brother's difficult birth on a farm where my parents were trapped as the frontline shifted: all remained powerful memories for them.

When Irene and Dimitri moved to the city it was a bustling port. They both worked in shipping, so their lives became intimately linked with the port and the Loire River on which it sat, about fifty kilometres upstream from the Atlantic Ocean.

When my sister and I visited in 2001, we looked in vain for the busy shipping scenes we had imagined. Walking along the river, the only waterfront activity we saw involved a row of fishermen on a wall, dangling lines into the murky depths below. In buckets behind them, splashes of water and glimpses of silver amid cooling beer bottles showed they had had some success. The men were happy to boast to a couple of curious strangers about their catches: eels and three other species of river fish. Behind the cracked concrete wall on which the men stood ran an old railway line overgrown with weeds, and beyond this, the ruins of a warehouse.

"We've got lots of time to fish," a small wiry man in a red checked shirt said. "We worked in shipping, but there's no work in that anymore."

CHAPTER FOURTEEN

He waved his arm to take in the Loire and its banks in both directions. The river flowed placidly by a scattering of warehouses, some apparently still in use, others derelict. On the opposite shore loomed a yellow crane, like a huge praying mantis perched over the river. But there were no vessels laden with cargo on to which the crane could pounce. Further upstream, a cluster of boats was tied to buoys, but these were clearly pleasure craft awaiting weekend sailors.

"The cranes used to run on those," the man pointed to the smothered tracks behind us. "But there are no more ships to load and unload." By this time, several other fishermen had encircled us, nodding forlornly.

"Shipping was the lifeblood here, and what's left now? Just ruins. Nantes is not the same any more."

The fishermen's declaration of the death of their city's maritime identity was not completely justified. There was still shipping work not far downstream and local tertiary institutions continued to teach maritime subjects.

But these did seem a pale shadow of the city's long nautical history. Nantes was the biggest merchant port in France in the eighteenth century. Cargoes from all over the world jostled for attention on its docks: from the French colonies in Africa and the Caribbean, from all over Europe and Asia. But silting sands overcame efforts to keep the wide, shallow river navigable for increasingly large ocean-plying vessels, and shipping activity moved downstream towards the coast. The word *quai* was still part of street names near the waterfront. But what was descriptive in my parents' time was now a reflection of the past (*).

It was hard to imagine the city of their stories, still vivid decades after they had left. These were suffused with fond memories of their meeting and decision to make a life together, but also of the terror of a tumultuous period.

Not long after my mother and then my father arrived in Nantes to begin their new jobs, they met in their company's offices. She worked as a secretary and he as a draughtsman. They were drawn to each other from the start.

The firm that employed them had done marine salvaging before the war, but after the Germans occupied the city, they took it over, along with all other shipping concerns along the coast. All the energies of the company were focused on war-related work. The designing of systems to protect naval craft from mines and bombs was a particular priority.

Their work provided Irene and Dimitri with unexpected contact with people from their families' homeland: some of the employees were Soviet prisoners of war brought there by the Germans. There were occasionally opportunities to communicate with them, but not surprisingly these Russians were too frightened to speak of anything beyond the job at hand.

Whatever my parents felt about working for the enemies and occupiers of their adopted land, they swallowed their misgivings. Under occupation, they believed that everyone who had a job was essentially working for the Germans, who controlled all aspects of the economy; yet they were acutely aware that their work was more directly linked to the German war effort than some other jobs. Their stories about this time revealed a range of conflicting emotions. They expressed contempt for French people who were too ready to kowtow to the occupiers, but were uneasily cognisant of their own acceptance of working for them. They were anxious, being subject to

CHAPTER FOURTEEN

a situation where arbitrary mistreatment was a constant possibility. On the other hand, they were resigned to the need to just quietly follow the rules no matter how humiliating. Constant fears over how the war would go and what the future would bring were mixed with a drive to survive the terrible times and try to help their relatives back in Paris.

My father's expectation that he would be better able to help his family with food supplies from Nantes and the farms surrounding it proved to be the case. Produce was meant to be sold to official organisations which distributed food to urban areas or shipped it to Germany. But the farmers held back a proportion; they had no great desire to cooperate with the occupation forces and also knew they could get more money for their products in unofficial exchanges. The location on the water meant there were also fish and seafood to be had. These black market options were much less expensive than in Paris. So even though rationing was strict here too, it was possible to supplement it, especially as my parents' employer paid well. Dimitri regularly set out on expeditions to gather food for parcels to send to the capital:

On the weekends I would go – sometimes with [your] Mom too – I would go on bike, make a big round of farms... I'd get some salted pork here, maybe half a kilo of butter in another place, and a few eggs elsewhere... It took a long long drive, because I had to go to many farms... Sometimes we could get a live chicken... or a live rabbit, so I had to kill the poor creature and then we had to feather it out or skin it if it was a rabbit, and then pack it up to send by mail to Paris. They ate everything we sent, even fresh meat like that...

[For] in those days, in spite of the war... a mailman had to bring the mail whatever happens... So they were getting our parcels in an average of... [a few] days. So in summer of course, the meat was not the freshest in the world, but treated with a little bit of vinegar it was edible.

When they married and pooled their salaries, one half of what they earned went on the Paris parcels. My mother's aunt and uncle also became regular recipients.

My parents' relationship was often dominated by such practical considerations. For instance, another regular activity when they were together was to darn and redarn their socks. There were not many possibilities for outings that in other times would have been typical for people of their age. But a few photos from the period show them enjoying picnics or swims with other young people from their work – often Russians from Paris like themselves. In one picture my father is doing a handstand, his muscled legs and arms on show. In another he is climbing a tree. There are pictures of my mother collecting wood for a bonfire or dangling her legs in the river. I imagine what a relief it must have been for them to share some light-hearted moments together, the war briefly pushed into the background.

Their courtship was not a long one. No doubt the constant anxiety over the war and the circumstances of the occupation helped cement the closeness of two people on their own. Also Irene said the precariousness of the times encouraged them not to delay their wedding; they did not want to find themselves in a tragic situation similar to what happened to a friend of hers, whose fiancé was killed just before their wedding date, after a long engagement.

Their haste does not seem unusual in the face of an uncertain

CHAPTER FOURTEEN

future; perhaps their unsettled existence since the Revolution had added to a sense that time might not wait. The war clearly did add urgency to my parents' planning, but at the same time they followed all the most important, long-established Russian Orthodox wedding customs.

An August date was chosen and Irene's aunt and Dimitri's mother took care of the formalities in Paris: the posting of the wedding banns and the booking of the town hall and church. My mother scraped together enough ration tickets to buy white crepe fabric for a gown. Meantime, my parents collected food and drink in Nantes for the reception, which they carted by train to the capital.

Due to France's strict separation of state and church, my parents effectively had two weddings: one to satisfy the civil authorities at the Town Hall of Paris' 15th *arrondissement*; another the next day conducted by a Russian priest. Irene said the need to prove that one was legally married under French law before the religious ceremony got underway was not the most romantic way to start:

You arrive, all in white, it is all so wonderful, and the first thing they ask is "where is your certificate, where is your paperwork?" This is not at all what you are thinking about!

The church was near the apartment of my mother's aunt, but across the city from the home of my father's family. Concerned an alert might shut down the subway for a few hours, Irene asked Dimitri to be sure to allow plenty of time to get there. He arrived long in advance, and to his surprise was admonished by those tidying up after the liturgy. This recollection always amused my mother:

They started cleaning and sweeping up and they asked him: "Who are you?" "I'm the groom," he answered.

"Well, wait in the corner there, out of the way," they told him. "We need to clean up for the wedding."

My parents were relieved there had been no alerts to delay my father, and there was none to interrupt the service or the gathering of friends that followed. But the studio hired to record the event was bombed soon afterwards. In the photographs which survived, Irene looks elegant in her flowing gown, her crisp veil above loose curly hair. Dimitri too looks smart in the suit he borrowed from a friend; he did not own one himself. They look young and vulnerable; it is hard to imagine them being ready to face the terror and hardships ahead. My father, a few years younger than my mother, was only twenty – not old enough to sign the official documents; his mother had to do this. They had a three-day honeymoon on the outskirts of Paris, then went back to Nantes.

But they did not have long to savour their new married life. In September 1943, the war hit the city with a vengeance.

Nantes, like other parts of France, had occasionally come under Allied bombardment since the start of the occupation. But the early raids on the city were infrequent and caused few casualties. From the start of the war until the end of 1942, there were some two-hundred alerts, but just a handful of these were actually followed by bombing, which killed a total of about two-dozen civilians.

From 1943, Allied bombing intensified in many parts of France and casualty numbers grew. Cities on the coast, with important German naval facilities, were among the areas to suffer major attacks. My father remembered that raids on St. Nazaire were so fierce that they were visible in Nantes, some fifty kilometres inland: "from our windows, we could see, far away, practically every night, the fireworks of the bombing of St. Nazaire."

On September 16th, less than three weeks after my parents' wedding, Nantes came under attack too, enduring its most deadly day of bombing in the war. The city's population had been boosted by the arrival of refugees from the raids on the coast, so every home was crammed full, multiplying the toll.

Alerts had become so frequent that people stopped rushing into shelters every time they heard the sirens. But late that afternoon, three waves of American planes flew over and this time the city was in their sights. The targets were the port and airport, but some of the planes missed their aim and the centre took the full force of their loads. My parents were among those who usually disregarded alerts, which till then had signalled bombings for somewhere else. Dimitri said on that day everything changed:

This time it was for us... there was an alert, [but] we didn't go to shelter, as usual. And we looked through the window, we saw the policeman in the street chasing as usual all the people out of the street – "go to shelter, go to shelter" – and in a point in time, we see the policeman just laying down by the sidewalk, completely laid down under the shelter of the sidewalk, so we said "my goodness, he's seeing something not normal", and just at that moment, a bomb exploded maybe one or two hundred metres from us. And the whole building shook, and all the windows fell down and doors were blown out, and we were in that office. So this time we went down to the shelter...

And when that was finished, this bombing, we went out into the streets and here we couldn't recognise that city where we lived for many months, and we knew every street, every corner, every nook – it was an old city, very old buildings, old narrow streets, some of the streets were so narrow that they were even dark. And here we walk in the streets and for the first time, we see those streets very light because all the buildings around were totally demolished...

About fifteen minutes of bombing had destroyed the heart of the city. Other witnesses spoke of the strangeness of the way the bright blue sky once again became clear and calm. On the ground, it was anything but calm. To the sounds of explosions and building collapses were soon added the terrible cries of people in pain and distress. My father saw members of the Civil Defence quickly begin the huge task of trying to get the wounded to medical centres:

Anything that could roll – whether it was a truck, a cart, a horse-driven cart, or even a wheelbarrow – they were all full of wounded people, but really badly wounded people... full of blood all over the place. They were transporting them to... hospitals. Very soon, all the hospitals were overfilled of course. There was no water, no electricity anywhere, and the fire began to start in the centre of that old city, with those narrow streets and old buildings; the fire started, and there was no water, no water anywhere... by nighttime, the whole downtown was burning – it was just like one big flame rising to the sky... So that was our first taste of real, real horror of war.

In spite of the now customary alerts, as well as shortages, curfews and other daily difficulties, until this event it seems the war had been somewhat distant in Nantes – the sense of unreality no doubt providing relief from constant fear and anxiety. The sudden confrontation with such devastation would have been all the more shocking: the emergence from underground to the disorientation of an unrecognisable physical landscape, then the assault on the senses – the sounds, the blood, the flames. As someone who had not had anything close to such an experience, I found my parents' vivid memories harrowing. It was hard to begin to comprehend that this type of incident was occurring in scores of other places, sometimes repeatedly and more destructively.

That evening a series of hospital trains arrived, which were filled – one after the other – with the wounded, then left for other towns. The city's facilities were particularly hard-pressed to cope with so many casualties, as the hospital earmarked to coordinate medical care in such a disaster had been hit and largely destroyed. Medical personnel operated non-stop for days on end, anywhere they could. Others dug through the destruction seeking victims. Up to a year later, bodies buried under rubble were still occasionally found. The toll in Nantes from that one day of bombing was about a thousand dead and nearly eighteen-hundred injured.

The apartment where my parents rented a room was badly damaged, with walls collapsed and windows blown out. As fire swept the city, they somehow managed to get to the building to grab a few belongings before the flames came too close.

A week later, when my father was away for work, there was another deadly day of bombing in Nantes. A morning raid caused widespread damage. Inaccurate targeting – partly the result of smoke screens sent up by the German forces – brought destruction to civilian as well as military targets. There had never been more than one bombing run a day, so there was shocked disbelief when in the evening the sirens began to wail once more. This attack by American planes was even more extensive, and again residential areas were hit.

There was no longer complacency and Irene, who had been in my parents' newly rented room when the alert was sounded, joined everyone else in running to a shelter. In a letter to Dimitri that she wrote two days later, she depicted the devastation that greeted them when they came out again. Well-known landmarks were in flames; there was the sense that everything familiar, that represented some sort of stability and continuity, was disintegrating. The letter is uncharacteristically untidy – written in pencil, the handwriting uneven – revealing how shaken she still was:

> *...I was afraid ... we sure felt them, these bombs. When we came out of the shelter, I saw that the Hachette [bookstore] was burning... The Decré [department store] was burning, at the same time exploding inside with strong detonations. I felt very alone and miserable in the middle of this crowd which was coming out of the shelter, seeing the damage, and starting to moan, to cry, to scream... These were the most painful moments... After a few minutes I made up my mind to go to [our office]. Everything was wrecked, torn down, and in a thousand pieces... Across the street, fire was burning more and more intensely... the spectacle of these fires... provided an unforgettable scene – it was so hideous.*

My father managed to reach my mother by phone; he heard her voice for a split second before the line was cut, enough to satisfy him that she was alright. Considering the destruction, it is amazing the

CHAPTER FOURTEEN

connection came through at all. The building into which my parents had just moved was badly damaged. For the second time in a week, they had lost their home.

The toll from September 23rd was over six-hundred dead and scores injured. Over the next year, my parents would witness other bombings but none as devastating as those in Nantes in September 1943. Many places across Europe would suffer much more horrific attacks. Irene and Dimitri were luckier than many to be spared worse and to remain physically unhurt. But in their terror, they shared feelings that millions of others were going through as the war dragged on.

Thousands of buildings in the city had become uninhabitable. Many people had fled or been evacuated after the first severe bombardment; now the departures became a flood. My mother too headed further inland. She was happy to leave "that hell, Nantes", but anxiously waited for my father to join her.

Irene and two co-workers cycled under heavy autumn rain to the historic town of Ancenis, about 35 kilometres upstream on the Loire River. She may have been relieved to escape Nantes and the threat of more bombing there, but her first days in Ancenis were difficult. The threesome had been sent ahead to requisition accommodation for other employees and their German managers, as the company was relocating its offices:

People treated us very badly. You'd arrive and start asking whether there were rooms, and I was told at first not to say what for – so they thought they were renting to refugees – and then they were requisitioned. It was very, very unpleasant. In a few places,

> *my co-worker Le Prêtre – who was a huge man – would stand between me and them, especially if it was a man [at the door], because they were very unhappy about it.*

She quickly gave up any deception in requesting rooms, but found the whole task harrowing. She had real concerns some people might physically attack her when they learned they had to house Germans. Whenever she recounted this episode half-a-century later, she shuddered with remembered fear.

Irene and her companions walked and knocked on doors for a couple of very long days. Beyond homeowners' reluctance to cooperate, there was a shortage of space in town, due to many who had fled the bombing in Nantes and elsewhere. When my mother completed the distressing assignment, to her great relief my father arrived. They were grateful for mutual support to face what lay ahead. And there was always danger in being apart; one never knew what might happen to prevent reunion.

Irene and Dimitri found much about Ancenis appealing. It was an attractive old town, and as a centre for the surrounding farming region, there was even more food available than in Nantes. This was particularly surprising at a time when so much of France was struggling with increasingly severe shortages. With many vineyards close by, even wine was readily obtainable. My parents found more sources for the food parcels they continued to post to relatives in hungry Paris, though these were sometimes now delayed as transport was disrupted amid increasing Allied and Resistance activity against the occupiers.

Ancenis is a quiet town, the pace of its old centre matching the peaceful flow of the Loire River which it faces. The population is nearly 8000. This is only a couple of thousand more than when my parents lived there – though at that time a third of the inhabitants were war refugees. Nowadays, the town swells with out-of-towners also, but only during the day, for in a newer section there are factories which attract workers from a wide area. Schools too bring in many from the surrounding countryside.

It is a charming town, with webs of streets crammed with historic buildings converging on a sixteenth century castle. In the area near the river, where my parents lived, the old stone houses face streets sometimes too narrow for cars. The townsfolk are extremely hospitable, as they were then, according to my parents, once the issue of forced accommodation was dealt with. When my sister and I visited in 2001, there was overwhelming interest in our reason for being there. In the library and archives of the *Association de Recherches sur la Région d'Ancenis* we were helped with information about 1944, then referred to the Town Hall for more.

There, an enthusiastic young man took us in hand and spent half the afternoon with us, as if his honour depended on satisfying our queries. He led us down narrow stairs to a basement storage area where huge musty binders of surveyors' cadastral maps going back a few centuries were stored on wide shelves. He extracted one from the mid-1800s. He told us that the drafting of such detailed depictions of the town was abandoned after that for about a century, but assured us that street names were pretty constant during that gap in time. It was only after the war, he said, that names were changed, with Resistance figures replacing some of the older notables on signboards. The war had changed much in the historical landscape of France; even in small places like Ancenis, there had been efforts to alter the symbolic landscape accordingly – in spite of there still being questions over the meanings of some of these symbols. Carefully opening the brittle, crumbling pages, our guide ran his finger above fading handwritten words, following every street until he found the one mentioned in documents relating to our parents' time there. It had become part of a longer street, which indeed had been renamed after the war for a new hero, General Leclerc. By coincidence he was the commander of the section of the Free French forces in which my father's older brother had served.

While Dimitri, in his positive way of relating the past, told about his and Irene's stay in Ancenis as if it were a holiday in the country, there is no question that the war continued to have regular, serious impacts. My mother travelled back to Nantes on a number of occasions to put her German to use to intercede at the *Kommandatur* for this person or another threatened with being taken to Germany to work. And eventually, attack planes appeared in the skies above Ancenis too.

My father described an incident when a train loaded with German tanks stopped in the town, making it a target. By then my mother was pregnant with my older brother:

> *Allied planes were trying to destroy those tanks…*
> *we were hearing those small planes, all the time,*
> *for hours… they were diving and firing small*
> *cannons and small bombs… And that was extremely*
> *frightening – to hear those small planes all the time,*
> *running around, and then suddenly you hear them*
> *diving, and "tat-tat-tat-tat", and then "boom!",*
> *a small bomb. They started to unload that train, and*
> *the tanks were passing in the streets of the village,*

CHAPTER FOURTEEN

just where we were hiding, in the ground floor – there was no basement... so we were in the corridor of the ground floor, listening to those planes, and [your] Mom was pregnant and we were standing for hours. And finally those tanks were unloaded and they dispersed in the country, and that bombing was finished. It was extremely frightening...

Some people had unusual ways of coping with such terrifying events. My parents spoke with awe about two of their co-workers who had a different view of where to go to escape raids. My father said their tactics almost cost them their lives when the train in Ancenis was attacked:

We had an accountant... an old Russian man who was a bibliophile – he was crazy about books. And everywhere he was travelling, he had a huge suitcase full of his most precious books... When that particular bombing took place, he fled the town and just ran across the fields with his precious suitcase of books – none of his other belongings... He ran into the fields with an engineer... And here they were, those two for some reason fleeing into that field with that huge suitcase, trying to save those precious books. And just where they were, a bomb fell... – a small bomb – and it made a big crater just near them... it was very close... But the two men were alright and the books were alright. It was so strange.

Another co-worker, an electrician, did not shelter when alerts were sounded. He had been told by a fortuneteller that he would die by hanging and he firmly believed in this prediction. So he refused to hide from falling bombs, in spite of others' attempts to convince him of his folly. Yet he survived the war uninjured. My parents did not know his subsequent fate, though they believed he was too gentle and kind a person to ever do anything to provoke the death penalty.

The company of such diverse characters provided distraction during the daily uncertainties over what the war would bring. These uncertainties preyed on my parents as they prepared for my brother's birth as best they could. They scrounged whatever fabric they could find for diapers, lined up an obstetrician, and booked a bed in a clinic. But developments in the war would render these preparations futile, for not long before the birth, they would find themselves cut off from Ancenis.

On Bastille Day weekend in July 1944 my parents decided to try to briefly escape the constant anxieties. In spite of the German censors, news of what was happening around the country was filtering into Ancenis, through word of mouth and forbidden radio broadcasts from Britain, so these anxieties were suffused with hope. The Allies had begun their invasion from across the Channel in early June and, along with efforts by the increasingly active Resistance, were putting the German forces to flight. The hope for a quick end to the occupation was mixed with fears over the violence this might entail: fighting and reprisals by the retreating troops. Dimitri said it was with such thoughts that he and Irene left Ancenis, with a group of friends, and crossed the Loire River to the southern bank:

> *[We wanted] some rest from the war. And the weather was fantastic... cloudless skies... we found meadows, little woods, and we found an old barn in ruin – a very small barn – and we sort of camped*

> *there... we made a fire with a big pot on the fire, and everybody who was coming was bringing something – either some vegetables, or a piece of meat, or a piece of lard, or something – and everything was thrown in that big, huge pot on the fire... and of course lots of wine... At night we were all sleeping in that old barn... and the roof was half-broken, so we could see the stars... the atmosphere was very good.*

But if the young people thought they could flee the war for a time, in the morning they awoke to discover that it had followed them. During the night Ancenis members of the Resistance had set fire to the bridge across the Loire, to help impede the movement of the German military. The original bridge had been destroyed earlier in the conflict and replaced by a temporary wooden structure. Now this too was impassable. A couple of weeks later, Allied troops arrived in the town. But while the northern shore celebrated its liberation, the southern side remained German-controlled.

My parents were among those who became trapped on the southern bank. It is not clear why they had not found another way to get back to Ancenis between the time the bridge was sabotaged and the Allies arrived. Perhaps they had feared there would be reprisals for the arson. About half the population fled because of bombing and other violent incidents during this time, so they were not alone in thinking it was safer away from the town. Then the choice was taken from them: the Loire which stood between them and home became part of the front line. A friend of theirs in the Resistance offered to get my mother back on a nighttime boat crossing to Ancenis. But he could not guarantee a pass for my father and my parents refused to be separated.

They found accommodation about two kilometres down the

road from the river, near Liré, a village amid vineyards. Most of the population there too had fled, but some farm families on the outskirts remained. My parents rented space in a smithy on one of these farms for what they expected would be a very short stay. But the Germans dug in. Dimitri and Irene heard frequent cannon and machine gun fire in the distance during the nights, reminding them of the dangers of trying to go back. My mother nervously watched the calendar, as the predicted date of their baby's birth approached:

> *Basically we got stuck there... Your father worked – at the time, they were collecting grapes, he did the wine harvest, he helped out. We paid – we had some money – we paid for the room and the food. It was hard to get food, but still, in the country it was not too bad... And the people were all very friendly... I think that besides [our landlady] they did not know how to write or read – they were very simple, but very wise, really nice people. They were very good to us, they directed us to a doctor and [helped in every other way].*

My mother felt the first signs one evening late in August. She reviewed with my father the German phrases she had been teaching him, and for good measure also wrote them out for him. The farm family pulled a bicycle out of a haystack, their one emergency vehicle they kept hidden from requisition or theft. Dimitri sped off to the doctor's home a few kilometres away as it got dark, hoping not to have to try out his German lessons. He met no-one on the road and soon was back with the doctor.

It was a long night. My parents had managed to obtain enough kerosene for one small lamp for the most crucial moments, and otherwise had only a hollowed-out potato with grease in it for light.

CHAPTER FOURTEEN

In the morning, when my brother finally decided to make an appearance, the doctor used strong drinking alcohol mixed with iodine for disinfectant. It was a difficult birth, with complications, and no anaesthetic. But the baby was born healthy, and all the women in the neighbourhood contributed whatever they could find of linen and other necessities.

Memories of the experience brought shivers to my mother whenever she talked about it decades later, or whenever she caught a whiff reminiscent of the concoction the doctor had used for disinfectant. Yet she also recalled with amusement his pride in the happy ending involving his first ever Parisian patient. If the doctor found her exotic because she came from the capital, it is hard to imagine what he thought of her Russian origins – though perhaps my parents did not share such inconvenient information. In spite of the trauma of that night and morning, the help and support provided by the farm families made it among the warmest contact Dimitri and Irene had with locals during their time in France. War built barriers of suspicion and fear, but also tore them down in such shared dramatic moments.

My parents gave their son a name with echoes in both families: Alexander, the name of Irene's father and Dimitri's paternal grandfather and older brother.

Crossing the bridge over the Loire at Ancenis with my sister in 2001, I reminded myself to appreciate the solidity of the metal structure beneath my feet. It was a rather ordinary bridge, finally erected in 1953 after a variety of temporary arrangements. I contemplated the shores from different points along it; even with sandbanks encroaching from both sides, the river's width was clearly not an obstacle easily overcome.

We walked past the houses on the southern bank, where the Germans had held out after losing Ancenis, and continued on to the village of Liré. This seemed rather too close for comfort to what had been part of the frontline when our parents sheltered here. The village was rather nondescript, its only claim to fame the fact that it was the birthplace of the sixteenth century poet Joachim du Bellay.

The district around Liré continued to be mainly dedicated to grape-growing. Rows of vines dangling on strings spread out in all directions, carpeting the low hills beyond the village; these were generously peppered with stone houses with terracotta roofs. New World residents used to expansive farms, we were not prepared for the small size and quantity of these holdings. With so many homes among the vineyards, and without any names or other clues about where exactly our parents had stayed, a search would have been futile, so we returned to Ancenis.

There, we decided we could not leave without a taste of the local product, so we visited the *Maison des Vins* to explore its small wine-making museum and buy some Liré *rosé*. The women on duty plied us with tastes of many local wines – and questions, their curiosity aroused by our French-Canadian accents. They were touched that their town had retained a prominent place in our parents' memories. They were too young to have experienced the war, yet seemed to feel that our quest was important; it was hard to gauge whether this was because their small town did not normally attract much attention from foreign visitors, or because they were among those in France still pondering that era and its significance. Then again, it was perhaps just another example of the hospitality and friendliness we had encountered here. These fit well with stories about Ancenis and Liré that had been so legendary in our family history.

CHAPTER FOURTEEN

While my parents lived through their own private drama on the farm, a wider drama was unfolding around them. The night after my brother's birth, Resistance forces moved to dislodge the Germans on the southern shore of the Loire opposite Ancenis.

Soon there was evidence that the attack had succeeded: the retreat down the road of the local occupation forces – along with some of their closest French allies. At one point my mother was shocked to see from a window some of the German officers she had had to deal with in past months, in a bedraggled state, asking at the farm door for water. The reversal of roles, with her former overseers now supplicants, did not give her any particular joy; some had behaved in ways that left her feeling no pity over what might happen to them, but others had been as decent as their positions and circumstances had allowed. This just reaffirmed her bitter and helpless feelings over war's absurdity and its entrapment of ordinary humans in brutal realities on all sides.

All over France, the Germans were retreating in the face of Resistance and Allied attacks. They surrendered Paris two days before my brother's birth, following a popular uprising. The next day, on August 26th, there was a triumphant parade down the Champs Elysées of Free French forces, with their leader General Charles de Gaulle, and heads of Resistance groups. Dimitri's mother Nadezhda, his sister Nadia and brother Seriozha were among the crowds that went to applaud them. They were also hoping to catch sight of the eldest sibling Sasha, who they believed was with a tank unit of the Free French.

My Uncle Sasha had been in Tunisia with the French Army at the beginning of the war. With the start of occupation, his unit had been disbanded but he had remained in North Africa. He had married the woman whose family was connected to the former tsarist naval fleet, who worked as a wartime ambulance driver. While employed in a German-run factory, Sasha had participated in sabotage; he fled after a colleague warned that he was about to be arrested, and found his way to the Free French forces in England. He crossed the Channel with them in the assault on occupied France. The family had had to decipher his wife's coded letters to guess his movements.

The Paris metro was not working, so on the day of the parade, Dimitri's family joined the thousands walking to the centre of the city. My Aunt Nadia said the long hike did not dim their excitement:

It was a very warm and beautiful day... There was great enthusiasm, masses of people, an unbelievable lot of people – communists, monarchists, anyone you like – there was a wonderful atmosphere... We were on the roundabout of the Champs Elysées... and the parade began. It was very beautiful... but we did not know if Sasha was there or not, because the tanks were going past, and he was in the tanks, but you can't tell who is sitting inside a tank. Then... [we saw] de Gaulle, General de Gaulle... of course there was a big ovation...

As the parade ended and the crowds started to break up, suddenly shots rang out from a number of rooftops. These snipers are believed to have been French people still loyal to the occupiers. Another theory is that they were political opponents of de Gaulle; the anti-German forces, while united in fighting the Nazis, were split along ideological lines. Everyone scattered for cover, running into building entranceways. When the shooting eased, Nadia and her mother and brother resumed their walk home, but then the sniping started again and they again ran for shelter. This happened several times, and though they saw many bullet holes in shop windows, they did not witness anyone being hurt.

Close to home, a neighbour ran to greet them, excitedly crying out that Sasha was waiting for them. He had received permission to miss the parade so he could get home faster, and had also walked a long distance in the absence of metros. He was amused that "along the way all the women stopped him – everyone wanted to kiss a French soldier".

The family went home to savour the reunion, but others wanted to contribute to the festive mood. A blanket covered an open window and every few minutes a hand would reach in under it: one held a bottle of wine, another a bit of some food, and so on. By this time, the city's food shortages were dire. A grim joke that was passed around asserted that the meat ration was so small it could be wrapped in a metro ticket. But the neighbours dug into their emergency stores to show their appreciation for Sasha, a "hero" of the Liberation.

But if Parisians thought the time of fear was over, there was another reminder, besides the earlier sniping, that this was not yet so. The Germans were not about to leave the city, whose capture had been such an important milestone, without a damaging farewell salvo. Indeed Hitler had ordered that if Paris was to be lost, there should be nothing but ruins left. So that evening, the Nazis sent in their bombers. Previously, raids – by the Allies – had targeted industrial sites or other strategic points. Many civilians had died nonetheless. My Aunt Nadia said now the German bombs seemed to be dropped anywhere, willy-nilly. The area where the family lived had no military importance and had never yet been hit; they had usually ignored alerts. Now they did the same, and for the first time, a bomb landed just two streets away. Sasha was horrified at their heedlessness. Before rejoining his unit, he made them promise to go to their designated shelter in future at the sound of the sirens. This they did, though no bombs came near them again.

The clashes and killings that had accompanied the end of the occupation in Ancenis were over by the time my parents returned there from the farm in mid-September. My mother said no-one was quite sure what to do, or what would happen next. She and my father felt going to Paris with the baby was risky, but they were also worried about their families. Eventually they got word that everyone was alright.

The war in Europe would continue until May 1945. Sasha would be among the French forces that marched into Germany not long before it capitulated to the Allies. France may have been trying to make up for the humiliation of its quick defeat at the start of the war during these remaining months. But the Liberation brought people face to face with other sobering realities: the need to repair the damage caused by the occupation, both physical and moral, and the sometimes vicious hunt for who was guilty of what under the Germans.

An atmosphere of revenge took hold, built on the horrors and deprivations of the preceding four years. The line between voluntary collaboration and forced cooperation was often blurred. The necessarily secretive nature of people's actions – along with a certain amount of score-settling – left the way open for errors. There were innocent individuals among thousands of executions that took place after quick and often arbitrary judgment. There were no doubt also innocent women among those whose heads were shaved and who were paraded in the streets, accused of relationships with Germans.

CHAPTER FOURTEEN

When more orderly and formal procedures were applied, over 160,000 people were tried. Some 1500 were executed, and thousands more were imprisoned.

Others would escape punishment through a variety of ploys. The new authorities contributed to many not being charged; they wanted to suppress divisions and begin building the peace, and introduced amnesty measures in the early 1950s. For a large part of the population, this suited their need to leave the traumatic era behind. It would be some years before renewed questioning attracted wider attention and rekindled efforts to untangle the anguished issues of guilt – personal and collective – and non-punishment.

My mother became nervous after the Liberation, when accusing fingers were being pointed in all directions. Her knowledge of German had resulted in her often acting as a go-between for the occupiers. But those who had been saved by her intercession from being sent to Germany were quick to assure her they would come to her defence should she be challenged.

My parents watched with dismay the way some relished the bloodiness of the initial vengeful reaction. But more disturbing were the knowledge that the bloodshed of the war was continuing elsewhere and the increasingly shocking revelations of atrocities.

Then came the nuclear bombings of Japan. My mother said that to her, this was like a portent of the end of the world; it was as if nothing was anchored any longer, that things could never return to normality again.

(*) Since our visit some of the docklands have been rehabilitated and converted into business and leisure space, attracting cultural and tourist activities. The crane we saw is now considered a Nantes landmark.

15
"The world is big…"

When I was growing up in Canada, my mother often told people that I was a "real *Parisienne*", born in the City of Light. To back up this assertion, she would point out that I came into the world in the same part of Paris as Maurice Chevalier. Ménilmontant was put on the map by that quintessentially French film star and crooner, whose accent and flamboyance, so very "Parisian", also took him to Hollywood.

Yet I was born just a few years after the city and all of France had gone through a decidedly unromantic period: the War and German occupation, along with the whiff of French collaboration. In other ways too, my mother's connection to the country of her youth was not a source of positive memories. Although I was born nearly thirty years after Irene and Dimitri arrived there, I was registered as a refugee to parents who were still refugees; I may have been *Parisienne* by geography of birth, but I was never French by citizenship. My parents grew up in Paris, were educated and started their working lives there, and married in the city. Yet my mother always felt that Paris and France never quite accepted them, and their refugee status pointed to their enduring position as outsiders. Invoking a familiar Parisian icon like Chevalier may have been useful for a migrant trying to break the ice with her neighbours in a new land, but her relationship to the country he represented had never felt completely secure or comfortable.

It was sometime in the first half-decade after the war that my

CHAPTER FIFTEEN

parents decided to try for a new life somewhere else. They made this momentous decision amid the many difficulties both they and their adopted country faced.

At the end of the occupation in France, there were those who got caught up in accusations and counter-accusations over collaboration, and the subsequent punishments and revenge. But for many others there was little energy to spare at this point to dwell on the recent past. For them, like for my parents, the need to survive materially was the top priority.

Still in Ancenis, wondering what to do next, they learned their old company was being revived in Nantes, with a new name, and new bosses replacing those tainted by having been too close to the Germans. Under its revamped identity, it was hiring many of those who had worked for it previously. Dimitri signed on and my parents went back to Nantes in early 1945. They rented a couple of rooms amid the ruins of a city facing a huge reconstruction task.

Restoration of the port was now the work of the shipping company. It was to be an important entry point for food and materials critically needed by France. But the harbour was blocked to shipping by submerged vessels. Just about everything that could float, apart from small fishing boats and rowboats, had been sunk, either in the bombings of the city, or scuttled by the Germans when they retreated. The scale of destruction is evident in photographs: the river is clogged with burnt out, smashed or capsized ships, and docks are jammed with acres of twisted metal from collapsed cranes and warehouses.

My father joined the salvage crews raising the ships. Then later he participated in the planning of such operations. The tides and weather dictated the long and irregular working hours. It was a dangerous occupation; some of the ships pulled up were the largest then plying the oceans and manoeuvring their broken, unevenly weighted hulls was tricky. Once in winter, Dimitri fell from a tilting wreck into the water. By the time he was fished out and rushed to a barge, his clothes were "like a wooden suit". But he warmed up in front of a fire, and was quickly back on the job.

In war my father had survived bombings and many other dangers unscathed, yet here, in peacetime, in another accident, he nearly lost his life. In going to the assistance of a man who had passed out in a newly-opened manhole on a refloated ship, Dimitri too lost consciousness, due either to toxic fumes or lack of oxygen. He was forever grateful for the courage and quick thinking of a co-worker:

> *To get me out of the hole, that was a very difficult process, because someone had to go into that hole in order to put a rope around my body, to get me up. They tried with a diving suit, because the idea was that the air was toxic in that hole, but the diving suit in those days was so huge and so cumbersome that he couldn't pass through that hole with the diving suit [on]. So that particular diver volunteered to go there without anything, just with a gauze mask in case there was something toxic, but he put a good rope around his own waist and he climbed [in]. By that time, it looks like the air renewed itself to a certain point, so he could stay inside enough time to put a rope around me, then climb back up, get me out... he was certainly responsible for the saving of my life.*

For the man my father had been trying to rescue it was too late – when he was brought up, he was already dead.

CHAPTER FIFTEEN

While recovering in hospital, my father had another close call: he had a bad reaction to medication:

I had a wound around the belt, because that's where they put the rope on me to pass me through the manhole... so since it was so dirty, and full of mud and oil and stuff, they gave me lots of shots at the hospital and a few days after, I developed an allergy. I started to inflate – in a couple of days I was inflated like a "bonhomme" Michelin, my face was like a football, even I could hardly open my eyes... that inflation began to go into the throat, so it was getting really critical. And impossible to find any antihistamines, because it was the end of the war, many things were not in proper production yet. Poor Mommy had to run all around the city of Nantes, from pharmacy to pharmacy trying to find that chlor-tripolon, and... she finally found some. And as soon as I got those pills, things started to improve.

By its very nature, my father's job in Nantes was finite. After a few months of work, enough of the harbour was cleared for ships to be able to again dock and unload. Within two-and-a-half years, the crews with whom Dimitri worked had refloated almost all the sizeable vessels. In spite of the dangers, he enjoyed the challenges involved in raising damaged, unstable ships – some of them enormous – amid shifting tides. He often told stories about this period, about the mishaps – and the achievements in the face of many hazards. Most of the vessels recovered were able to be repaired and put back into service. After witnessing so much destruction, there was satisfaction in reversing the damage.

But my father felt it was time to move on, to "put some sort of regular life together".

When my parents considered their future, Paris, the home of most of their relatives and friends, was their natural first choice of destination. It was mid-1947 and they found the capital struggling to come to terms with the occupation and its fall-out. Shortages continued, with many goods still rationed. There was a dearth of housing, so they moved in with Dimitri's mother Nadezhda and brother Seriozha. His sister Nadia had left the apartment after marrying a Russian from Finland at the end of the war.

Nadezhda's apartment was small, though there was the advantage that my baby brother could be cared for there while my mother worked. She quickly found an interesting, hectic job in a grain brokering company, involved in France's efforts to obtain supplies while its own agricultural sector recovered. Just before my birth two years later, my parents "bought" an apartment. That is, they did a deal with the former tenant, whereby he claimed they were his relatives. This circumvented bureaucratic complications, not to mention a big hike in rent. The man my parents paid was emigrating to Argentina, part of the flow out of war-shattered Europe.

With a new baby due, my mother quit work. My father was unsettled, staying only briefly in his first three jobs, which provided few challenges. For a couple of these he had turned to relatives, the family network helping him overcome his limited experience in fields outside shipping, which was not very applicable in Paris. After stints in an electronic tube factory, repairing elevators, and in a metal workshop, Dimitri seemed to find his niche in a company involved in air conditioning and ventilation. He said his superiors were lazy,

CHAPTER FIFTEEN

spending their days in bistros, but for him this was a windfall: they gave him increasingly responsible roles, encouraging him to learn quickly and gain new skills. This knowledge and what he picked up in another brief position he held just before emigrating would provide him with a foundation to launch himself into his working career in Canada.

My father's restlessness in his work perhaps foreshadowed a desire for more fundamental change, but a decision in mid-1948 suggests that he and Irene did not yet have any firm ideas about leaving France. In the face of continuing housing shortages, my mother said they decided to buy a property in a tiny village just outside Paris amid farmland and orchards.

> We decided to build ourselves.... in Paris, it was impossible to get anything, at that time apartments weren't being sold – when we "bought" it was just giving a bribe. Apartments weren't sold – it was very rare, there were no condominiums or anything like that. We bought some land outside town – in Cœuilly – and planned to build there.

The piece of land was cheap because there was a huge crater of unknown origin on it. They spent every spare moment there, shifting soil to fill the hole, building a shed, and planting trees and a garden. Travelling by metro and bus from the city, Dimitri regularly carted as much timber as he could carry and Irene juggled my brother, and then the new baby: me. Eventually my father bought an old car and rebuilt it into a station wagon; the trips became easier.

There is a puzzling discrepancy between this laying of the groundwork for an eventual permanent home, and thoughts of leaving, apparently already in the background. In a letter he wrote just before emigrating, my father said he had been contemplating an "escape" from France for years. Yet preparing to sell the cottage had been "a heavy page to turn: so many memories, so much work, hopes and sweat; this little house in which each bit of wood was arranged with such care." All the family became very attached to it – my mother did not tell my seven-year-old brother it had been sold until they were halfway across the Atlantic because she knew the news would devastate him.

Their time there was the subject of many nostalgic stories in later decades. Yet only two years after they had bought the land, they were already actively planning to quit France. And less than four years after they had begun working on it, they pulled up the roots they had started to establish. In the same letter, Dimitri wrote that when this was finally done, he felt a certain relief, crediting his family's legendary "gypsy blood" for helping him break this tie. The proceeds from the much-improved Cœuilly property were exchanged for ship tickets and my parents prepared to leave their cherished cottage and Paris for good.

If there is some mystery surrounding the place of Cœuilly in their plans, my parents' motivations to emigrate, at least as they expressed them when they looked back many years later, are less difficult to fathom. As with many migrants, there was a combination of factors that accumulated and shaped their thinking. The main reason they gave was the ongoing regime of restrictions on foreigners in France, which particularly irked my mother:

> *I was so sick of it – 10%, 10%... it was 10% at work, it was continuing, even after the war...10% only in each company could be foreigners. There was nothing*

> *official, but that's how it worked... Also, the constant need for a "permis de travail" (work permit), "permis de séjour" (residence permit), constant, constant, constant. Then the question came up of us getting citizenship, it was so expensive. And you had to prove all sorts of things – I went around to find out about it, and in the end we gave up...*

Some bureaucratic hurdles for migrants were gradually being eased. But there were still limitations, for instance in mobility among occupations. Work permits stated: "It is... forbidden to employ a foreigner in a professional category or a profession other than that cited on the... card". Changing this designation was difficult. After the war employers were often flexible and overlooked the details on documents of long-term residents like my parents. But the official restrictions were there, to be applied as it suited, whether by employers or government officials.

The sort of absurd situations this could create – and the arbitrariness in handling them – were demonstrated when my Aunt Nadia started an office job. When she went to renew her work permit, the government official told her it was not possible that she was employed in an office, because her document said she was a shop assistant. My aunt burst into tears and the official became uncomfortable. So he changed the work category noted on her card. This incident occurred towards the end of the war, but several years later, the type of employment that foreigners were meant to do was still spelt out on their permits. This is evident in the renewals obtained by both Dimitri and Irene in 1948, documents that remain in the family archive.

My parents were also well aware of – and sometimes subject

to – discriminatory procedures that had been applied in wartime. Compared to people who had been detained in French camps, or worse, shipped to German ones, they had fared well. But while they had shared the daily hardships and fears of the war and occupation with the rest of the population, as foreigners they had not always shared equal treatment, whether under the French or the Germans.

For instance, Irene said pregnant French women were issued cards to give them priority in long food queues. When she was pregnant with my brother and feeling poorly, she did not receive any special treatment. At least not until her pregnancy became obvious, when she was moved forward in the lines. But this was often only due to the goodhearted concern of others also waiting.

Other émigrés told of struggling to get Russian children out of Paris, away from possible attacks at the start of the war, in government evacuations; the plans had neglected to include children of migrants. They had been left out once again when gas masks were first distributed. And my parents knew of widows of Russian men killed while in the French forces being denied the compensation given to others who lost husbands in the fighting. Many émigrés were left with the feeling that the government saw them as being good enough to die for France, yet not worthy of the benefits and rights afforded citizens.

This revived bitterness over the lack of recognition for older émigrés. Many had served in the First World War in the Russian Army on the side of the Allies, and in actions that had saved France casualties. Yet they had found that this counted for little when they arrived in the country.

Some of the reactions to German occupation had added to my parents' disillusionment. Yet their misgivings were ones of nuance rather than substance, and no doubt hindsight played a part in how they looked back. For in many ways Dimitri and Irene had held similar views to the bulk of French people. Such views had evolved from acceptance of the armistice and occupation as unpleasant necessities, to approval or support for the Resistance as Nazi rule became more repressive and cruel. But my parents decried the extremes they witnessed: the enthusiasm and hastiness of some to collaborate, and the vicious settling of scores that came with the punishment meted out after Liberation.

The émigrés were sometimes among those scapegoated amid the atmosphere of revenge. Historian Robert Johnston quotes a 1945 community newspaper describing posters that appeared in Paris which carried the words: "Frenchmen! Do not forget that your enemies are Germans, White Russians and collaborators!" He also writes of the thousands of pleas for help addressed to the main representative of the émigrés in dealings with the French government. Vasily Maklakov sent off more than four-thousand letters from mid-1945 to late 1946 to intercede for Russians he believed were accused of collaboration only because of their ethnic origin.

Community leader Sofia Zernov was also flooded with appeals to intervene for Russians arrested with seemingly little justification. Some who came to her sought help for women who were attacked and had their hair shorn off amid false accusations of relationships with Germans. In one instance, when she went searching for a woman detained at a Resistance office, she was threatened with having her head shaved too. It seemed her crime was purely that she was from the White Russian community. Her fury was such that she found the courage to confront the officials, accusing them of never standing up to the German occupation and of knowing nothing of the role of the

White Russians in it. Her vehemence so took them aback that they released her with her hair intact.

She did receive some cooperation from more sympathetic officials and eventually gained access to prisons, the Drancy camp in Paris where suspected collaborators were held, and court hearings. Zernov helped to get many Russians released (though she did not deny that there were certainly others guilty of collaboration).

All this built on the catalogue of hurts – from the petty to the serious – that had accumulated before the war: the quotas in education and the professions, the continuous obligation to satisfy a multitude of bureaucratic requirements and the sense of insecurity this fostered. It stoked feelings of being excluded in some way, both officially and socially. While it was clear that their generation had suffered much less than that of their parents, my father said he and my mother dreamed of living in a place where their rights would be the same as those of everyone else:

> *You know, we'd always been foreigners in France... Many, many French people at that time never travelled, they stayed in their village or in their town, even in Paris – in their district. So they were very – I don't know if it's the right word – parochial. So foreigners for them were something strange... and they were suspicious, and sometimes it came even to hostility... In that atmosphere, when the war was finished... we said what the hell – the world is big, why not try elsewhere? There are countries that are new, where people are more equal, where Europeans arrived only a few hundred years ago, and not a few thousand years ago. So why not? The world is open*

CHAPTER FIFTEEN

to everybody, and from the moment we thought that way, we decided to go somewhere.

My parents hoped that in the New World they might in future have a better chance of escaping wars, a hope shared by many others who left Europe. In my father's case, this had a particular personal dimension: in spite of hailing from a family with a long tradition of military service (his grandfather had risen to general, his father was highly decorated for his role in the First World War) Dimitri had become a pacifist. He was sixteen when the war started. It is unclear when his pacifism emerged, but due to the quick defeat of the French Army, he had not had to deal with the consequences of being called up and refusing to go. He now had a son and the prospect of his child being required to serve in the armed forces was an added incentive to leave.

My father's views are demonstrated in a letter he wrote to a Montreal newspaper soon after arriving in Canada. In it he passionately described the results of "hatred, this damned essence": the devastation and death he had witnessed during the war. His beliefs had not changed nearly fifty years later when he wrote to a magazine about the "orgies of killing" during the war and the Russian Revolution, expressing gratitude that he had been "lucky enough to never have to touch a firearm".

Dimitri and Irene were not alone among the Russian émigrés preparing to leave France; the community was falling apart. During the war, differences over whether, and to what extent, to support the Soviet Union in any fight against fascism had split the already politically fractious community (*). The role of Stalin, first as a partner of Hitler's, then on the side of the Allies, had added further bewilderment. After witnessing the Soviets in action, it was clear to any who may still have harboured dreams that the regime would collapse, that this was a pointless hope. Moscow was showing anything but weakness, now flexing its muscles over other Eastern European nations. The determination to stay relatively close by, ready to return to their homeland if communism was defeated, evaporated as a reason to remain in Europe.

Generational change also contributed to the disintegration of the community. Older members, among them many of the political and cultural leaders in exile, were dying. "Russia Abroad" would leave many traces in Paris, its capital in the West, but its heyday was over.

As members of the community moved on, or increasingly integrated in their adopted countries, a new cohort of Russian refugees was settling in Western Europe. The upbringing of these "displaced persons" in the Soviet Union meant they had little in common with the post-revolution migrants, beyond a hatred of communism. But while they may not have become active in the old émigré community, they were able to convey to it the horrors of the regime they had fled.

In spite of these reports, there was a small number of émigrés who, like some of their counterparts in the late 1930s, were having a change of heart. For them, the realisation of the permanency of Soviet rule was a signal that it was time to return and learn to accept – or just to die. They were tempted by an offer of "amnesty" from Moscow to those who had opposed the regime. They became more prepared to recognise, in historian Robert Johnston's words, that "the Revolution and Soviet power were now an organic part of Russian history". This was often bolstered by hopeful expectations that the war – and time – meant that a more open regime would soon evolve there. While not all returnees were so optimistic, shades of similar ideas, along with weariness over their status as outsiders, added up to a powerful magnet. Johnston writes:

*The chance to die in Russia for the old,
an opportunity to make something useful of their
lives among their own people for younger refugees;
for both, the wish to identify with a powerful,
apparently forgiving motherland and thus end their
drab existence under alien skies – all these motives
played a part in the decision.*

Many of those who went back would later regret it. Some ended up in labour camps and did not survive the experience, many were punished in other ways by the regime. (**).

The fragmentation of the community, with some members going back and many more moving to different countries twice or even three or four times since the Revolution, was reflected in my family. Various relatives who had lived in Western Europe went to Brazil, Argentina, the United States, or Canada. Some who had settled in Eastern Europe became trapped when the Soviets moved in. But others managed to get away, including my great-uncle Sergei (whose memoirs are cited earlier in this book). Having lived in Serbia before the war, he and his family ended up in New York afterwards. Meantime, my Uncle Sasha, who had gone to Tunisia to join the French Army, stayed in Africa, where he worked in various parts of the continent, only returning to France in his later years. Many émigré families found themselves scattered even more widely across the globe.

My parents never considered going to the Soviet Union, but they pondered various other destinations. As so often happens with migration, family connections played a part in their decision-making. Their first choice was Brazil. A cousin of my father's had emigrated there with his French wife soon after the war and wrote glowing letters, contrasting it to the devastation and greyness of Europe. He offered to help our family get papers and then in every aspect of settling in a land he believed had great prospects:

> *Here, you see, things are not the way one pictures them to be in Europe: here, this is America, need I say more?... neither must you think that Brazil is a backward country – far from it. There are certain aspects here, that are much superior to Europe... Do not worry... there is no shortage of work especially for those who have initiative and energy... From the point of view of the political situation... it is certainly more stable than in France, the government is elected for four years and good or bad it remains; the Communist Party is banned. As concerns the economic situation... one thing I can say is that Brazil is a rich country and that I live well.*

Dimitri's cousin had grown up in great poverty; this was also the cousin who had been taken to Germany to work in terrible conditions during the war and then had nearly become trapped in the Soviet zone. His enthusiasm for his new home matched the ideas many had of life in the New World; his past experiences led him to appreciate even more keenly the opportunities before him. He suggested he and my father could start a business, and become prosperous together. Later, he did indeed start his own company and became wealthy. However the political stability he vaunted

CHAPTER FIFTEEN

turned out to be illusory; ahead for Brazil in the next few years was much upheaval, culminating in military rule that would last more than two decades.

My parents applied for visas to Brazil, which were granted in early 1952. But they began to have doubts. They met a number of people who had moved there, then returned, which my father said disturbed him and my mother:

> *I spoke with people who... were so happy to escape, so to say. Because of the very hard climate, and mentality. They said it was hard to live within a society which is divided into several classes – the Europeans at the top, then the rich Brazilians in the middle, and then the poor Brazilians. Even the poor Brazilians had divisions, according to the colour of their skin, or something else. Anyway, we had very pessimistic reports.*

Clearly they were considering Canada at the same time: the visas for both countries were approved just days apart. In favour of Canada was another family link: his sister Nadia and her husband had decided to go there. My uncle was a deacon in the Russian Orthodox church, and a Montreal parish had offered him a position. My aunt said she did not take to heart as much as my parents the restrictions on foreigners in France, seeing them as inevitable for refugees. But her husband was among many who had become "infected" with the thought of emigrating to better their lives.

If my aunt's plans influenced my parents' choice, there was much more to their decision. While many others with a similar background clung to class distinctions they had carried from Russia, in spite of their impoverished situation, my parents had rejected such views. An improvement in material circumstances was a strong motive, but social values were at least as important – as their doubts about Brazil demonstrated. There were other aspects, among them the perhaps unconscious lure of a place which echoed their ancestors' homeland in climate and geography. After reading widely and speaking to people who had been to Canada, Dimitri said he and Irene concluded it would be more suitable for them than Brazil:

> *Finally… we said, what the hell, why should we go to such a hostile country, when Canada is so close to us, matter of fact they speak French in a good part of eastern Canada. And it seemed to us closer to our minds. Also the fact that it is a cold country was not a bad idea, for me at least, because in Paris, the trouble is when winter comes, you have rain, rain, and sometimes there is a tiny bit of snow, and you always have that hope that this snow will cover everything, everything will be nice and white and it will be cold, and freeze. And… next day it rains again, everything is washed out in the dirt, and the mud and so on. So we said, there at least we'll see some real snow… And of course Canada had the reputation of a civilised country, where we'd have no problem in terms of educating our children. And also it's a new country with lots of opportunity, a huge area with very little population.*

The knowledge that we had almost immigrated to Brazil added another destination to my escapist childhood daydreams about what might have been. Having even less of a realistic idea of the South

CHAPTER FIFTEEN

American country than I did of Russia did not stop me fantasising about the life we might have had there. My imaginings were made up of Amazon jungle and extravagant Carnival festivities, scorching heat and white mansions full of servants, which owed more to clichés of the old American south than to any knowledge of Brazil. The exoticism I pictured would provide occasional distraction from reality in Canada, which – besides being literally very cold – was at times chilly in other ways.

People of Slavic origin had never been among Canada's most favoured immigrant groups. When our family joined the post-war wave across the Atlantic, there were misgivings about Russians for reasons beyond wariness over difference. The Soviet Union's role in defeating Hitler had been overshadowed by the ever-icier Cold War. The general apprehension was reinforced by Moscow's aggressive actions towards its neighbours. In the years following the Revolution, there had been fears Russians might import bolshevism. Now too there was a tendency to identify Russian migrants – whatever their trajectory and political background – with communist ideology. This was something of a paradox considering most who did arrive at this time were, if anything, more anti-communist than most Canadians.

The search in the United States for left-wing "subversives" was at its greatest intensity precisely around the time my parents first stepped onto North American soil. Canada itself had not fully recovered from the Igor Gouzenko spy scandal; in 1945-46 this defector from Moscow's Embassy had pointed the finger at a list of Canadians, resulting in a royal commission and a series of trials. The government subsequently tried to resist being infected by the extremes of the McCarthyite witch-hunts south of the border, not always successfully. According to political scientist Reg Whitaker and journalist Gary Marcuse, Ottawa chose "...a particular kind of Middle Way: Canada practised only restricted witch-hunting." The Gouzenko affair, along with the inevitable influence of its powerful neighbour, set the scene for Canada's anti-communism.

When I started school in the mid-1950s, this atmosphere was sometimes reflected at recess or after classes, when children in the yard would call out at me: "Commie! Commie!" It did not happen often, and of course they had no idea of the meaning of their taunt and of the strength of its potential to wound. I too lacked understanding, in this case, that the children were just parroting what they picked up from their parents and the media. I would react with rage, though also with the righteous certainty that youngsters possess: I just knew their insults were wrong.

After the war, Canada had been slow to open its doors to "displaced persons" and other migrants if they were not northern or western Europeans. But as in the past, pragmatic considerations changed that. In preceding decades, the government's desire to settle the west and get the cross-Canada railroad built helped members of less favoured ethnic categories get permission to enter the country – including Slavs. Among them were large numbers of Ukrainians who went to farm the Prairies. Post-war labour shortages encouraged the government to again start opening the doors wider. In 1947 Prime Minister Mackenzie King announced less restrictive policies, though he emphasised that "the people of Canada do not wish, as a result of mass immigration, to make a fundamental alteration in the character of our population."

That translated to an order of preference which kept eastern and southern Europeans low on the list. But over the next decade

CHAPTER FIFTEEN

or so, barriers against most Europeans would gradually fall away; non-Europeans would remain the applicants facing the most restrictions, a situation which would continue until 1967 when the last remnants of race or ethnicity-based discrimination were officially dropped from immigration regulations.

Dimitri and Irene were still labelled as Russian refugees on their identity papers when they applied for Canadian visas. But any qualms over their Slavic origins were tempered by the fact that they were coming from the country which had provided one of Canada's founding peoples. Their fluency in French also helped, as did my father's diverse technical experience. The result was that in some ways they were treated as though they were French, something of an irony considering they were migrating mainly because of not being seen that way in France. They were given more leeway than many refugees from the recent war – both in the application process and later when they settled: people who came from "displaced person" camps in Europe were often required to do labouring or agricultural work for a time, regardless of their qualifications. They also had more difficulty achieving permanent residence.

In contrast, my parents found the procedures to obtain landed immigrant status bureaucratic and time-consuming, but not overly difficult. They filled out the expected mountain of forms, chased various French government departments, schools and employers for certificates proving milestones from their past, and underwent a slew of medical tests. My mother went to the police for a "certificate of good conduct". She also procured a document reaffirming that in spite of having been born in France, my brother was not a citizen, clearing him of any future obligation to do military service there.

My father was granted his visa first, and he was required to find work and accommodation in Canada before the rest of the family could follow. He had to enter the country within two months, so five weeks later Dimitri set off, in April 1952. He left to Irene the stressful task of "selling" their apartment, as well as the packing and many other preparations to complete.

Dimitri sailed on a British ship, the "Scythia". He was awed by the immensity of the ocean, appreciating it even when rough as tangible evidence of its power. And he found shipboard life liberating:

I was so lucky, my trip was such a fantastic trip. When I was leaving it was very suspenseful, because I was leaving my wife with two children, I was going to the unknown and stuff. And suddenly, the ship departs, and here you're stuck in that small world of the ship for eight days, because it was a very old ship, she was going slowly, and it took eight days. And those eight days were one of the best vacations that you could dream of. Because about the second day, all your troubles sort of began to vanish at the horizon – oh, they existed still, but very back in your mind. Because everything was so different in that little world that is the ship.

He was impressed by the onboard services and the copiousness of the food – though on landing, in a letter to Irene, he would extol a meal he had in a Russian home, saying how tasty it was after the blandness of the ship's fare. Some of the other travellers he met – also migrants – would remain firm friends. Dimitri wrote that British and Canadian passengers were in the minority, while:

At the opposite end, there are the immigrants who on

CHAPTER FIFTEEN

their own make up a whole world, all the languages, all the classes of society. In general, [they are] of very modest appearance, with rather scruffy clothing: Germans in large part, French, Polish, etc...

After initial misgivings, he felt that the obvious social distance between the first class passengers and the cohort of less well-heeled immigrants was mainly overcome, through mutual respect. He hoped this levelling reflected Canadian society and was very encouraged. But he conceded to Irene that his poor English – in spite of ongoing efforts at sea to study it – was often a barrier. The "Scythia" docked in Quebec City in early May. My father took a train to Montreal, about 250 kilometres to the southwest.

From the relaxing ocean trip, he launched into the frantic chase for work and a home so my mother could follow.

(*) Some émigrés went so far as to join the German military, when Hitler turned against Stalin, in their fervent desire to see the communist regime defeated – even though this meant they fought against their adopted country.

(**) The voluntary returners followed the numerous Soviet citizens who found themselves outside Soviet zones at the end of the war but were repatriated by the Allies, whether they wanted to return or not. It's thought France sent back over a hundred-thousand POWs the Germans brought to work in France and others who had managed to flee westwards. There are also claims that among those repatriated were Nansen passport holders who had been living in France and other western countries for years.

16

New World

Everything is different, but absolutely different from that which we know. To such an extent different that one experiences almost a physical suffering...

So wrote Dimitri to Irene on arrival in Canada. Coming to a new country, a new continent, is always daunting. In the days before television and the internet, access to information about foreign lands was more limited. Throwing oneself into a new world would have been even more overwhelming – especially knowing there was not much likelihood of ever going back. But Dimitri could not dwell on how lost he clearly felt – he had to urgently find a job and housing for our family.

My parents were rarely apart during nearly sixty years of marriage. Thus there were few letters between them. But in this period when my father went ahead to Canada, they wrote to each other frequently. Four decades later, they spoke about their emigration in interviews that I conducted with them. Dimitri's letters from the 1950s amplify those stories. They contain impressions that had not been overlaid by later experiences or reworked in memory. Yet his overall observations in the 1990s did not differ radically from what my father wrote in his letters all those years before. These included feelings that are not unexpected in such a break from the past: sadness at leaving relatives behind, an initial bewilderment over the unfamiliarity of things and apprehension over an uncertain future.

CHAPTER SIXTEEN

Though their numbers were relatively small, Canada had a long history of Russian immigration: explorers and fur traders, religious and political dissidents, poor farming families seeking land. Some came during a surge of immigration early in the twentieth century; the Depression decade before the Second World War put a stop to that influx. But after the conflict, as the government gradually eased restrictions, numbers climbed quickly.

In 1952, the year in which our family made the move, a total of nearly 165,000 migrants entered Canada, to join a population of some fourteen million.

Even transplanted across the Atlantic, Russian community links from Paris were a help to my father when he landed. Other émigrés were also choosing Montreal as their destination, their knowledge of French an incentive. They joined a small, but well established Russian community in the city. With the injection of new immigrants, activities begun before the war gained new impetus. Reinvigorated, the community was keen to welcome newcomers.

One family related to acquaintances in France provided Dimitri a bed until he could rent a room. He also frequented a Russian Orthodox church, a magnet for new arrivals. The priest too came from France and my parents had known him and his wife there. They hosted gatherings in the church basement after Sunday liturgy, and teas during the week. My father told me this provided the opportunity both for social interaction among lonely people in a new country, and for the exchange of practical advice and information:

[Father Oleg's] basement was always full of recently arriving people, who were meeting there... to talk, to share experiences, to share tips, and sometimes to play chess and cards. And Father Oleg had always

> *at his table several of those immigrants, that he was trying to either console or guide or whatever.*

But when it came to finding employment, Russian contacts were not able to help. My father knew that if he did not get a job quickly my mother would lose her spot on the ship they had booked for her. There were only a couple of weeks between the date of his arrival and when Irene needed to confirm the booking. With streams of migrants sailing, room on vessels with good reputations was scarce and reservations had to be made well in advance. If he failed there could be a long wait for another berth. He did not want to be apart from his family for many months. Besides, Irene's approval from the Canadians was only valid for three months.

Dimitri's growing alarm as the days went by and he still did not have work was fresh in his memory many years later:

> *I was desperately looking for a job, and I soon realised that in spite of my good certificates, the whole situation is different, the work is different, the equipment is different, everything is so different... and since there were thousands and thousands disembarking every day in the harbours of Quebec and Montreal, and Halifax in winter, that were looking for jobs, the employment offices had queues in the street. I spoke with some people, they said "oh, we've been here already for two or three months and still looking for a job, it's so hard to come by."*

My father was determined to remain optimistic over his prospects and to keep an open mind towards this new society. But doubts crept into his letters to my mother in Paris:

> *It is difficult to find work because of a certain suspicion which exists vis-à-vis immigrants*

CHAPTER SIXTEEN

> *since they are so numerous and some have left bad impressions... The people here are very private and mind their own business and do not help out unless they are certain this will benefit them.*

Dimitri pored over the telephone book in the evenings for potential employers, and plotted out itineraries with maps and streetcar timetables that kept him rushing around throughout the working day. He also joined long lines outside various agencies trying to match newcomers with work. Finally, in a Catholic Church office assisting immigrants, he convinced an employee of the urgency of his quest. She gave him letters which allowed him to avoid waiting hours in queues outside government employment offices, taking him directly to specific individuals. It is hard to imagine why he received such special treatment. He could be charming and was also very determined, but he was not pushy. Years later he was still amazed at the efforts these people took to try to find him work:

> *So I went to the first office and it worked – I passed all those crowds, and went straight with that letter, and saw the guy immediately... He really worked for about half an hour to try to find a job for me, and phoning and consulting his files and so on. I don't know if he was a kind of, little bit of a chief of department, or something. And finally nothing could work for an immediate job... So I went to the second office and the same scenario. And the guy made a few phone calls, and [consulted] a few files, and finally he found a job for me.*

The position was with a kitchen equipment manufacturer. It was not his preferred occupational area, but Dimitri told me he

launched into it as though it was the job of his dreams:
> *I can tell you I was working with enthusiasm, I can tell you that! It was about ten days from the moment I landed in Canada to the moment I started a real, well paid, one dollar an hour job. But it was a real serious job... with a real company who gave me a certificate of employment immediately so I could go to the immigration authorities.*

Dimitri had a letter from a Russian family declaring there was space for all of us in their home. He never intended to live there, but it took care of the second major official requirement.

Irene received a telegram from Dimitri with the news just days before she had to pay for the ship cabin they had reserved for her. She rushed to the Canadian Embassy to get the document required for confirmation of her booking. She feared difficulties as the official papers from Canada had yet to arrive by mail. But she found my father's message was enough to set in motion the finalising of her papers. When all the documents had arrived, my mother again set off to the Embassy. After often unsympathetic treatment in years of dealing with French officialdom and the bureaucratic tangle she had had to navigate with the Canadians until then, she was surprised at their friendliness. When an official applied the final stamp and said "Welcome to Canada" she felt he meant it.

About a week later, in mid-June, my mother farewelled more than twenty-five years of life in France and boarded the Panama-flagged "Atlantic" with us children, aged seven and three. This vessel too was packed with migrants. Her voyage took just five days, but at times the ocean was rough. And for Irene it was not a relaxing escape as it had been for Dimitri – two small children kept her busy, especially my brother who was always running away, giving her many nervous moments:

> *You felt bad, but you weren't sick. As for Alex! He'd disappear. I wasn't sick – I couldn't allow myself to be sick... And there were lots of kids, maybe as many as 200. The first couple of days, I managed to get into first class with you both, to watch a film and so on. Then they said the first class had started complaining, that all the kids were very noisy. So we were no longer allowed to go to first class.*

She was lucky to have a sympathetic waiter, who gave her fresh fruit, juice and other food items that were not meant for economy passengers. And there was another unexpected food bonus – this came from some of the other travellers, when they learned about quarantine regulations in Canada:

> *...the last couple of days, the Italian passengers found out that it was forbidden to bring in any sausages. They all had them and they found out they would be taken away. So they walked around with knives, they would get bread from somewhere... and they would cut it for you and give you such wonderful things: gorgonzola [cheese], all sorts of salamis, and so on and so on – it was "formidable!" So hardly anyone ate [ship meals] because we were all filling up on the Italian food.*

It is hard to imagine what my mother expected when she arrived, considering the letters she had received from my father. Dimitri had tried to be positive, reassuring Irene he would get settled quickly and well, in anticipation of her joining him, though he was clearly worried that this was not happening as easily as he had hoped. His first impressions of the city that was to be their home must also have given her pause. While trying to maintain an optimistic tone in what he wrote her, Dimitri seemed baffled and at times apprehensive at what he encountered:

> *Montreal is a strange city... Some neighbourhoods of the city are very mixed. A veritable salad of tenements, beautiful houses, factories, stores, etc. The big arteries... are full of stores of every sort with displays of neon lights that are absolutely blinding. Every little store is saturated with panels of moving light... All this is in the most gaudy tones: yellow, green, orange, red, blue, etc., in dreadful taste... The city itself is not very clean and certain densely inhabited areas are made up of what one could really call hovels where very dirty children play in the gutters. It is a very curious mixture of opulence and misery exactly as one knows it from novels about American cities. However other neighbourhoods are well defined: residences, low modern buildings... very spaced and airy with large lawns and parks.*

He liked the convenience of shops, open long hours. He found their unfamiliar products peculiar, such as factory-made sliced bread, but enthused that these made meal preparation quicker and easier. The novelty of pre-packaged food would quickly wear off for both him and Irene. They would soon lament the absence of affordable European-style products. Their European sensibilities would also

CHAPTER SIXTEEN

contribute to their enduring distaste for the flashy; they had misgivings over what they saw as excessive materialism, and a perception that appearance was more important than substance. But the openness and greenery in many residential areas would continue to appeal to them, even if, my father told me, he often found the designs ugly: "the apartment buildings... looked like cubes, the architecture... a bit simplistic, shapeless...". The abundance of accommodation in these unattractive buildings impressed him though, after the shortages of post-war France.

The disorientation Dimitri clearly experienced at first could not be suppressed in his letters to Irene, though he tried to temper such feelings with reassurances that he was overcoming it:

> *I had a meal with some French companions from the trip across. This did me good because they are demoralised to the point of crying, really at zero. I did my best to cheer them up and in fact I am the one who became cheered up when I saw how ridiculous their attitude was. And today, while I was hiking around I suddenly realised – that's it, I am accepting it. The sight of the houses no longer hurts my eyes. I am beginning to get used to the language (which has the sound of the most ugly of provincial patois that one can imagine...). And in fact this transition now made, I have noticed that this city does not lack charm.*

The letters Irene sent before she set sail, in answer to these mixed and sometimes disconcerting impressions, emphasised the positive too. She counselled patience, writing that it was natural for things to be tough at first, but reaffirming the belief that all would go well for them. There is a feeling that she was trying to respond to what she sensed he needed to calm his apprehensions – which she no doubt fully shared. As she would so often do in the face of difficulties in the coming years, she masked her own concerns over what lay ahead. It is hard to find the line between how much she really believed in what she was writing, and how much came from her attempts to bolster his – and at the same time, her own – morale.

There is no record of my mother's reactions to her new home when she joined my father in Canada. Looking back later, she said she'd been "horrified" by some aspects:

> *...I must admit, it took me more than three years to get used to being here, but I had no way out – we had arrived... we could not do anything about it. First of all, it was the climate, not just that it is so cold, but that it changes so quickly... And I also did not understand the Quebeckers at all, I understood absolutely nothing [of their French]... I was totally confounded by the high prices [of food]... and there was still the apartment to pay for.*

It was not just the accent that Irene found so different. There were certain basic practices in France that she had assumed would be similar among French Canadians. For instance, she had not anticipated that the Catholic Church could play such a prominent role in daily life, compared to the highly secularised society left behind. She also felt that the French in Canada had adopted many customs that she saw as Anglo-influenced; she found this surprising among people who so vaunted their uniqueness in opposition to English or American ways.

CHAPTER SIXTEEN

One trait which my parents feared might be shared among the French on the Canadian side of the Atlantic was narrow-mindedness towards immigrants. They found that there was hostility among some people towards newcomers but also that such views were rare. At one of the companies where my father sought employment in his first days, the engineer he approached, a French Canadian, told him there were no openings. He then promptly invited Dimitri to his home for dinner that evening, a spontaneous warmth my father found touching.

Many did not quite know what to make of my parents; they seemed to be – but were not – French. Besides, Quebeckers had ambivalent feelings towards the mother country. My parents came to realise that some of the wariness towards foreigners was the result of concerns that the French-Canadian language and culture could be swamped and disappear amid the arrival of many immigrants likely to integrate into the English part of society.

Over time it would indeed be the English side where my parents felt most at home. This was a sentiment shared by many immigrants to the province, much to the chagrin of separatist French-Canadians in later years: in the independence referendums of 1980 and 1995 there was little support among the so-called allophones (neither francophones nor anglophones) for aspirations to Quebec sovereignty.

After the loss of the 1995 referendum by a very slim margin, the provincial Premier and leader of the separatist Parti Québecois, Jacques Parizeau, famously blamed *"l'argent puis des votes ethniques"* – money and ethnic votes. The comment caused a storm and he resigned – though this may have had as much to do with internal party rivalries and a brewing conflict-of-interest scandal as it did with the unacceptability of his words. But what he said did sting for immigrant Quebeckers, especially those who had shown confidence in the province by choosing to stay in spite of the separatist movement. Many others had fled around the time of the first referendum.

Official discrimination was what Irene and Dimitri had most wanted to escape, and this they achieved: as landed immigrants, they were subject to the same regulations as other Canadian residents in terms of work and movement. My mother said they could not avoid being seen as different. But they did not feel they faced the sorts of barriers with which they had grown up:

> *So you can't really say it was discrimination...*
> *in general, later I got used to it – we were seen as*
> *kind of odd people, a bit odd. But that did not really*
> *bother me. We were free to go wherever we wanted,*
> *even outside the country. In France, every time you*
> *went away for more than 24 hours, you had to go*
> *tell the police.*

My father never felt discrimination at work based on his ethnicity. But in the beginning he did have a major handicap: language. This was partly why it had been hard for him to get his first job. Much business in Montreal was conducted in English – not surprising perhaps in the context of a largely English-speaking continent – though it was a bone of contention for French-Canadians. Dimitri attended government night classes to study English, and he quickly picked up vocabulary at work. Unlike many other immigrants, he did not face rejection of his qualifications. But then his official qualifications were modest. His experience and eagerness to learn meant he often did work usually performed by those with higher levels of training. He was rarely paid to match.

CHAPTER SIXTEEN

Irene's summers in England had given her a basic foundation in the language. The issue of schooling meant she needed to apply this knowledge more quickly than she had expected. At the time education in the Province of Quebec was divided along religious lines. Language split roughly parallel: Catholic schools were mainly French, while under the Protestant Board, the majority were English.

My parents quickly realised that an education in the English sector would probably be more suitable for us children since the Catholic system put a lot of time into religious teaching. Our family was Russian Orthodox, and besides, Dimitri and Irene did not feel religious instruction should be a large component of classwork. Even French-Canadian work colleagues of my father's envied the fact that we had a choice and suggested going for the Protestant Board to avoid the "endless" catechism. The basically non-denominational Protestant schools included children of all religions and ethnicities, and were generally more welcoming to those of diverse backgrounds.

The choice they felt they had to make was a blow to my parents, because it would see us moving increasingly into unfamiliar cultural territory, far from their own experience. It also set back my brother. He had been at school already for a couple of years in France, and needed to not only catch up with different ways of teaching, but also to learn an entirely new language. The conundrum surrounding language, one of the last aspects in which my parents had anticipated problems in a French-speaking land, left them, as my mother put it:

> *...between two chairs. Because, no matter how you look at it, by upbringing... [we] had come through the French system... and you [children] all ended up on the English side.*

By the time I started kindergarten, my parents made sure I had been exposed to English, to add to the French and Russian with which I had grown up. This made the start of my education easier than what my brother had had to endure. I did not have an opinion on which system was better, though I do remember Russian friends of mine who went to French schools having to memorise prayers and other religious texts on the weekends. If only for that reason, I was happy that we were in English school.

In later years my parents did not regret their choice, believing it better prepared us for the future. But the French language had been a large factor in their decision to emigrate to Canada. They had filled precious space in their ship trunks with books they had probably chosen with our education in mind: dictionaries, the classics, a gazetteer, a huge atlas, and so on. These stood yellowing on the bookshelf as we, unpredictably but inexorably, drifted towards the English side of Quebec's tortuous – and tortured – divide.

It is no small irony that some twenty years later the Quebec Provincial Government passed legislation obligating children of immigrants to attend French schools. New arrivals had consistently preferred English education for their children, for the purely practical reason that most of North America operates in English. But other factors, applying even in the case of French-speaking families like ours, had contributed to a history of integration, via children, into the English side of society.

One of the hardest aspects of emigrating is the separation from kin. On leaving France, my parents did not know if and when they would see their relatives there again. While there were no political barriers to them returning, as had been the case with their parents when they left Russia, they knew the voyage would be too costly for them for some time to come. Indeed, my mother would never again see the people who had become her replacement family after the untimely deaths of Alexander and Natalia: her father's close friend "Uncle" Mikhail and her mother's sister Evgeniia and her husband. My father was more fortunate; sent to England for work a few times, he crossed to France to visit his mother and brother.

My grandmother Nadezhda came to North America once. She seemed very old to me, a shrivelled dour woman exuding profound sadness. I found it hard to relate to her. As I was thirteen this is perhaps not surprising. I could not know the significance of her visit: this was the last time I was to see her. By the time I got to Europe ten years later, she had passed away.

During my childhood, letters arrived regularly from Europe. Among them were fond notes for me, from people I knew only by name and through photographs. There were also parcels containing Russian storybooks, scarves, embroidered handkerchiefs, stationery, chocolates. I enjoyed the chocolates of course, but found it hard to appreciate old-fashioned hankies or scarves covered in flowers or pictures of the Eiffel Tower.

I was instructed to respond, a tedious chore as these relatives had no substance in my reality. Now I wish I had put more effort into my correspondence. I can only imagine how much greater the sadness of not being close to loved ones must have been with so little prospect of reunion.

It would only be when I grew older and witnessed other children's relationships with their grandparents and extended families, that I began to understand what I was missing. In Canada, our family – grown to five with my sister's birth – clung to the tiny group of relatives around us: at first my Aunt Nadia and her family, until they moved to the United States. Then my father's second cousin and his family, who arrived after a failed attempt to settle in Argentina (this was a son of Anna, whose memoirs appear in earlier chapters of this book). In spite of the fragmentation that had resulted after the Revolution, Irene and especially Dimitri had grown up with comparatively numerous relatives close by. The absence of this type of supportive network – both practical and emotional – would have been particularly felt during the period of adjustment to a new and confusing environment.

My parents struggled in their early years in Canada for other reasons. My father was paid little, and their financial situation was precarious. Often Dimitri had two jobs or worked many extra hours to earn enough for the family. Yet in spite of the hurdles, I believe he and Irene ultimately did not regret having settled in Canada. They worked long and hard, they scrimped and saved. But we children all received a university education – a crucial aim for them, as they had always keenly felt having missed out on this themselves. And we established ourselves in good careers. My parents even made up for the little house they had abandoned on the outskirts of Paris: they built another small cottage, in Ste Agathe in the Laurentian Mountains north of Montreal. They also eventually fulfilled the dream of many Canadians, buying a house in the suburbs.

And as soon as the five years of residence stipulated by the then law had passed, they applied for citizenship. In their thirties, Dimitri and Irene finally became citizens of a country for the first time.

17

"Citizens of the world…"

When I was a child, our family regularly travelled to New York to see my Aunt Nadia and her family. Every time we approached the American border, we were all apprehensive. While Canadian citizenship provided a feeling of security, it did not mean that my parents' origins passed unnoticed. Just as my father had provoked suspicions whenever he had had to declare during the war that he was born in Germany, my mother's place of birth being Russia was often greeted with misgivings. She was sometimes marched into the border post for further questioning. The diverse list of our places of birth – four countries among five people – probably made the officials additionally wary.

But on one occasion, on hearing our surname, the US guard broke into a smile; even more surprisingly he broke into Russian. Having recognised the origins of the name, he plied us with friendly questions, comparing the answers to his own immigration experience. When a queue of cars formed behind ours, he reluctantly sent us off with a heartfelt "Welcome to the United States!"

My mother was astounded that an American border guard could be from Russia. The Cold War was far from over, and there would be more hostile receptions at the crossing, but Irene never worried about these encounters in quite the same way again.

Unease with officialdom is not uncommon among migrants, many having suffered at its hands. Nor was Irene's unhappy response to the way history and bureaucracy combined to infringe on her idea of her identity. This time it was Canadian officials and their approach to her place of birth that created contention. In her eyes, she was born in Russia, since Mogilev had been, at the time, in the Russian Empire. It was still under Moscow's control. But she was offended by the designation in her Canadian papers: Soviet Union. Besides, she argued, she could not have been born in a country that did not then exist. She would no doubt be equally dismayed that now her birth country is known as Belarus.

My parents were happy to be seen as Canadians, or Russian-Canadians. They felt that their ethnic origin was a crucial part of who they were, but a part among others. My Aunt Nadia saw her identity as more strongly Russian, but of a Russianness from the past. It was a point of view that was reinforced when she visited the land of her ancestors in 1996, after the collapse of communism:

I am Russian, of course I'm Russian.
But unfortunately that Russia no longer exists,
so this is a very complicated question. It does not
exist. That Russia that I saw – you know some
people have said to me, on returning from Russia:
"Oh I immediately felt myself at home, I want
to move there"... But not me... Russia is entirely
different now... All those years of communism
have made the people completely different...
they have a different way of life, everything is
completely different from us. I think it shows on you,
the country in which you live, and what you take
from its psychology.

My father concurred that the place from which his parents hailed would no longer have suited the person he became. He retained affection for the culture and traditions of his ancestors' homeland. He saw them as important elements in having formed him, but not as part of a current reality that could hold him. Having seen the torment his parents' homesickness had brought them, in later years he did not regret his own distancing. On the contrary, Dimitri felt it had provided a certain freedom – the silver lining perhaps, of not belonging:

> *Our parents suffered much more than us… because they left a home, they left a country without wanting to leave it. They had a home, they had a country of their own, something that we, their children, never knew what that meant, because we never had a country of our own, we were wanderers, we were citizens of the world always. Which in a way, it's better, because many people suffer a very acute nostalgia simply of the land where they were born, and where their parents were born, to which they have an extremely strong attachment. So, many of those Russian refugees were extremely miserable for those reasons.*

For some, this attachment would continue to tear at them, their years in their adopted homes not able to submerge their affection for the land they had fled. Even with communism still in place, Russia continued to exert a strong attraction. In the immediate post-war period, those who went back had had to face the terror regime of Stalin. But soon after my parents left for Canada, the Soviet leader died, and again, there were hopes for changes for the better. In 1956, my mother's "Uncle" Mikhail decided to leave France and return to the land of his youth after an absence of over thirty years.

Whether he was influenced by the leadership change or by another of Moscow's periodic campaigns enticing émigrés, it seems his main motivation was yearning for family. The misery of being away from the homeland was compounded by the departure of my mother, whom he considered as his niece; he had no other close relatives in France. He had a big family in Russia, but had lost contact with them two decades earlier. He now asked the Soviet Embassy in Paris to trace them.

Mikhail was overjoyed when they got back to him: five of his siblings were alive. Letters from them started to pour in and he learned that he had some forty close relatives in the Soviet Union, all of whom had prospered. He responded to their warm invitations and went back. Three months later he wrote to Irene:

> *Finally I am at home, in my land, among close people. Around me are Russian faces, I hear the Russian language, I experience the life... of my immense homeland. It does not seem strange to me, that right after my arrival I simply and easily entered into this life. It is as if there had not been 36 years spent abroad. It is as if I had never abandoned my native land. I immediately merged with everything, with the local life, and if by chance I remember anything of Paris, it seems to me like something absurd, unnatural, like a bad dream, like an event which one wants to destroy in one's memory.*

Mikhail wrote that he had been entrusted with a responsible job, and praised the government for recognising his skills. He insisted that western beliefs about shortages were wrong, that everything was available and much of it more affordable than in France. He rejected other ideas in the West, and particularly among some of the émigrés, about the Soviet Union. They had a "false concept about... coercion", based on either "ignorance" or "malice". He stated he was free to go anywhere and do what he wanted, that life there was "wonderful".

Perhaps Mikhail was catering to the censors, perhaps he was influenced by propaganda or by the happiness of being with family. But it was an optimistic time in the Soviet Union, the period of new leader Nikita Khrushchev's "thaw" (though later that year the crushing of the Hungarian uprising put question marks over the extent of the change). Mikhail's ultimate fate is unknown, because this is the only letter from him after his return that remained among my mother's papers. Whether there were more that were not kept, or whether they stopped, is not clear. Perhaps Mikhail did not write again because Irene was apparently reluctant to respond, either too upset over his move, or fearful over any communication with the Soviet Union. It was a strong apprehension she long retained, even if contact would likely have been more risky for him than for her. But perhaps propaganda again – this time from the western side of the Cold War – had an impact, bolstering her already deep disquiet over the Soviet regime.

For members of my grandparents' generation to feel such strong homesickness for their homeland that some decided to chance a return was perhaps not surprising. What was less comprehensible was the continuing pull on people of my generation.

When I decided to visit the Soviet Union on my first overseas trip in 1973, I was among numerous descendants of refugees heading to explore the land of their ancestors. Still, I made my plans with no small amount of trepidation. I had been subject to years of Cold War rhetoric and the deep-seated fears of Russian immigrants, and my nervousness was not helped by the Canadian Department of External Affairs. They warned me that if the Soviets wanted to keep me, their Embassy would be hard pressed to help; I may have been Canadian but, they reminded me, my mother was born in what was Soviet territory. I could not imagine why Moscow might want to claim me, but then there was much about this land that was mysterious to me.

To be on the safe side, I denied any connection, not that that would have fooled anyone. To questions by Soviet officials about any family there, I always responded with emphatic negatives. This was of course not strictly true, but I believed that contacts had ended years before. If challenged I could say that my relatives there had died long ago – for all I knew, they had.

On this first visit I came away amazed at the splendour and lavishness of the pre-revolutionary palaces and churches – so much richer even than I had imagined. I was both stunned by their beauty and squeamish at such excessive opulence. But I was disappointed by the impossibility of contact with ordinary people. My naïve attempts to start conversations in shops, museums or on the street received the cold shoulder; people clearly wanted to avoid troubles that could result from communicating with foreigners. Interactions were largely limited to people employed in tourism and well-schooled in dealing with visitors. All were polite but distant. I enjoyed – for once – having my name pronounced with ease, while every other visitor's was garbled, usually my fate. But this was an insignificant chink in the invisible wall that stood between the local people and me.

On my only other visit during Soviet rule, in 1978, my experience was quite different. I was offered warm hospitality everywhere I went and had many opportunities for meaningful contact. This was because I was sponsored by a family my sister had met during a study exchange. Many doors opened for me, and in time-honoured tradition, every home offered a table laden with food and drink – in spite of the ongoing shortages of many goods.

My host family and their friends put themselves out for me financially and also placed themselves at risk. I was still a dangerous westerner, and worse, by then I was also a journalist. I was sometimes followed – something I myself would never have noticed but which my hosts pointed out. In case I thought they were being paranoid, on a couple of occasions when we were walking they led me through charades that felt like something out of a spy movie: sudden 180 degree turns or quick moves into dead-end lanes, which confused the followers. Their reactions gave them away.

As it happened I visited at a very sensitive time, just after a period of labour unrest about which the government had banned reporting (*). The refusal of my hosts to allow all this to dampen their welcome moved me deeply – though it did make them very careful in expressing any opinions divergent from the official line. This heartfelt reception left me with a strengthened feeling of some fundamental connection. But paradoxically, a feeling of distance grew simultaneously, the result of the better understanding I gained of the differences between our societies.

During both trips which took me to the Soviet Union I also visited France. I had heard many fascinating stories about my parents' lives there. But when it came to cultural legacies, the emphasis was always on the Russian one, with France's contribution secondary. Beyond appreciating the advantages of speaking the language, I had not given that part of my family background much room in my identity.

This is curious perhaps, considering this was the country where I was born, where my parents had been brought up, and where I still had numerous relatives. The society too was not unlike the one I had become part of in Canada. Yet even after travelling there, I felt little change in what I saw as the superficiality of my links to it. It would only be in later years, when I explored more thoroughly venues and events of importance to my parents, that France began to work its way into a more prominent position in the place I gave it in my family's history.

With my visits to the Soviet Union largely satisfying what had seemed a critical need to see the place from which my family originated, the pull of the past weakened. Yet just when I started to feel that links to my ancestors' homeland were becoming remote, something happened to rekindle my interest in them: from behind the fraying iron curtain came word from the descendants of Annochka, my paternal grandmother's sister who had gone back in 1937 after the Ignace Reiss spy scandal.

When I had declared to the Soviet authorities that I had no ties to the country, I had felt that in a concrete sense this was true. Now I learned that when I first visited, one connection had still been very much active and ongoing: correspondence between Annochka – and after her death, her daughter Anika – and relatives in Europe and the United States. With all mail monitored, the Soviets would have known about this, but perhaps they did not discover the link to me. Sometime after my trip, the letters from Moscow had stopped.

With the new freedoms of the Gorbachev era in the late 1980s, Anika's daughter, an actress, was allowed to travel abroad with a theatre company. In Paris, she found someone at the church her grandmother had attended in the 1930s who had my Aunt Nadia's address in the US. Renewed correspondence resulted in Anika and her husband coming to North America in 1990. She obtained the permission her mother had craved for so many years and had never been given: to see relatives outside the Soviet Union. Among those she visited were her cousins: Nadia in New York and my father in Canada.

When she arrived at my parents' home, it was as if a large missing piece of a torn photograph had been stuck back on. Anika brought family photos from before the Revolution which matched or complemented those we had in our albums, as well as more recent ones of her parents and of some of the relatives who had always remained there. She filled in gaps in the stories of the lives of these relatives, providing substance for people who had become ghosts to us. What she told us about life in the Soviet Union over the preceding half century did not match the glowing observations in "Uncle" Mikhail's letter to my mother. Well beyond the Khrushchev era, she said, life had been difficult, especially for people with the wrong social pedigree.

Anika recounted her parents' return in 1937 to the Soviet Union, her own birth just as the Second World War was beginning, and soon after, her father Vadim's death from tuberculosis. She and her mother were left in Moscow without official residence documents or the means to make a living. Annochka's brother Sergei took them in, but they were constantly evading the authorities because of their lack of papers:

> *In Moscow there was always this vicious circle –*
> *you couldn't work without a right of residence,*
> *but you couldn't register for a right of residence*

if you didn't have work... And so we slept in the metro... because everyone who was afraid of bombings slept in the metro. And there they never checked anything. Because people would run, they wouldn't have time to grab their papers when bombings began, so it was possible to calmly spend time there... Plywood sheets were laid right on the tracks and people slept there, all of them. [We] lived at [my uncle's] but slept the nights there – because for all those who harboured people without the right of residence, it was very dangerous.

Anika's mother did a quick wartime nursing course. When she began to work with the wounded she was finally given the right to be in the city. They were then able to live openly with Sergei.

Anika described the fate of some of our relatives, who had been sent to prison or exile in remote areas after the Revolution. Sergei too had been imprisoned – twice, but fortunately only for short periods. But the possibility of further arrest constantly preyed on him:

And so all his life he had this fear, that they would take him away – this I remember. Once – even though he was a very kind person – once he yelled at me terribly, because in the morning when he was sleeping a friend of his came, and I woke him and told him there was someone to see him, and he couldn't forgive me because I didn't say who it was and why. He jumped up as if scalded – this was incomprehensible to me and I was very hurt – he yelled at me "never say that to me, that someone's come for me."

While his stints in custody left Sergei nervous forever afterwards, the impact of time in jail on his first wife was even more severe and she never recovered her shattered mental stability. Soon after the Second World War, hearing someone at the door and thinking they had come to rearrest her, she had jumped out of a window. She fell to her death on the pavement four storeys below.

Daily life was often hard, amid poverty, and with shortages frequent. Accommodation was always cramped, with Annochka, Anika and Sergei sharing small rooms in overfull communal apartments. In spite of all this, Sergei had always insisted he could never have left Russia. Annochka too, even after nearly twenty years abroad and with her sadness at being apart from her relatives there, came to feel that her place was in her homeland, no matter how difficult life was there:

She used to say [about her time in France]:
every minute, you suffered from not being in
Russia – everyone annoyed you, everything
was repulsive to you, and there was
no spiritual connection there, never.

Anika's mother and uncle provided as secure an environment as possible for her as she grew up. But the family's social origins were never forgotten and she fought the odds – both financial and political – to get a good education. Later, when she had established a career as a university English instructor, her past came to haunt her once again and she was overlooked for better jobs. Anika had the qualifications and skills, but it was more important to be "morally steadfast" and "politically literate" – code words, she said, for having the right lineage and politics. She was also repeatedly refused permission to go abroad – until then.

I had glimpsed Soviet life during my travels, I had read and heard a great deal about it. But Anika's descriptions of her experiences and those of other family members provided a very personal and moving perspective; they also brought into sharper focus what might have been had my grandparents chosen a different path. The fate of many relatives – including those on my mother's side – remained a mystery. But there was now some insight into what they too might have gone through – if they had survived the early tumultuous years. There had been hardships on both sides of the east-west divide, though played out in radically different ways. There were striking and sometimes surprising parallels in terms of beliefs and values, but also many divergences born of such different life experiences.

The year after Anika's visit, the Soviet Union ceased to exist. The fervent desire of those who had fled Russia in the 1920s had finally been fulfilled, but it came too late for them. As for their children, they had moved on, and most had no interest in going back. Visiting was a different matter. Before, they may have been fearful or not able to stomach the idea of going to the land run by the enemies of their parents. But many now saw an opportunity. My Aunt Nadia travelled to the new Russia, and in 1997 my father followed.

Seventy-seven years after his parents had sailed away from their homeland, Dimitri set foot onto Russian soil for the first time. His parents Nikolai and Nadezhda were long dead, as were all the others of the family group which had crossed the Black Sea in 1920, three years before his birth: his older brother Sasha, his mother's sister Annochka, and his paternal grandmother Varvara.

My father's Russian background had been an important element in his life. His parents' attachment to the language and culture in which they had grown up, and his youth in France amid a large and vibrant exile community, had shaped his upbringing, and indeed his whole life. My mother had carried the Russian part of her identity even more tenaciously than my father. Just as adamantly, she had held on to her hatred of the Soviet system, and even after its collapse, refused to go to Russia. So my father travelled with his daughters – my sister and me – on a visit to his cousin Anika.

When we stepped out of a plane into the poorly-lit gloom of Moscow's Sheremetevo Airport, the only thing mirroring Dimitri's parents' departure was the congestion – crowds of people shoving and pushing impatiently as officials plodded through the paperwork of the throng of arrivals. Finally, the three of us stepped out into weak spring sunshine, into the startling chaos of touts and vehicles swarming at the exits, jostling and cajoling for trade.

This visit was very different to the ones my sister and I had made in the days when this was the Soviet Union. Then we had assiduously avoided admitting to family connections. Now, in Moscow, we stayed with Anika. Following her directions we found the cream coloured building where Dimitri's mother, as a 19-year-old widow, had mourned her first husband, killed in the opening weeks of World War One. Around the corner, we looked up to the fourth floor of another building, from which the first wife of my father's Uncle Sergei had jumped to her death after the end of the Second World War.

In the city once again named St. Petersburg, we went to the Peter and Paul Fortress and in the museum read Dimitri's father's name in the list of commanders in 1917. We discovered where the poet Aleksei Apouchtine was buried. We found an imposing memorial at the cemetery, a large bust looking down from it. A man who helped us find the gravesite told us that he was a singer, and that when he had work – all too rarely in those post-communist days – he liked to perform those verses of our poet relative which had been put to music.

People marvelled that my father, who had never before been to Russia, spoke the language nearly unaccented. Some said it sounded like it came from literature of the past, with expressions no longer used; people quickly picked him for a foreigner. When we visited museums, galleries and historic buildings, we were always charged tourist rates. When my father asked his cousin how he could make himself sound more like a local, she told him he was too polite. "Don't say 'please give me three tickets' when you go to a museum," Anika suggested. "Thump the counter and demand tickets – no 'pleases', no 'thank yous.' They're an immediate sign you're not from here." This sort of behaviour would have been completely out of character for my soft-spoken father, so he never took her advice.

Many people we met were touched by Dimitri's knowledge not only of the language, but also of Russian history, folklore and customs. One museum attendant burst into tears when she learned of our origins, thanking us profusely for coming back to the land that had treated our forebears so harshly. She and others welcomed us to return to live there, as though we were long lost relatives.

The traces of our family that had survived the turbulent twentieth century provided concrete evidence of what had seemed an impossibly distant past. But any thoughts of returning to live there were another matter. The many links to the place, which my father's parents had told him so much about, could not counter his perception that this country bore little resemblance to their memories. He had closed the circle by returning to their homeland, but this did not feel anything like "home" to him. He was devastated that instead of the strong bond with people that he had anticipated, he found it hard to relate to them.

Any nostalgia for the past continually collided with the bleak realities of early post-Soviet Russia. The quick political changes had brought disruption, along with poverty and cynicism. There was disillusionment that the collapse of communism had not lived up to the huge expectations of those who had so long hoped for this change. It was again a fractured society.

My father left Russia deeply disappointed, his hopes for some sort of meaningful connection dashed. But at the same time, the visit provided additional validation for the path his family had taken all those years before – and for his own evolution into what he aimed to be: a "citizen of the world".

(*) Although the family which sponsored me was Russian, they lived in Abkhaziia, a region in Georgia long unhappy with being part of that republic. At the time of my visit in 1978, there had just been a spate of strikes to back demands for the area to be transferred to the Russian Republic. During my stay a witch-hunt was underway to punish the leaders and instigators of the separatist unrest.

Epilogue
Moving on

Nearly six decades after my grandparents fled Russia and twenty-six years after my parents sailed away from France, I left Canada. I had not been forced to leave by historical upheaval, or to seek a place free of restrictions on rights and opportunities. I had joined the waves of young people in the West heading off to "see the world".

The discoveries that I made went much beyond exotic cultures and geography: they resulted in another migration. I did not return to live in Canada and am now a resident of Australia.

I arrived in Sydney as a tourist in 1979. It was a hot October day with dazzling sun – that immediately appealed to me. From a dirty, rattling suburban train, I marvelled at the lush greenery, even in what looked like poorer or more industrial neighbourhoods. I was equally shocked at the squalid, decrepit housing in some areas. The streets were mostly deserted, at a time when everything stopped at midday on a Saturday after the shops closed, so different from the crowded, vibrant towns in Asia I had come from.

After a few months, when I decided to stay, it became evident that I had climbed considerably in the immigration hierarchy. The authorities did not pay much attention to my unpronounceable surname or my family origins in a country considered the enemy of the West. They were no less aware of the Cold War than Canadians. But the layer of my identity acquired in Canada had obscured my origins. My arrival in North America with my family after the war had seen me categorised as an "ethnic", my Russian background a major defining aspect. But in Australia, I was seen in another way: I was white, I spoke English with an acceptable accent, I was university educated, I had skills and experience to offer. This exempted me from being an "ethnic" of Russian extraction. I was welcomed as a Canadian, hardly different at all.

This applied officially, as well as informally. From 1973, with the repudiation of the last elements of the White Australia Policy, all would-be immigrants were meant to be treated equally. Yet those responsible for the practicalities worked in ways that clearly made distinctions. My First World credentials allowed me to skirt government rules. On landing in Australia I faced the requirement put to all foreign arrivals – the need to show evidence of funds to support myself during my visit. I had a total of just fifty dollars but had no difficulty in bluffing my way through, even though the money barely covered transport to the house of the friend with whom I went to stay. Within a few days I had office work, my lack of papers no obstacle. I was not from a "visible minority" so no-one in the job agency or among my employers thought to question my right to work. And I was able to convert my tourist visa to permanent residency without leaving the country, something that was officially forbidden.

After the sixty-year legacy of my family's experience as exiles and refugees, I had been "promoted" to being the "right type" of immigrant. It was a relief that my passage through the formalities was so lax, yet I was acutely aware of my privileged position and somewhat uneasy, knowing others were put through much more arduous procedures.

As I settled in to my new life in Sydney in an impossibly warm climate, the bitterly icy lands of my past faded into the background.

Yet when cultural nostalgia struck, it was my Russian heritage as much as my Canadian one that came to haunt me. This had a great deal to do with homesickness for my family: there had always been an inextricable link between Russian customs and the relatives I had left behind. But the importance of Russian roots in my sense of identity also played a role. They had remained a major strand, in spite of my birth in France and my years in Canada. I found myself seeking out others with similar origins.

As in Canada, Slavs had not traditionally been among the immigrants most favoured by Australia. But in spite of that, and with restrictions eased after the Second World War, a sizeable Russian community had developed in Sydney. Here I once again found evidence of a determination to hold on to the culture of origin. This retention of Russian ways had also resulted in the first generation – and sometimes the second – being reluctant to get very involved in the host country. There was much in common with the community in which I had grown up.

Parallel to my experience in Canada, I found that a scattering of Russian Orthodox churches in Sydney provided meeting points. But here too disagreements over the position to take towards the Soviet branch of Orthodoxy had split and fragmented the church-based community. There were other associations, centred on cultural and social pursuits, which were in any case more appealing to me.

In my search for a compatible group, I encountered both poles of political opinion. One club I attended for a while was focussed on showing film adaptations of classic Russian novels. But these came with a heavy dose of Soviet propaganda through short films that preceded the features and through the conversations of the members. I did not last long with this outfit.

My attempts to link up with other groups were equally ill-fated, for similar reasons, though opposite politics. In Canada, I had grown up in a primarily "White" Russian community, among which were numerous members with conservative beliefs, not surprising considering the impact the Bolshevik victory had had on their families. There was a similar inclination in Australia. I found the deeply conservative views no more palatable than the Communist Party line I had come across at the film screenings.

I understood that perhaps I just had bad luck. The people I met were probably not at all representative of the wider, no doubt more diverse membership. But then someone at a social function – to general approval – seriously expressed the opinion that the Australian Labor Party leader Bob Hawke was as dangerous as Stalin. I decided to give up on my attempts to pursue my cultural legacy through organised activities.

For many years after they left Russia, my grandparents pined for their homeland and found solace among others with a similar past. For my parents, double displacement made the community abroad – whatever their political and other disagreements with it – an important supportive presence, a place of belonging. It did not define them but they could turn to it. For me too, in my younger years, community groups provided a sort of refuge, a place where my difference felt at home.

My inability to come to terms with the organised elements of the community I encountered in Australia, whatever and whoever they represented, had little to do with any failings of theirs. It was more about shifts in my own identity. I now sought connections to the past in different ways.

I did not negate my origins, in spite of frequent severe discomfort over the actions of my ancestors' homeland. Rather I focused on their positives. Indeed, I now appreciate my good fortune in having a multiple identity more than ever, and my inheritance from generations past. I carry what I know of their stories as part of my personal history.

I value the legacy of tradition, language and customs that my grandparents and parents have bequeathed me, and the access it gives me to a different cultural kaleidoscope, past and present. I appreciate the unplanned corollary of that legacy, that of helping me aim to be, as my father put it, "a citizen of the world". My Russian identity increasingly jostles for space with the many other identities that have become part of who I am, but it will always be there.

Charting a symbolic voyage in parallel with the travels of my family in the twentieth century, through writing this book, has changed my perceptions in many areas. I have gained a better understanding of my own origins, and insights into the wider histories of peoples, eras and places. The journey that I have taken has been one of discovery – in both anticipated and unexpected ways.

Acknowledgments

I am eternally grateful to my predecessors in my grandparents' generation who left behind memoirs or dairies. Without their prescience in recording their times, this book would not exist. The words of Nadezhda Apouchtine, Sergei Apuchtin, Olga Tretiakow (neé Apouchtine) and Anna Voeikoff revealed to me a different time and world.

Many thanks are due also to those of my parents' generation who agreed to be interviewed, often at great length. My recordings of Irene Apouchtine, Dimitri Apouchtine, Nadezhda Svetlovsky, Anika Vladislavov and Olga Levchine gave me insights into their lives and enhanced my understanding of their parents' times.

My parents Irene and Dimitri were helpful and supportive in many other ways. They enthusiastically became involved in my project, digging up lots of useful material. I remember a time when every few days there would be a large brown envelope from Canada jutting out of my mailbox when I got home of an evening, with some new gem in it. Travelling with my father and sister to Russia after the collapse of Communism, I witnessed Dimitri's struggle to comprehend this strange land of our ancestors, while always maintaining his good humour and courtesy in the face of never-ending surprises. Sadly both Dimitri and Irene passed away before I completed the manuscript.

My sister Helen Apouchtine was a constant and keen companion on this journey of discovery. She travelled with me to venues of importance to the family in France and Russia, read and made myriad suggestions on the

ACKNOWLEDGMENTS

various drafts of my writing, found many valuable sources of material and organised searches of archives in Moscow. Her assistance and faith in the project were vital to it.

My Aunt Nadezhda Svetlovsky passed on useful material, agreed to be interviewed on numerous occasions, took me on a tour of her – and my father's – childhood stomping grounds in France, read drafts and offered much useful feedback. She was a crucial link to my grandparents' generation, her memories bringing to life people who were gone. Sadly she too has now passed away.

Thanks are due to other relatives who provided access to their own archives and offered additional information. Particularly helpful were Nikita Tretiakow, Maria Fedorowsky, Nicholas Voeikoff and Helen Fotopoulos.

Many more people helped in various ways, among them:
Mary Besemeres, Inga Brasche, Jo-Anne Duggan, Susanna Egan, Elena Govor, Paula Hamilton, Andrew Jakubowicz, Vadim Kukushkin, Vera Lopatnikova, Marvin Lyons, Kiril Ostroukhoff, Andreas Patzer and Nadezhda Rashba.

I am grateful to the University of Technology, Sydney, which awarded me a scholarship and study space to research this family history for my doctoral thesis, research which forms the foundation of this book.

The Women Writers' Network of Writing New South Wales provided feedback and support through several versions of the manuscript. The group workshopped all of it and urged me on with expressions of faith in what I was doing.

Many thanks are due to my publisher Jacqueline Buswell for also constantly believing in this project.

Last but certainly not least, I am grateful to my partner Peter Harlow, who has helped me in ways too numerous to list. He also travelled with me to Russia, joining in my attempts to understand my fascination about my past and this always baffling country. Most importantly, he was always there for me, through the highs, the lows and the in-betweens.

SOURCES AND FURTHER READING

FAMILY SOURCES

Written Memoirs/Diaries/Other Written Material
Apouchtine, Nadezhda
Apuchtin, Sergei A.
Svetlovsky, Nadezhda (*née* Apouchtine)
Tretiakow, Olga (*née* Apouchtine)
Voeikoff, Anna
Voeikoff, Nicolas N.

Taped Memoirs/Interviews
Apouchtine, Dimitri
Apouchtine, Irene
Levchine, Olga (*née* Tretiakow)
Svetlovsky, Nadezhda (*née* Apouchtine)
Vladislavov, Anika
Voeikoff, Anna

Letters
1920s to 2000 (Russia, Serbia, France, Brazil, Canada, Uzbekistan)

Documents
1914 to 1951 (including passports and other identity and travel documents, birth and marriage certificates, educational certificates, work permits and contracts, residence certificates, death notices, etc.)

OTHER ARCHIVAL MATERIAL

Rossiiskii Gosudarstvennyi Voenno-Istoricheskii Arkhiv (Russian State Military History Archive), Moscow (RGVIA) (military records)

SECONDARY SOURCES AND FURTHER READING

RUSSIA

Acton, Edward, Vladimir Iu. Cherniaev and William G. Rosenberg, eds. *Critical Companion to the Russian Revolution 1914-1921.* London: Arnold, 1997.

Bertaux, Daniel. "Transmission in Extreme Situations: Russian Families Expropriated by the October Revolution", translated by Nora Scott. In *Pathways to Social Class: A Qualitative Approach to Social Mobility*, edited by Daniel Bertaux and Paul Thompson. Oxford: Clarendon Press, 1997.

Boym, Svetlana. *The Future of Nostalgia.* New York: Basic Books, 2001.

Browder, Robert Paul, and Alexander F. Kerensky, eds. *The Russian Provisional Government 1917.* Stanford: Stanford University Press (Hoover Institution Publications), 3 volumes, 1961.

Corin, Chris. "Police, Spies and Double Agents: Russia 1881-1914." *History Review*, 2009: 34-39.

Dmitrovskii, I. *Dubrovitsy: znatnoe selo, imienie Kniazia S. M. Golitsyna (Dubrovitsy: noble village, estate of Prince S. M. Galitzine).* Moscow: A. A. Levenson Press, 1908.

Engelstein, Laura. *Russia in Flames: War, Revolution, Civil War 1914-1921.* New York: Oxford University Press, 2018.

Figes, Orlando. *A People's Tragedy: The Russian Revolution 1891-1924.* London: Pimlico, 1996.

Figes, Orlando. *Natasha's Dance: A Cultural History of Russia.* London: Penguin Books, 2003.

Fitzpatrick, Sheila. "Russia's Twentieth Century in History and Historiography." *The Australian Journal of Politics and History* 46, no. 3 (2000): 378.

Freeze, Gregory L. *Russia:* A History. Oxford: Oxford University Press, 2002.
Lazarski, Christopher. "White Propaganda Efforts in the South during the Russian Civil War, 1918-19 (the Alekseev-Denikin Period)." *Slavonic and East European Review* 70, no. 4 (1992): 688-707.
Lyons, Marvin. *Biographical Dictionary of the Corps of Pages: An Outline of the Project.* Vancouver, private publication, 1984.
Lyons, Marvin. *Russia in Original Photographs 1860-1920.* London: Routledge and Kegan Paul, 1977.
Merridale, Catherine. *Night of Stone: Death and Memory in Russia.* London: Granta Books, 2000.
Nabokov, V. D. *The Provisional Government*, translated and edited by A. G. E. Spiers and Andrew Field. Brisbane: University of Queensland Press, 1970.
Nikitine, B. V. *The Fatal Years: Fresh Revelations on a Chapter of Underground History*, translated by Douglas Hastie Smith. Westport, Connecticut: Hyperion Press Inc., 1977 (first published in 1938).
Pares, Bernard. *The Fall of the Russian Monarchy.* London: Phoenix Press, 2001 (first published 1939).
Pipes, Richard. *A Concise History of the Russian Revolution.* New York: Vintage Books, 1996.
Porietskii, N. A. *Selo Vlakhernskoe: imienie Kniazia S. M. Golitsyna (Vlakhernskoe Village, estate of Prince S. M. Galitzine).* Moscow: no publisher given, 1913.
Reed, John. *Ten Days that Shook the World.* London: Penguin Books, 1982 (first published 1926).
Schakhovskoy, D. *Société et Noblesse Russe (Russian Society and Nobility)*, Vol. 2. Rennes: Université de la Haute Bretagne, 1979.

Schwartz, Stephen. "Intellectuals and Assassins – Annals of Stalin's Killerati." *The New York Times*, 24 January 1988. Available at https://www.nytimes.com/1988/01/24/books/intellectuals-and-assassins-annals-of-stalin-s-killerati.html? (Accessed 8 July 2023).

Service, Robert. *A History of Twentieth-Century Russia.* Cambridge: Harvard University Press, 2003.

Shukman, Harold, ed. *The Blackwell Encyclopedia of the Russian Revolution.* Oxford: Blackwell Reference, 1994.

Smith, Douglas. *Former People: The Final Days of the Russian Aristocracy.* New York: Picador (Farrar, Struass and Giroux), 2012.

Smith, Steve. "Writing the history of the Russian Revolution after the fall of communism." *Europe-Asia Studies* 46, no. 4 (1994): 563.

Swettenham, John. *Allied Intervention in Russia 1918-1919, and the Part Played by Canada.* London: George Allen and Unwin Ltd., 1967.

Timchenko-Ruban', Vl. "K Piatidesiatilietiiu Boia na Stokhode 15-go iiulia 1916 goda" ("On the fiftieth anniversary of the Battle on the Stokhod, 15th of July 1916"). *Vestnik gvardeiskogo ob'edineniia (The Bulletin of the Guards Association)*, no. 16 (1966): 6-8.

Waldron, Peter. *Between two Revolutions: Stolypin and the politics of renewal in Russia.* London: University College London Press, 1998.

Welch, Frances. *The Russian Court at Sea: the Voyage of HMS Marlborough, April 1919.* London: Short Books, 2011

Wildman, Allan. "The Future of Russian History." *Russian Review* 60, no. 1 (2001): 9.

Zygar, Mikhail. *The Empire Must Die: Russia's revolutionary collapse, 1900-1917.* New York: Public Affairs (Hachette Book Group), 2017.

FRANCE

Anglade, Jean. *La vie quotidienne des immigrés en France de 1919 à nos jours (Daily Life of Immigrants in France from 1919 to the Present Day)*. Paris: Librairie Hachette, 1976.

Azéma, Jean-Pierre. *From Munich to Liberation, 1938-1944*, translated by Janet Lloyd. Cambridge/Paris: Cambridge University Press/Éditions de la Maison des Sciences de l'Homme, 1984.

Azéma, Jean-Pierre and Olivier Wievorka. *Vichy 1940-1944*. Ligugé-Poitiers: Librairie Académique Perrin, 1997.

Blumenson, Martin. "Politics and the Military in the Liberation of Paris." *Parameters, US Army War College Quarterly* xxviii, no. 2 (1998): 4-14.

Burrin, Philippe. *France under the Germans: Collaboration and Compromise*, translated by Janet Lloyd. New York: The New Press, 1996.

Collins, Larry and Dominique Lapierre. *Is Paris Burning?* New York: Simon and Schuster, 1965.

Cross, Gary S. *Immigrant Workers in Industrial France: The Making of a New Laboring Class*. Philadelphia: Temple University Press, 1983.

Efimovsky, Olga. *Il était une fois... Brunoy... Quincy (Once upon a time there was... Brunoy... Quincy...)*. Paris: self-published, 1991.

Fricero, Emmanuel and "team work". *The Russian Orthodox Cathedral of St Nicholas in Nice,* translator unnamed. Florence: Casa Editrice Bonechi, 2001.

Johnston, Robert H. *"New Mecca, New Babylon": Paris and the Russian Exiles, 1920-1945*. Kingston/Montreal: McGill-Queen's University Press, 1988.

Kunzi, Daniel and Peter Huber. "Paris dans les années 30: Sur Serge Efron et quelques agents du NKVD" ("Paris in the thirties: On Serge Efron and a few agents of the NKVD"). *Cahiers du Monde Russe (Journal of the Russian World)*, no. 32-2 (1991): 285-310. Available at: https://www.persee.fr/doc/cmr_0008-0160_1991_num_32_2_2282 (Accessed 4 July 2023)

Lagrou, Pieter. "Victims of genocide and national memory: Belgium, France and the Netherlands 1945-1965." *Past & Present*, no. 154, (1997): 181.

McMillan, James F. *Twentieth-Century France: Politics and Society 1898-1991*. London: Arnold, Hodder Headline Group, 1992.

Menegaldo, Hélène. *Les Russes à Paris, 1919-1939 (The Russians in Paris, 1919-1939)*. Paris: Éditions Autrement, 1998.

Miller, Michael B. *Shanghai on the Metro: Spies, Intrigue, and the French between the Wars*. Berkeley/Los Angeles: University of California Press, 1994.

Nora, Pierre and Lawrence D. Kritzman, eds. *Realms of Memory: Rethinking the French Past*, translated by Arthur Goldhammer. New York: Columbia University Press, 1996.

Noiriel, Gérard. *The French Melting Pot: Immigration, Citizenship, and National Identity*, translated by Geoffroy de Laforcade. Minneapolis: University of Minnesota Press, 1996.

Paxton, Robert O. *Vichy France: Old Guard and New Order, 1940-1944*. New York: Columbia University Press, 2001.

Raeff, Marc. *Russia Abroad: A Cultural History of the Russian Emigration, 1919-1939*. New York: Oxford University Press, 1990.

Rousso, Henry. *The Vichy Syndrome: History and Memory in France since 1944*, translated by Arthur Goldhammer. Cambridge: Harvard University Press, 1991.

Struve, Nikita. *Soixante-dix ans d'émigration Russe, 1919-1989 (Seventy Years of Russian Emigration, 1919-1989).* Paris: Librairie Arthème Fayard, 1996.

Taylor, Lynne. *Between Resistance and Collaboration: Popular Protest in Northern France, 1940-45.* London/New York: MacMillan Press/St. Martin's Press, 2000.

Thiévin, Joël, and Génica Cuisnier. "5 Août 1944 – 5 Août 1994: 50e anniversaire de la libération d'Ancenis et de ses environs. Délivrance et souffrances (5th of August 1944 – 5th of August 1994: The Fiftieth Anniversary of the Liberation of Ancenis and Its Vicinity. Deliverance and Suffering)." *Histoire et Patrimoine au Pays d'Ancenis (History and Heritage in the Region of Ancenis), Ancenis Association de Recherches sur la Région d'Ancenis,* 9th edition (1994): 2-44.

Thomas, Patrick. *Nantes: Les Bombardements (Nantes: The Bombings), Collection Mémoire d'une Ville.* Nantes: Editions C.M.D., n.d.

Torpey, John. *The Invention of the Passport: Surveillance, Citizenship and the State.* Cambridge: Cambridge University Press, 2000.

Weber, Eugen. *The Hollow Years: France in the 1930s.* New York: W. W. Norton and Company, 1994.

Zernov, N. M. and M. V. Zernov, eds. *Za Rubezhom: Belgrade, Parizh, Oxford (Khronika Semyi Zernovykh, 1921-1972) (Abroad: Belgrade, Paris, Oxford [the Chronicle of the Zernov Family, 1921-1972]).* Paris: YMCA Press, 1973.

CANADA

Bélanger, Claude: "The Language Laws of Quebec (1969-1998)"; Marianopolis College, Quebec History (1998). Available at http://faculty.marianopolis.edu/c.belanger/quebechistory/readings/langlaws.htm (Accessed 4 July 2023).

Broadfoot, Barry. *The Immigrant Years: From Europe to Canada 1945-1967*. Vancouver: Douglas & McIntyre, 1986.

Burnet, Jean R. with Howard Palmer. *"Coming Canadians": An Introduction to a History of Canada's Peoples*. Toronto: McClelland and Stewart/Ministry of Supply and Services (Canada), 1988.

De Brou, Dave and Bill Waiser. *Documenting Canada: A History of Modern Canada in Documents*. Saskatoon: Fifth House Publishing, 1992.

Herberg, Edward N. *Ethnic Groups in Canada: Adaptations and Transitions*. Toronto: Nelson Canada, 1989.

Jeletzky, Tamara F., ed. *Russian Canadians: Their Past and Present*. Ottawa: Borealis Press, 1983.

Kaprelian-Churchill, Isabel. "Rejecting 'misfits': Canada and the Nansen Passport." *International Migration Review* 28, no. 2 (1994): 281.

Li, Peter S. *The Making of Post-War Canada*. Toronto: Oxford University Press, 1996.

Magocsi, Paul Robert, ed. *Encyclopedia of Canada's Peoples*. Toronto: University of Toronto Press, 1999.

Okulevich, G. *Russkie v Kanade (The Russians in Canada)*. Toronto: The Federation of Russian Canadians, 1952.

Palmer, Howard. "Mosaic versus Melting Pot?: Immigration and Ethnicity in Canada and the United States." In Mandel, Eli and David Taras. *A Passion for Identity: Introduction to Canadian Studies*. Toronto: Methuen, 1987.

Suyama, Nobuaki. "The Evolving Pattern of Canada's Immigration Policy-Making." *Australian Canadian Studies* 15 & 16, no. 2 & 1 (1997-1998): 115-41.

Whitaker, Reg and Gary Marcuse. *Cold War Canada: The Making of a National Insecurity State, 1945-1957*. Toronto: University of Toronto Press, 1994.

AUSTRALIA

Collins, Jock. *Cohesion with Diversity? Immigration and Multiculturalism in Canada and Australia.* Sydney: University of Technology, Sydney (Working Paper Series, No. 28), 1993.

Collins, Jock. *Migrant Hands in a Distant Land: Australia's post-war immigration.* Sydney: Pluto Press Australia, 1991.

Govor, Elena. *Australia in the Russian Mirror: Changing Perceptions 1770-1919.* Melbourne: Melbourne University Press, 1997.

Hawkins, Freda. *Critical Years in Immigration: Canada and Australia Compared.* Sydney: New South Wales University Press, 1989.

Jakubowicz, Andrew and Nathalie Apouchtine, eds. *Making Multicultural Australia* (CD-ROM). Sydney: Board of Studies New South Wales et al, 1999.

Jupp, James. *Immigration.* Melbourne: Oxford University Press, 1998.

Jupp, James, ed. *The Australian People: an Encyclopedia of the Nation, its People and their Origins.* Sydney: Angus and Robertson, 2001.

Lack, John and Jacqueline Templeton. *Bold Experiment: A Documentary History of Australian Immigration since 1945.* Melbourne: Oxford University Press, 1995.

Martin, Jean I. *Refugee Settlers: A Study of Displaced Persons in Australia.* Canberra: ANU Press, 1965.

McNair, John and Thomas Poole, eds. *Russia and the Fifth Continent.* Brisbane: University of Queensland Press, 1992.

Wilton, Janis and Richard Bosworth. *Old Worlds and New Australia: The post-war migrant experience.* Melbourne: Penguin Books, 1984.

MEMOIRS/BIOGRAPHIES

Benckendorff, Paul. *Last Days at Tsarskoe Selo,* translated by Maurice Baring. London: William Heinemann, 1927. Also available at: http://www.alexanderpalace.org/lastdays/intro.html (Accessed 4 July 2023).

Berberova, Nina. *The Italics are Mine,* translated by Philippe Radley. London/Harlow: Longmans, Green and Co. Ltd., 1969.

Bezobrazov, Vladimir Mikhailovich. *Diary of the Commander of the Russian Imperial Guard 1914-1917*, translated and edited by Ivan Stenbock-Fermor and Marvin Lyons. Boynton Beach, Florida: Dramco Publishers, 1994.

Botkine, Tatiana. *Au Temps Des Tsars (In the Age of the Tsars).* Paris: Bernard Grasset, 1980.

Chang, Jung. *Wild Swans: Three Daughters of China.* London: Flamingo, 1993.

Chong, Denise. *The Concubine's Children: the Story of a Chinese Family Living on Two Sides of the Globe.* Toronto: Penguin Books Canada, 1994.

Christesen, Nina. "A Russian migrant." In *The Half-Open Door: Sixteen modern Australian women look at professional life and achievement,* edited by Patricia Grimshaw and Lynne Strahan. Sydney: Hale and Iremonger, 1982.

Dorfman, Ariel. *Heading South, Looking North.* New York: Penguin Books, 1998.

Farmborough, Florence. *Nurse at the Russian Front – A Diary 1914-18.* London: Constable and Co Ltd, 1974.

Fraser, Eugenie. *The House by the Dvina: A Russian Childhood.* London: Corgi Books, 1984.

Galitzine, Alexandre A. and Christine H. Galitzine, eds. *The Princes Galitzine: before 1917... and Afterwards.* Washington, DC: Galitzine Books, 2002.

Goshtov, Georgii. *Dnevnik Kavaleriiskago Ofitsera (The Diary of a Cavalry Officer)*. Paris: E. Siial'skoi Books, 1931.
Grow, Malcolm C. *Surgeon Grow: An American in the Russian fighting*. New York: Frederick A. Stokes Co., 1918. Available at: https://babel.hathitrust.org/cgi/pt?id=nyp.334 33070300243&view=1up&seq=359 (Accessed 4 July 2023).
Heresch, Elisabeth. *Blood on the Snow: Eyewitness Accounts of the Russian Revolution*. New York: Paragon House, 1990.
Horsbrugh-Porter, Anna, ed. *Memories of Revolution: Russian Women Remember*. London: Routledge, 1993.
Hsu Accomando, Claire. *Love and Rutabaga: A Remembrance of the War Years*. New York: St. Martin's Press, 1993.
Humbert, Agnès. *Résistance: Memoirs of Occupied France*, translated by Barbara Mellor. London: Bloomsbury, 2008 (first published 1946).
Ignatieff, George. *The Making of a Peacemonger: The Memoirs of George Ignatieff*. Toronto: University of Toronto Press, 1985.
Ignatieff, Michael. *The Russian Album*. New York: Elisabeth Sifton Books, Viking, 1987.
Knox, Alfred. *With the Russian Army 1914-1917: Being Chiefly Extracts from the Diary of a Military Attaché*. London: Hutchinson and Co., 2 volumes, 1921.
Koestler, Arthur. *Scum of the Earth*. London: Jonathan Cape, 1941.
Koulomzin, Sophie. *Many Worlds: A Russian Life*. Crestwood, NY: St. Vladimir's Seminary Press, 1980.
Krasil'shchikov, A. P. and V. D. Safronov. *Fabrikanty Krasil'shchikovy (The Manufacturers Krasil'shchikovs)*. Moscow: self-published, 2000.
Kulyk Keefer, Janice. *Honey and Ashes: A Story of Family*. Toronto: Harper Perennial Canada, 1998.
Kuzmina, Nina Dimitrievna. *Prince Sergei Mikhailovich Galitzine (1843-1915)*. Moscow: self-published, 2009.

Manstein-Chirinsky, Anastasia. *La Dernière Escale: Le siècle d'une exilée russe à Bizerte (The Last Stopover: The Century of an Exiled Russian Woman in Bizerte)*. Tunis: Suds Éditions, 2000.

Moustafine, Mara. *Secrets and Spies: The Harbin Files*. Sydney: Random House Australia, 2002.

Nabokov, Vladimir. *Speak, Memory: An Autobiography Revisited*. New York: Vintage International, 1989.

Nash, Gary. *The Tarasov Saga: From Russia through China to Australia*. Sydney: Rosenberg Publishing, 2002.

Orwell, George. *Down and out in Paris and London*. London: Penguin Books, 1940 (first published 1933).

Ouspensky, P. D. and C. E. Bechhofer. *Letters from Russia 1919*, translated by Bechhofer and Paul Leon. London: Routledge and Kegan Paul Ltd., 1978.

Paléologue, Maurice. *An Ambassador's Memoirs*, translated by F. A. Holt. London: 1923.
Available at: http://www.alexanderpalace.org/mpmemoirs/ (Accessed 4 July 2023).

Poretsky, Elisabeth K. *Our Own People: A Memoir of 'Ignace Reiss' and His Friends*. London: Oxford University Press, 1969.

Porter, Anna. *The Storyteller: Memory, Secrets, Magic and Lies – A Memoir of Hungary*. Toronto: Anchor Canada, 2000.

Saranin, Alex. *Child of the Kulaks*. Brisbane: University of Queensland Press, 1997.

Schmemann, Serge. *Echoes of a Native Land: Two Centuries of a Russian Village*. New York: Alfred A. Knopf, 1997.

Slezkine, Yuri and Sheila Fitzpatrick, eds. *In the Shadow of Revolution: Life Stories of Russian Women from 1917 to the Second World War*, translated by Yuri Slezkine. Princeton: Princeton University Press, 2000.

Stone, Norman and Michael Glenny, eds. *The Other Russia*. London: Faber and Faber, 1990.

Sukanov, N. N. *The Russian Revolution 1917: Eyewitness Account*, translated and edited by Joel Carmichael. New York: Harper and Brothers, 2 volumes, 1962.
Teffi (Lokhvitskaya, Nadezhda). *Memories: from Moscow to the Black Sea*, translated by Robert Chandler, Elizabeth Chandler, Anne Marie Jackson and Irina Steinberg. London: Pushkin Press, 2016 (first published in 1930).
White, Richard. *Remembering Ahanagran: Storytelling in a Family's Past*. New York: Hill and Wang, 1998.
Williams, Stephanie. *Olga's Story*. New York: Doubleday, 2005.
Wrangel, Peter N. *Always with Honour*. New York: Robert Speller and Sons, 1957.

FICTION

Apukhtin, Aleksey. *Three Tales*, translated by Philip Taylor. Madison, NJ: Fairleigh Dickinson University Press, 2003.
Bulgakov, Mikhail. *White Guard*, translated by Michael Glenny. New York/St Louis/San Francisco: McGraw-Hill, 1971.
Ignatieff, Michael. *Asya*. London: Arrow Books, 1992.
Nabokov, Vladimir. *The Gift*, translated by Michael Scammell. London: Panther, 1966.
Troyat, Henri. *Aliocha*. Paris: Editions J'ai Lu, 1991.
Tsvetaeva, Marina. *A Captive Spirit: Selected Prose*, translated by J. Marin King. London: Virago, 1983.
Viat, Denys. *Un monde en marge (A World on the Fringes)*. Paris: L'Age d'Homme, 1989.

ORAL HISTORY, BIOGRAPHY AND MEMOIR

Benmayor, Rina and Andor Skotnes, eds. *Migration and Identity (International Yearbook of Oral History and Life Stories*, Vol III). Oxford: Oxford University Press, 1994.

Bertaux, Daniel and Paul Thompson, eds. *Between Generations: Family models, myths and memories (International Yearbook of Oral History and Life Stories*, Vol II). New York: Oxford University Press, 1993.

Besemeres, Mary. *Translating One's Self: Language and Selfhood in Cross-Cultural Autobiography*. Bern: Peter Lang, 2002.

Curthoys, Ann and Ann McGrath, eds. *Writing Histories – Imagination and Narration*. Clayton, Vic: Monash Publications in History, 2000.

Darian-Smith, Kate and Paula Hamilton, eds. *Memory and History in Twentieth-Century Australia*. Melbourne: Oxford University Press, 1994.

Egan, Susanna. *Mirror Talk: Genres of Crisis in Contemporary Autobiography*. Chapel Hill: University of North Carolina Press, 1999.

Kuhn, Annette. *Family Secrets: Acts of Memory and Imagination*. London: Verso, 1995.

Perks, Robert and Alistair Thomson, eds. *The Oral History Reader*. London: Routledge, 1998.

Popkin, Jeremy D. "Historians on the Autobiographical Frontier." *American Historical Review* 104, no 3. (1999): 725-48.

Stone, Elizabeth. *Black Sheep and Kissing Cousins: How Our Family Stories Shape Us*. New York: Penguin Books, 1988.

Thompson, Paul. *The Voice of the Past: Oral History*. Oxford: Oxford University Press, 2000.

www.ingramcontent.com/pod-product-compliance
Lightning Source LLC
LaVergne TN
LVHW010252260326
834688LV00044B/1247